Frederic Carrel

The Adventures of John Johns

Frederic Carrel

The Adventures of John Johns

ISBN/EAN: 9783337179526

Printed in Europe, USA, Canada, Australia, Japan

Cover: Foto ©ninafisch / pixelio.de

More available books at **www.hansebooks.com**

THE ADVENTURES OF JOHN JOHNS

By

FREDERIC CARREL

Author of The City

LONDON:
BLISS SANDS & CO.
MDCCCXCVII

NEW 6/-
NOVELS.

LADS' LOVE
By S. R. CROCKETT
With 16 Illustrations
By Warwick Goble

CHARITY CHANCE
By WALTER RAYMOND
With a Frontispiece
By H. T. Robinson

MR. PETERS
By RICCARDO STEPHENS

ADVENTURES OF JOHN JOHNS
By FREDERIC CARREL

BELINDA'S BEAUX
And other Stories
By ARABELLA KENEALY

OUR LADDIE
By OLIPHANT SMEATON
With 8 Illustrations
By Anthony Fox

TRISCOMBE STONE
By PORTLAND BOARD AKERMAN
and NORMAN HURST

I DESIRE to say, by way of preface, that my sole endeavour in writing this story has been to mirror, and not to preach.

F. C.

CONTENTS

	PAGE
CHAPTER FIRST	1
CHAPTER SECOND	18
CHAPTER THIRD	34
CHAPTER FOURTH	51
CHAPTER FIFTH	65
CHAPTER SIXTH	82
CHAPTER SEVENTH	102
CHAPTER EIGHTH	117
CHAPTER NINTH	132
CHAPTER TENTH	147
CHAPTER ELEVENTH	163
CHAPTER TWELFTH	178
CHAPTER THIRTEENTH	194
CHAPTER FOURTEENTH	209
CHAPTER FIFTEENTH	225
CHAPTER SIXTEENTH	239
CHAPTER SEVENTEENTH	255
CHAPTER EIGHTEENTH	274
CHAPTER NINETEENTH	287

*THE ADVENTURES
OF JOHN JOHNS*

CHAPTER FIRST

THE train from Tilbury steamed into Fenchurch Street at four o'clock, and John Johns, carrying a black portmanteau, alighted from a third-class carriage. He stood for a moment on the platform of the dingy terminus, amid the crowd of passengers and porters, realizing that he was back again in London, after six years' absence in Australia. Then, as he resented being elbowed, he crossed over to the cab-rank, opened the door of the first hansom he found vacant, and thrust his only piece of luggage into it.

Whither, in search of lodgings, should he tell the man to drive? That was a question which he had debated on the journey up. With only five pounds and a few shillings in his pocket, and very uncertain prospects, he needed a cheap neighbourhood. After a moment's hesitation, therefore, he decided to try Bloomsbury.

As the cab passed through the City—still full of life and of activity—the spring sun was shining on the walls of its classic buildings, illumining the streets and the faces of the passers in them. Overhead, the pale blue sky was cloudless, and the outlines of the houses were unusually distinct. London looked bright enough, Johns thought, that afternoon.

Passing slowly through Cheapside—congested by the traffic —the hansom made its way through Newgate Street and along Holborn. As it passed a colossal draper's shop a few yards from the "Circus," a girl with a slight figure and a pretty babyface was leaving it. She gave a sidelong look at Johns, and, when he smiled engagingly, she returned his smile. This put him into a good temper, and, instinctively, he cast a glance at his attire, which consisted of a well-worn, lightish overcoat, of

B

more or less colonial cut, half covering a brown tweed suit of doubtful quality. Then he drew his soft felt hat a little forward, adjusted his red necktie, and looked at the people in the streets with calm assurance, twirling the rather long and dark moustache which relieved, to some extent, the snubness of his nose and the somewhat excessive breadth of a face lit up by a pair of keen black eyes of extraordinary expressiveness and penetration. He was thinking that he was back again in England furnished with a stock of roughly-bought experience. He was about to test himself in earnest, and to find out whether he possessed the quality which carries a man along to fortune. He was six-and-twenty, and he calculated that he had ample time before him—the great thing was to make a lucky start.

What had he not been in Australia? Tramp, and cow-boy, broker's clerk, evening lecturer, journalist, and schoolmaster. He had drifted, as most men do who go out "on spec," from one calling to another in search of the main chance, which he had not found. Still he had managed to enjoy himself sufficiently in spite of his vicissitudes, and of his amorous adventures there was no end. Thanks to the attraction he possessed in women's eyes, his love adventures had been many. Twice he had managed to elude the vengeance of a father and an elder brother, and he had been once victorious in an encounter with a weakly rival who had proved to be no match for him. For although he was below the medium height, he was strongly built and muscular; his roving life had given him a good physique. On the whole, he had taken life out there much as he had found it, and though he had landed almost penniless, he had contrived, by one means or another, to earn a livelihood.

The hansom entered Russell Square, which he remembered vaguely, for he did not know London well, having only spent a few months there after leaving school while seeking an employment.

He looked around in search of houses where apartments were to let, when, presently, the words "Bedford Place" caught his eye, and he told the cabman to drive slowly up what seemed to be a long, wide street. Here there was no lack of window cards bearing the inscription, "Apartments to let furnished." Causing the man to stop before the first he saw thus labelled, he alighted.

The red-faced woman who answered to his knock looked at him suspiciously, as if his somewhat foreign costume made her diffident There was a bed-sitting room just vacant, she said in answer to his enquiry; but how much did he want to pay? Well, he didn't want to pay much, just then. Six or seven shillings weekly would be about his price, and he didn't care how high up it was.

Oh, there was nothing for *that* in the whole neighbourhood. He might save himself the trouble of going farther. *She* wanted double for her room. But as he seldom believed any assertion which he had not checked, he walked along the street and knocked at other doors, with much the same result. For a few moments he debated within himself whether he could afford ten shillings, at which price he could have a room on a third floor back. But as he had made a resolution that he would husband his resources, he decided to consult the cabman as to the whereabouts of cheaper quarters. The cabman knew a street off Tottenham Court Road, called Grafton Street, where prices did not run so high, and as the name caught his fancy, he told him at once to drive there.

Passing out of the quietude of Bloomsbury into a long, noisy thoroughfare, of which Johns had very little recollection, the cab at length turned off to the right, and stopped before one of a row of houses in a quiet street, built in a style which seemed pretentious for the neighbourhood. Johns pulled a bell which was so loose that he drew out a foot of wire before it offered the least resistance. After a few moments, a stout woman, middle-aged, appeared.

Could he have a room for seven shillings? he enquired. Yes, that was the price she wanted for a nice front room on the third floor. Whereupon, as he asked to see it, she began to roll slowly up the somewhat narrow stairs, requesting him to follow. There was a complex odour in the house, one of those indefinable smells of London lodging-houses composed of emanations from greasy kitchens, defective drains, and mustiness of furniture. The stair carpets were threadbare in many places, and here and there the wall paper of the staircase was unstuck.

The stout woman turned the handle of a door on the top of the third flight, and requested Johns to enter. He found himself in a large, low-ceilinged room, in which the musty smell was stronger. In one corner there was a small washstand in mahogany, with a marble top, and in another a chest of drawers of painted deal.

Between the two windows was a much worn horse-hair sofa. A round table, covered with a green cloth stained with ink, stood in the centre, and a large iron bedstead occupied nearly the whole of the small back room. A few dissimilar chairs were dotted here and there upon a much soiled carpet.

Johns's first act after casting a look around was to open one of the windows to relieve the stuffiness. He next turned to the woman who was waiting near the door, and said, "All right, this will do, I'll take it."

Then he went down, paid the cabman, and returned quickly bearing his portmanteau, which he put upon a chair, and began unpacking. He placed his linen in one of the drawers of the chest of drawers, which he noticed was unsteady on its legs, distributed his toilet requisites about the room, and threw a night-shirt on the bed. This done, he drew a volume of Shelley's poems from the pocket of his overcoat (which he had not taken off), and placed it on the table. Then he sat down on the sofa, took a cigarette from a case he produced from an inner pocket, lit it, and began to smoke.

Here he was at length in London with a long task before him, and but a very hazy notion as to how it was to be begun. For a man who had no footing in any of the professions, and who wanted money badly, there were only two things open —journalism or business. One or the other he must adopt. His taste inclined to letters, for which he had a bent, but then business offered a better chance of becoming rich, and his aim was to become rich. But yet, again, how could he do anything in business without capital, and what means had he of obtaining any? None whatever, whereas in journalism the case was different: he *might* make his head supply the capital, and journalism led to other things.

Presently, after turning over the question in his mind, he rose, and, taking a sheet of paper from his wallet on the table, began to write a letter to his parents. He had not written to them for a long time, and his return would be a piece of news for the old retired fisherman and his wife in their Guernsey village. No doubt they would be disappointed when they found that he had come away without having accomplished anything, especially as they had stinted themselves sorely, first to give him an education at the College, and then to send him to Australia. He commenced, therefore, with a little explanation of his motives for leaving, and ended by promising that his next letter would contain good news. And they wouldn't, he said, have long to wait for it. When he had finished, he folded the letter, placed it in an envelope, and addressed it in a bold, clear hand to Mrs. David Johns, St. Martin's, adding in the right-hand corner, "Guernsey." This done, he lit another cigarette and looked at his watch. It was half-past five. He rose, put on his hat, and left his room. His landlady, whom he met at the bottom of the stairs, handed him a well-worn latch-key, and having now a roof to shelter him, he sallied forth to post his letter, and to seek a restaurant, for he was feeling hungry, not having eaten since the morning. He walked along Tottenham Court Road, looking at the shops, full of middle-class commodities, which the last rays of the setting sun were unable to idealise; at the tawdry women stopped before the windows of cheap bonnet shops; at the ragged females issuing from palatial public houses; at the workmen returning from their work with a jaunty air of self-complacency; at the pale-faced urchins playing on the pavements; and at the ceaseless traffic in the road. Into the first pillar-box he saw, he thrust his letter. Then he began to make his way down Shaftesbury Avenue. "This looks dismal," he said to himself, as he noticed the dirty walls of the high buildings and the mean side streets. But he had seen much the same aspects previously in Sydney, and he pursued his way westward, seeking a place at which to dine.

When he arrived at Piccadilly Circus, and beheld an open space towards which several ends of streets converged at all angles incoherently, and in the centre of which stood a ponderous metal fountain surmounted by a winged figure which, balanced on one leg, was shooting grotesquely with a bow and arrow at the little crowd of arabs gathered round the base, he laughed. "A pretty mess they've made of this," he said, for he was not without taste, and he had acquired as much culture as he was able in the sedentary intervals of his roving life. He crossed to the island add looked about him. Presently the words "Café Monico," in large white letters, on a house, attracted his attention.

Could he afford to dine at a big restaurant? Well, no, he couldn't, certainly; but as this was his first day in London, he was inclined to celebrate the circumstance a little lavishly. So he crossed the road again, and entered the place with a firm step and an air of dignified assurance. Passing through the café where drinks were being served by Continental waiters to somewhat showily dressed people seated at round tables, he found himself in a vast dining hall, which he recollected for having once had dinner there before. He seated himself on the divan before a vacant table, next to one at which a lady was finishing her dinner, and ordered *Soles Colbert*, an entrecôte, and sweets, as well as a half bottle of Chateau Lafitte. While he was waiting for the meal, he cast a glance at the lady near him, who was looking in his direction smiling, but seeing that her face was faded, even jaded, and far from pretty, he took up an evening paper and read it until his dinner came. Then he ate heartily, finding the dishes excellent, and the wine grateful, after the coarse fare he had had on board the liner as a third-class passenger. When he had finished, he called for coffee and a cigar, and sat for more than half an hour watching the diners, and trying to weave plans for future action. When the waiter brought the bill it amounted to seven shillings. Drawing out his purse, he threw a sovereign upon the table with the air of a man accustomed to spend freely. The waiter quickly produced the change, and Johns left a shilling on the table for him. The man bowed and helped him deferentially to put on his coat. "One gets a lot of politeness in this country for a shilling," he thought, "much more than in Australia."

As it was still early, he drifted along Piccadilly, making his way against a stream of home-going shop assistants of both sexes. Many of the shops were already shut, and others were being closed, as the noise of rolling shutters indicated. Johns stopped before what seemed to be a French provision shop, with sides of white marble, and a rich collection of braised edibles in the window. A little blonde serving girl had caught his eye, and she seemed so piquante in her black frock and snow-white apron that he debated with himself for a few moments whether he should enter and order something, to have an opportunity of making her acquaintance. But, when he thought of the bill he had just paid, he decided that it would be imprudent, and he resumed his walk with a feeling of annoyance and regret. Certainly he might have entered without buying anything, but of what use would it have been, since he couldn't afford to pursue the adventure further? And he liked pursuing his adventures to the end.

When he reached Burlington House, something unusual seemed to be taking place. A little crowd was gathered on either side of the high archway, looking at the private carriages which were entering in quick succession, filled with people in evening dress. Evidently a banquet or a reception was being held. He stood for a few moments amid the crowd, looking also, and the people in the carriages appeared to him so disdainful in the display of their wealth that he grew angry with them for possessing it, while he, with a capacity for pleasure as great as theirs, and with brains as good as theirs, was in want of a ten-pound note. This was altogether wrong and contrary to fitness. It must be remedied, and soon. Thinking thus, he took advantage of an interval to cross, and continued his way up Piccadilly. Broughams and hansoms passed him, full of people going out to dinner or to the play, and the lights were lit in the club-houses of St. James', down which he paused to look a moment. When he arrived at the Berkeley Hotel he paused again, for he could see into the dining-room, which was full of men and women in evening dress, dining at little tables, lighted by red-shaded candles. And the same feeling of irritation came over him which he had experienced a few moments before. They looked so surfeited with well being, so comfortable, so calmly, masterfully happy in their luxury, so brilliant, that they excited in him mingled feelings of envy, admiration, and a kind of scorn. Quite close to him, so close that, had the window been open, he might have touched her, a lady was seated with her back towards him, and he looked with admiration at the fresh white flesh to which the subdued light of the shaded candles lent a tint of exceeding softness. He could not well see her face, but he noticed that she had light-brown hair, and that she was young and shapely. He scrutinized the others at the table, wondering which of them was her husband, or if she had a husband, or if she was in any way related to the middle-aged, bejewelled lady on her right, or to either of the two men of elderly appearance who made up the party. But, as he was eyeing the stouter of the two—a man somewhere between fifty-five and sixty—he fancied he had seen that physiognomy before. He looked again. Yes, certainly, he *had* seen the man before. But where? He searched his memory for a few moments, when suddenly he recollected. The stout man was the newspaper proprietor from England whom, during his brief career as a journalist in Melbourne, he had been deputed to pilot round the city. There could be no doubt about it. He remembered the double chin, the fat neck, and the little peering eyes, and he told himself that this was an opportunity which was too good to be missed. " By God," he said, "what luck!" But how was the gentleman to be approached? He couldn't present himself at that moment while they were in the middle of their dinner! He would wait till they had finished.

He paced slowly up and down in front of the hotel, keeping his eye upon the little party, and noticing the progress they were making with their dinner by the dishes which the waiters served. The *menu* seemed inexhaustible, for, when he had been pacing fully half an hour, fresh dishes were still arriving. He muttered, "They take a long time filling!"

At length, when his patience was almost at an end, he saw the sweets arrive. It was time to prepare for action. He vaguely remembered the name of the man he was going to address. Something like Lawson; or was it Dawson? Yes, Dawson seemed to be the name. At any rate it was good enough to try. He waited a few more minutes until the waiters brought the dessert, and then he walked up Berkeley Street to the main entrance. The hall porter scanned him narrowly, and asked him, somewhat gruffly, what he wanted. But he drew out his pocket-case, and selecting the cleanest of the few cards he had left, he wrote underneath his name, "*of Melbourne, would like to speak to you on urgent business.*"

"There," he said; "send that in to the gentleman sitting at the table in the left-hand window, opposite a lady with light hair."

The man looked at the card, and then again at Johns, whose appearance did not seem to please him. "Send it in," Johns repeated, firmly, and with authority; "it's urgent." This time the man obeyed, though churlishly.

The waiter who had been sent in with the card returned presently. The gentleman, he said, didn't quite remember Mr. Johns, but would see him later in the hall.

Johns took a seat, congratulating himself on the success of his first move. He waited for nearly half an hour watching the diners leaving the dining room in groups, until at length his man appeared accompanied by the remainder of the party.

Johns rose at once.

"I think you must remember me," he said; "I took you round in Melbourne."

"Ah, yes, I recollect," the stout man answered, stiffly. And then saying that he had only a few moments to spare, he led Johns to a small parlour which was already occupied by the remainder of the party. "And what, may I ask, is the urgent business?"

"There isn't any," Johns said, flatly, and with an intonation peculiar to him, "except that I wanted to see you, and I didn't know how to manage it."

The stout man frowned. But Johns continued quickly, noticing that the lady with light hair was looking at him.

"It *does* seem a strange proceeding, I admit, and I apologise. But the fact is, I've just arrived this morning from Australia, and, as I don't intend to go back again, I want work here. You, sir, I believe, own newspapers, and therefore you can give me work. Pray, don't say you haven't got a vacancy. There are always vacancies, and I'll put life into your paper; life, sir, and you won't regret it if you take me on."

The stout man looked at Johns with evident surprise, while

the fair-haired lady, who had been listening, smiled encouragingly, Johns thought.

"You've a good opinion of yourself, at all events, young man; but the question is whether others will have the same of you."

"Try me, and you'll see."

Again the stout man surveyed Johns, this time with more interest.

He reflected for a moment, then he said—

"I don't believe it will be of any use, but if you like to call to-morrow at the office of the *Planet* at half-past twelve, I may *show* you to the editor."

"Thanks, that's all I want. Your name, sir, is Mr. Dawson, I believe."

"That's my name, and I wish you a good evening."

Johns rose. He made a bow to the fair-haired lady, including Dawson in it, and the couple who seemed to be the hosts. Then, without more words, he left.

He was pleased with himself, and he walked towards Hyde Park Corner with a light step, for he felt that in a few moments, by a lucky chance, the outlook had changed greatly for the better. Dawson, he deemed, was sent him from the skies. He didn't regret his expensive dinner now that he had got so suddenly upon the right tack. It seemed, somehow, to have led to it.

When he reached the Corner, as the empty park did not look inviting, he turned and retraced his steps, wondering how he was to pass the evening.

There was a lull in the street traffic. The dinners were over, and London was digesting. The shops were shut, and the streets had assumed their nightly aspect. Johns strolled along until he found himself again before the fountain, where he bought a *Planet*. Then he crossed to the further pavement, and continued his way to Leicester Square. An evening's entertainment was offered him at the Empire Theatre, before which he stood reading the long programme displayed upon the walls. Once or twice he was on the point of entering, but when he put his hand into his pocket, and felt the thinness of his purse, in which the sovereigns took up so little room, he abandoned the idea. "No," he said; "I must stick to them like glue."

Still, the evening had to be spent somehow; so he walked up Regent Street, and, noticing the Café Royal, entered it. Here he would be able to pass the time. He took a seat in the gilded room, full of foreigners, called for a glass of maraschino, and became much interested in watching two

Spaniards, next him, playing dominoes. Then, when the clock above the counter was pointing to a quarter before twelve, and the Café was emptying, he left.

As it was a fine night, he thought he would take the longest road home by Regent Street, and he strolled leisurely up the Quadrant, where his seemingly provincial costume singled him out to the nightly promenaders of many nationalities, by several of whom he was accosted.

But Johns had no taste for deteriorated charms, and he walked along without responding to their overtures, until at length, as he wanted to think, and their chatter prevented him from doing so, he grew impatient, and, when a stout enamelled damsel caught him by the arm, he turned round upon her and told her roughly to be off. She answered with a volley of invectives, which ended with—"You little pauper; you can't even buy yourself a decent coat." He only laughed, and continued on his way, followed, until he was out of hearing, by more abuse of the same kind.

"They're all alike," he said, "when they're not appreciated."

In Oxford Street, again, he had to run the gauntlet; but as he grunted something like a "No" as soon as he was approached, he was not much molested, and he reached his quarters half an hour after midnight.

The door of the house was being opened by a rather pretty, fair-haired girl, sufficiently well-dressed, who was followed in by a young man. Johns was the last to enter, and, as he was shutting the door, he heard the lady say, "This way," and saw the couple disappear into a room on the ground floor.

He shrugged his shoulders, and, without thinking more about it, took a candle from the table, lit it, mounted the three flights of stairs rapidly, and went to bed.

The next morning, when he awoke, the sun was shining brightly. He rose quickly, and, in dressing, selected the best of his four shirts, cutting the frayed edge of one of its wristbands with a pair of scissors. Then he brushed his clothes, and erased, as best he could, a spot upon the overcoat with the aid of a wet towel. After this he left his room, and hurried to a bread shop in New Oxford Street for breakfast.

It was scarcely nine o'clock, and the shop was empty. A woman with bare arms was sweeping the floor, while the serving girls were arranging cakes and buns in the high, wide window. On the counter the coffee-urns were smoking fragrantly. Johns ordered a modest breakfast, and began to read the copy of the *Planet* which he had bought the night before, concentrating his attention on its contents, so that he might become familiar with its policy.

His first impression was that it was well written, and he saw some articles which surpassed anything he remembered in his Australasian experience, though that, it was true, had not lasted longer than a fortnight. There appeared to be a place for every interest in the yellow sheet, from football to bimetalism, and he noticed that the City Article was long and prominent. As for the paper's politics, he could not quite unravel them, but he gathered that they were radical.

When he had finished his breakfast and the paper, as he had much time before him, he sauntered slowly towards the Strand, enjoying the fresh morning air. Feeling stimulated by the bustle of the busy streets, he spent the hours before his interview exploring the land of newspapers in the vicinity of Fleet Street, until his watch told him that it was time to present himself at the office of the *Planet*.

This was located in the Strand, in a large house possessing a façade on the street, bearing the name of the journal in large, gilt letters in German text. When he reached it, he pushed one side of the swing door, and entered a long room in which thick parcels of papers were being handed over a counter by clerks to a crowd of newsboys.

"Could he see Mr. Dawson?" he enquired.

"First door round the corner."

Johns repaired to the side street, where he found a narrow doorway, above which he read *The Planet, Editorial Offices*. He ascended the flight of steps before him, and, entering the first room he saw, he told an old man, who was sitting at a table in a small office strewn with papers, that he had come to see Mr. Dawson.

"Have you an appointment?"

"Yes."

"Then it's the last door on the right, at the bottom of the passage."

Johns hastened down the corridor, and found himself in an ante-room filled with people who seemed to be waiting for an interview. A young man with a pale face was seated at a table, writing. Johns gave him his card, saying that Mr. Dawson was expecting him.

"If you'll take a seat, your card shall be sent in."

Johns looked round the room. All the seats were occupied. So he took up a position near the window, and, leaning against the wall, observed the visitors. They were mostly men approaching middle age, pale, and wearing their hair longer than it is generally worn. They had a tired, nervous look, and there were well-marked lines about the lower portion of their faces. Their clothes were rather crumpled, as if they had been travelling or sleeping in them, and their neckties were negligently tied. They sat there without speaking to each other. One, a man whose hair was beginning to be silvered, was turning over the pages of a manuscript; the others were either reading the first edition of the paper, fresh from the printer's hands, or looking on the floor reflectively. There was one woman among them, neither young or old, but singularly plain and eccentrically dressed. She appeared absorbed in the perusal of a letter. But they all wore an expression which seemed to Johns so peculiarly intense and eager, that he reflected, "they take it seriously at all events."

It was a little time before his card was handed in—not until a clerk returned, whose duty it seemed to be to arrange the interviews. And when, at length, after a long wait, his turn came, he was conducted to a room on the other side of the lengthy passage.

Here Dawson was seated at a desk in the middle of a spacious, though plainly-furnished room, reading the first edition of the *Planet* also. As he did not look up or make any sign to welcome him, Johns, after a moment's pause, said in his deep voice—

"Well, Mr. Dawson, I'm here."

The stout man started, and put down the paper.

"I hear you are," he said. "What is it that you really want?"

"I want to write, as I told you yesterday."

Dawson smiled.

"That's not done as easily as you imagine. Who are you? What are you? Where did you get your education, and what do you fancy you can do for us? Tell me as quickly as you can, because I'm busy."

"My name you know. At present I'm not anything in particular. I was educated at Guernsey College, and I can do whatever there is to do."

Dawson adjusted his glasses, and inspected Johns anew. Then he said, "It's quite unusual for me to see would-be contributors, but as you appear to have some sort of an idea that you can do something, I suppose I must take you in to Mr. Boyd. *He'll* pretty soon get your measure."

Upon this Dawson rose, and requested Johns to follow him. They re-crossed the passage, passed through the ante-room again, and then into the editor's room, through a baize-covered door.

This was a long wood-panelled chamber, with a skylight in the ceiling. A middle-aged, somewhat red-faced man, with a short light beard, sat at the head of a long table. He was looking at a golf stick which a younger man, with rather long dark hair and a shaven upper lip, was showing him. Two others—young also—of the journalistic stamp, better dressed than those whom Johns had seen in the ante-room, were apparently engaged in a discussion. Book-shelves, filled with books, ran around the room, and on a side-table stood four empty glasses which diffused an odour of stale spirits, mingling with a combined smell of paper, printer's ink, tobacco—a curious indefinable smell, peculiar to the offices of journals.

Dawson said, addressing the editor at the head of the table—

"Here's a man, Boyd, I wish you'd try. He fancies he can work for us—says he can do anything."

The editor put down the golf club, and said discontentedly, "But we're full—ten times over."

"I know we are, but we're not so crammed with excellence that we couldn't dispense with one or two if we found better. I didn't know whether he might or might not be useful. At all events, I would be glad if you would ascertain."

The last words sounded somewhat like an order, and so the editor, visibly annoyed, and looking at Johns for the first time, said carelessly—

"Very well, then, will you be good enough to write me, say, a column on Parker's Education Bill. We slate the Board."

Johns, who had not followed English questions closely in Australia, neither knew who Parker was nor what his Education Bill might be; but he answered promptly, "Certainly," adding immediately, "I'll slate the Board."

Then, as he was preparing to withdraw, Boyd said, turning to one of the young men who had ceased talking, and were looking at Johns—

"Coulston, would you mind showing Mr. Johns to the reporters' room?"

Johns asked, "Do you wish me to write it in the office?"

"I should prefer it."

Seeing that there was no alternative, Johns expressed his readiness to follow Coulston, and they withdrew together.

The reporters' rooms were on the floor above, and as they ascended the stairs, Coulston, a short, stoutish man, of about thirty, with a round face and light, curly hair, remarked, "I suppose you're new to this sort of thing?"

Johns answered with assurance, "No; four years on the *Melbourne News*."

"Indeed," said Coulston, with consideration. "Are you an Australian?"

"No, I'm English. What is your position on the paper?"

"Sub-editor."

They had reached the reporters' room. This was a long, bare room, somewhat resembling a class-room in a school, with a leather-covered table in the centre, at which four individuals of unkempt appearance were writing as if for life, bending over the paper, their arms spread upon the table. One of them was wearing an Inverness cape and a soft felt hat, as if he had come in to write a brief report and were going out again.

He alone looked up when Johns and Coulston entered.

"Take a seat here," said Coulston, pointing to a vacant chair, and I'll send you in some paper. If you want Boyd to like your 'stuff' you'd better make it strong."

Saying this, he left, and a boy in uniform, a moment afterwards, brought the paper.

Johns sat looking at the sheet of foolscap, wondering what he was going to fill it with. His mind was a complete blank upon the subject of Parker's Education Bill, and it was very evident that he couldn't draw on his imagination. He must either confess his ignorance or ask assistance of one of the four reporters so fanatically busy. Of course, he might have told the editor at once that he was unacquainted with the question, but it would have made a bad impression at the outset, and that must be avoided at all costs. He did not take a pen lest the four reporters should notice his hesitation; but he leaned back in his chair and twisted his moustache as if he were focusing his thoughts, though he knew very well that if he reflected until midnight he would find nothing to say about Parker's Bill. He must be put upon the track by someone. But by whom? The four reporters did not seem helpful people, and they were eyeing him suspiciously, every now and then, as they dipped their pens into the ink.

Just as he was beginning to think the situation rather desperate, a man entered with a Wellingtonian type of face. He was slight, and rather short, though dignified, with a kind of secretarial air, and he was wearing a long frock coat. Johns recognised him as the old man who had directed him to the ante-room on his arrival.

"Some more little jobs for you, my boys," he said to the reporters, who, upon his entrance, had immediately looked up. "Maskelyne, you've got to go to the Millwall docks to do the strike. Boyd wants *you*, Thomas, to interview Prince Hanawaï, who's staying at Long's Hotel. There's a guinea for the interpreter if you can find one. You, Simson, must go to Islington to do the Cattle. There, you won't complain of slackness now."

"No," said Maskelyne, the gentleman with the Inverness cape, "it's always like that. Nothing to do one day, and twice too much the next."

"Work, my friend, and don't grumble, and bless your stars that you've got the work to do. Take me as an example. I'm going to work right on to the very end. Why? Because I respect my body, and the bits of gold I get here allow me to keep it clean and nourished. If they ceased to-morrow I should become an animal, feeding upon garbage. No, no, you can take my advice for it, my boys, work is the only chance we have."

Saying this, he left.

"He's in one of his moralising fits to-day," said Maskelyne, and the others acquiesced.

"I beg your pardon," said Johns, "but who is that old gentleman?"

"That's old Tarte."

"Is that his real name?"

"Yes, we have no nicknames here. They're not allowed."

Johns rose and went out quickly. Descending the flight of stairs rapidly, he overtook the moralist just as he was entering his room.

"Mr. Tarte," he said, "I would like to speak to you."

"Step in, sir, step in."

"Do you know anything about Parker's Education Bill?"

"My dear sir, of course I do. Who doesn't?"

"Well, I don't mind telling you that I'm in the dark, having just come over from Australia, and as I'm going to write about that Bill, I want some help. If you will give me a hint or two, I shall be obliged to you, and depend upon it, I'll remember it, especially if you don't tell anyone you helped me."

Tarte smiled.

"Don't make promises, young man. They're never kept. Boyd's trying you, I suppose."

"That's it."

"Well, I'm always ready to do a good turn. Parker is the member for North Aldgate, and he brought in a bill the other day to reform the Board and to give the little urchins more to learn. Of course, they've far too much already; but then we're Radicals who cry for progress, and we side with Parker. Do you understand?"

"Perfectly."

"Here's an article about it by Boyd himself, and here's what was said in the House last night. Now you can set to work."

Johns seized the cuttings eagerly, and feeling himself on the right track now, he thanked Tarte hurriedly, and left.

But as he did not want the reporters to see how he got his information, he stopped upon the stairs and read the extracts carefully, repeating the names of the men who had taken a part in the debate so that he might fix them in his memory. When he had done this, he went on to the landing, and there he tarried a few minutes longer to reflect upon what he was going to say. Then, when he had decided, he re-entered the reporters' room, resumed his seat at the table, and began to write.

Having been a schoolmaster, the subject of education was familiar to him, and now that he possessed his facts, it was not long before he had filled three sheets singularly free from errors or erasures. Parker's scheme, he wrote, was perhaps the most perfect model of legislative skill that had ever been invented. It provided for the boy from the budding of his intellect to the age of adolescence, when it left him fitted for every walk for which he had capacity or taste. The greatness of a nation consisted in the place it held in the van of progress, and England, if she wished to retain her place at the head of nations, should spend more on public education than any other country. The result would be an increased measure of advancement. It was ridiculous to fix a limit to gratuitous instruction, which must be free to extend and to develop to the utmost. If it was the duty of the citizen to educate the children of the citizen, who could say that that duty ended when a mere modicum of learning had been bestowed? And it was not entirely upon the public that the increased expenditure would fall. It must be partly met by an increased economy in the administration of the funds, and in an entire reconstruction of the Board, who had shown themselves to be hopeless blunderers of the worst stamp it was ever the misfortune of education to be burdened with. All this must be changed, and Parker was the man to do it.

After a great deal more in the same strain, he put down his pen and read his article. It pleased him, for he thought it clear and trenchant. The slating of the Board was about as forcible as he could make it. One adjective only he thought it necessary to change, finding it too strong.

Then he put the sheets together with the air of a man

who has done creditable work; while the reporters, who by this time were preparing to leave, glanced at him curiously.

The next thing to be done was to take his manuscript to Boyd, and he started for the purpose. He found Coulston in the ante-room, giving directions to the clerk.

"The editor's gone out," said Coulston, "but you can give me your 'stuff,' and I'll show it to him when he returns. It's too late for to-day, you know, even if it were golden."

Johns handed him the little roll, remarking carelessly, "You needn't be afraid of it—*it's good*. I'll call again to-morrow."

Then he returned to Grafton Street, and spent the remainder of the afternoon in his bed-room, reading a packet of journals he had brought to study their contents. In the evening he dined at a cheap Italian restaurant in the Tottenham Court Road.

CHAPTER SECOND

THE next morning Johns reached the Strand shortly before mid-day, just as the first editions of the evening papers were making their appearance in the streets, and the news-boys were proclaiming them in cavernous and strident tones. The *Star*, the *Evening News*, the *Globe* were being borne in piles upon the backs of ragged urchins, some of whom were racing with each other in their eagerness to reach a favoured corner first. The *Planet* was late that morning, and Johns, as he looked for it, felt his pulse beat faster. Either it contained his article or it did not, and for the moment his prospects were considerably bound up in that. He entered a tobacconist's, bought a cigar and lit it, and as he was leaving, he perceived a man hurrying down the street with a bundle of papers under his arm, holding the contents bill of the *Planet* before him like an apron. Johns made a sign to him to stop, and bought a copy. Then, with a frown to defy disappointment, he opened it, and the first article which caught his eye was *Retrogressive Education*—his own article printed in large type on the front page.

He gave a little whistle, and suddenly became conscious of a sense of increased importance. New vistas seemed to open, new possibilities to dawn. He had got his foot in the stirrup of the horse he meant to ride! How he would ride that horse!

"They must have thought it deuced good," he said, "to put it first."

As he walked along smoking his cigar, he read his article, noticing with satisfaction that it had been printed as he wrote it, without a single alteration, and pleased with its composition which struck him as forcible and clear. Journalism seemed to him an excellent profession.

He walked down one side of the Strand and up another, feeling that he had already played a part in the general activity by providing literary food that day for thousands. When he reached the office he entered it with a firm step, as if his place in it was now assured. In the corridor, he met Coulston, who said at once, "You see, we've printed you. Our leader man dried up, and so we shoved you in. I suppose you want to see the editor?"

"I do," said Johns, without noticing the first part of Coulston's sentence.

"Then step in there."

Johns entered the ante-room and took a seat. Several of the callers were reading the *Planet*, and the one next to him, his article on Parker's Bill. He felt conscious of a certain feeling of superiority over the crowd of postulants, a superiority acquired since his visit of the day before, and he was inclined to say to his neighbour, "*I* wrote that column, and I flatter myself it's good. I mean to write a great many more in the same style." But he refrained, and said, as soon as the visitor had finished, "What, sir, do you think of *that* article?"

The reader looked up at Johns suspiciously, with a slight start, and said, with an acidulated smile, "I should call it startling, most decidedly."

"Yes," said Johns, "it *is* startling. The public requires to be startled."

His neighbour replied with a smile of incredulity, and Johns thought, "the fool's jealous."

After he had waited a long time, and the ante-room showed no signs of emptying by calls from the editorial room, Johns, whose patience was exhausted, went out to look for Tarte. He found him seated before his table, engaged in the vague kind of paper-sorting which seemed to constitute his usual employment.

"Well," said Tarte, "what can I do for you to-day?"

"You can take me in to Boyd. I want to see him about my article."

"What article?"

"The one I spoke to you about yesterday. Surely you read the paper; it's on the front page!"

Tarte smiled.

"Ah, my friend, when you've journalized for a few years, you'll find that one doesn't trouble one's mind with too much reading. Life is a poor little game for scribblers, and we must make the best of it! So they put you in, did they?"

"Yes; and, as I don't care to stay in the ante-room all the afternoon, I want you to take me in."

"Well, I've no objection. I'll take you in to Cæsar."

Saying this, he rose and led Johns to the editorial room by a private door.

Boyd, whose face was redder than the day before, was dictating to a female typist with a pretty face and delicate, tapering fingers. A large empty glass stood on the table at his side.

Tarte said, apologetically, "I've brought in Mr. Johns, who would like to say a word to you."

"Well, sir," said Boyd, turning his red, moist eyes on Johns; "you wrote a damned bad article for the paper yesterday."

Johns felt the blood rise quickly to his face, and longed to strangle the brutish editor, but he restrained his temper with an effort, and replied—

"Pardon me, it was good enough for the front page."

For a moment the two men looked at each other, measuring each other. Boyd glanced down first.

"If you knew why you appeared in that position," he replied, "you wouldn't be quite so pleased with your performance. But that's nothing to do with the question. You want to know what you are to do. If you wish to work for us, you must join the reporters' staff."

"The reporters' staff?" repeated Johns, concealing his disappointment with great difficulty.

"Yes, the reporters' staff. You didn't imagine you were going to fill the first page *every* day, did you?"

Johns saw that there was nothing for it but to submit. Evidently Dawson had instructed Boyd to make the offer, such as it was, and his chief aim, after all, was to gain a footing.

He answered, "Very well then, Mr. Boyd, I will."

Upon this the editor went on dictating without taking any further notice of the new reporter. Tarte, however, who had been listening, touched Johns upon the arm, and made a sign to him to follow. As soon as they were in the corridor he said, "It's the old story. You've done something good, and they want to let you down. Sublime humanity, dear sir, is constituted so."

Johns said, "They'll find, maybe, that they're mistaken."

He now applied himself to win the friendship of Maskelyne by inviting him, two days following, to a wine shop in the Strand, where wines from the wood were served, and by amusing him with stories of his adventures—stories which he told well, and with a kind of humour somewhat in the manner of Mark Twain. At first Maskelyne was reticent, but at length he yielded to the fascination which Johns, when he liked, was able to exercise, and he was soon willing to impart his knowledge. Thus he confided to Johns the best methods of obtaining interviews, and the ablest means of keeping the interviewed from wandering, and of leading him on by apt suggestion to clear and pertinent replies.

Some of them, he said, were difficult to tap, and even when tapped afforded but a poor result. Others gave more than was required. Then there were those who thought interviewing an impertinence, and who hadn't realised that they could say just what they liked, and create exactly the impression which they chose upon the public. These must be delicately told that a strict adherence to the truth was by no means indispensable. Again, there was the great question of obtaining interviews with exalted or busy people who had no interest in publicity. Opinions were divided as to the way to deal with them. Some thought it better to "plump" down on them just as they were leaving home or reaching it, others preferred to send an eloquently-worded letter before calling, in the paper's name. But the characters of interviewables were so divergent that no rules could be well laid down. Sometimes a man would prefer to write the interview with himself, himself, and in such cases it was wise to let him. It saved time and trouble, even paper.

"I've always had a great ambition to do a king," said Maskelyne; "but in kings I never got beyond a nigger. No one ever has. But that nigger was the only man I ever found who spoke the truth! You've no idea how people lie before a note-book. But I can't be telling you anything you didn't know before. You must have seen all this in the *Melbourne News*."

"No," said Johns, with gravity, "I wrote leaders only."

The next day Maskelyne, over a second glass of port, was in a particularly communicative mood, and Johns asked him what he knew of Dawson.

"Dawson," he answered, "was once a wholesale grocer in Upper Thames Street, who retired with a fortune and bought the paper for a song from the man who started it. He's the nearest file on earth. He's had a machine made for him, which we call the columetre, to measure printed matter almost to a pennyworth. Only a few years ago the old devil married a pretty girl, and it won't be long before he gets into Parliament. So you see what grocery can do."

Johns listened carefully to Maskelyne, and before a week was over, he possessed all the information that he needed—he had taken, as he himself expressed it, all his bearings. Unfortunately, although he was nominally upon the staff, he was without fixed salary, his earnings depending wholly on the number of the "jobs" that were given him to do. But as those that fell to his share during the first fortnight did not exceed two—a brief report of an Exeter Hall meeting and an account of a prize fight held at Islington; and as these, measured by the columetre, represented little more than half a sovereign, he began to feel that he was being trifled with, and he suspected that Boyd was trying to discourage him by giving him as little work as possible. It was irritating to sit all day in the reporters' room and to see himself passed by in the distribution of the work, and he was determined that he would not stand it. He had made several attempts to have an interview with Dawson, but the great man was always busy, and referred him to the editor, who was even busier. When he spoke to Coulston about his want of work, Coulston told him that new men always had to wait.

"And supposing they starve in the meanwhile?" Johns said, bluntly.

"That's *their* business," was the answer.

The reporters also were beginning to smile when Johns entered the room; but he fixed one of them one morning as he caught him in the act, and the expression of his face was so much like that of a bull-dog about to spring that the scribe desisted quickly. To make matters worse, Tarte, for some reason he did not explain, had expressed himself unable to introduce Johns again to the editorial room. In fine, the situation was intolerable.

One afternoon, however, as he was leaving the office, resolved to assert himself in some way the next day, and to either obtain more recognition or else "chuck the thing" altogether, he saw a landau stopped before the office door, and in it a lady whom he at once recognised as the wife of the proprietor—the lady who had smiled encouragingly that evening at the Berkeley. She was reading, and was evidently waiting for her husband. Johns reflected for a moment. He had been accusing his luck pretty harshly for the last few days, but suddenly he felt inclined to bless it. A woman, young and pretty, to whom he had a right to speak! What could be more fortunate? A door seemed opened to him at once.

Buttoning his coat, because it looked fresher so, and ascertaining that his necktie was in place, he stepped forward to the carriage door and raised his hat. The lady looked up enquiringly, and as soon as she recognised him, gave him a little nod.

He said, somewhat deferentially, "I trust you have been well, Mrs. Dawson, since we met."

"Oh, quite well, thank you," she replied, smiling blandly.

But he fixed his penetrating gaze upon her, and, before it, she looked down. Then, in the deep tone that lent a strange importance to the most commonplace of his remarks, he said—

"It is not often you grace us with a visit!"

"As it was so fine to-day," she answered, "I thought I would call and take my husband for a drive."

"Yes," he said, earnestly, "to-day there is a fine, clear sky in London, a sky which reminds me of the pure blue stretches of Australia, where life is vigorous and free."

"You're fond of Australia, I see."

"Yes, fond of it for its vastness and its beauty; but glad to return to England, where beauty in its human form is so complete." And, as he said this, he looked at her admiringly.

"Really," she said, laughing, "you are appreciative. And yet, I thought the Australian ladies ——"

He shook his head, and, waving his hand deprecatingly, exclaimed—

"Comparison is quite impossible!"

She laughed again, and, closing her book, smoothed the folds of her brown cloth dress upon her knee. As she did so, he observed her well, deciding in his mind that her face was fairly pretty, although the nose was a little long and the lips a little pale. Upon the whole, though, an attractive blonde, whom he judged to be about thirty.

"My husband told me you had joined the paper," she said presently; "I hope you like it."

"Charming," he replied, "skilfully conducted—admirable."

"I hope, then, that we shall see you soon at Princes Gate. I'm 'at home' on Sundays."

He said, with fervency, "I will not fail to call"; and as he judged that he had prolonged the interview sufficiently, and produced a good effect, he raised his hat again and bowed impressively.

This meeting seemed to him to alter the position of affairs. He had now a means of attack, which a few minutes before he certainly did not possess. For he did not doubt that in Mrs. Dawson he would find an ally, and women, he thought, were the surest channels of success.

As he walked along the Strand, he reflected that it was then Friday, and that Mrs. Dawson had said she would be at home on Sunday. He was quite determined he would go to see her; but he was confronted by a difficulty. The whole of his wardrobe was on his back, and a black coat was not included in it. It would be fatal to present himself in a suit of tweeds. What was to be done? His fortnight's living had reduced his little store by nearly half, and the *Planet* paid but once a month.

He stopped before the window of a cheap tailor and inspected its contents, although he knew that, to purchase even the cheapest garment ticketed, would have emptied his purse completely. And yet he *must* have a black coat somehow. Again he looked at the sartorial display in the large plate-glass window, in which coats of many shapes were stretched on blocks, without a crease or furrow, exhibiting an apparent excellence of cut, notwithstanding their excessive cheapness. Presently, without exactly knowing what he was going to say or do, he entered the establishment.

A man, with a coat as creaseless as the models in the window, and an air of bombastic half gentility, asked him what he might require.

"I want a coat, but to pay for one at once is not convenient ——"

"We only sell for cash," the tailor interrupted.

"Listen, my friend. I'm on the *Planet's* staff, as you will ascertain if you send a messenger to inquire at the office. If you let me have what I want, I'll manage a street accident near your shop, which will give you a thundering advertisement. Something like this: A gentleman fell, in an apoplectic fit, as he was entering the tailoring establishment of Messrs. Townsend Brothers, in the Strand, at whose hands he received every attention, and who were able, as he was a customer of theirs, to have him conveyed to his own home as soon as medical aid had been obtained."

The tailor thrust his thumbs into the armholes of his waistcoat, and remarked, "You're a 'cute one, there's no mistake about it, and I don't say we won't come to business. Give me your name, and my brother 'll go and ask about you,"

Johns gave his name, and an individual of the same type as his brother started for the office.

While he was gone, Johns smoked a cigarette. The tailor gave some finishing touches to the arrangement of his window blocks.

Presently the messenger returned, and whispered something to his partner, who then said—

"If we let you have the goods, we must have something down. How much can you pay?"

"Well, say ten shillings down."

The brothers consulted together, and informed Johns finally that if he would take a "misfit frock" he might have one on those terms.

Johns asked to see the garment, and he was brought a coat

of a somewhat ancient cut, though sufficiently presentable, which chanced to fit him fairly well. It was without a waistcoat, but, as long as it was kept buttoned, no one would be the wiser. He could wear his tweed vest and his trousers of the same.

The bargain was forthwith concluded, and Johns, after signing an acknowledgment and promising that the advertisement would appear soon, left the shop, carrying the coat in a brown paper parcel under his left arm. He counted this, as he walked home, as not the least piece of good fortune he had had that day. Now he was properly equipped for the visit to the Dawsons! He said nothing at the office the next day of what had happened, for he knew that none of the reporters were received at Princes Gate, and he thought it useless to excite jealousies too soon. But he told Maskelyne that in a week or so things would be going well for him.

When the Sunday came he stayed in bed, reading and smoking cigarettes, till mid-day. Then he dressed with extreme care, shaving closely. His coat, though large, looked well enough when it was pulled down from the waist, as he discovered by several trials before the glass in standing and sitting postures. Late the night before he had bought a tie, a pair of gloves, and cuffs from a hosier in New Oxford Street who was selling off, and he thought, as he surveyed himself for the last time before going out, that his appearance was by no means bad. No doubt his low soft hat did not quite suit the costume: he would have to leave it in the hall.

He dined or lunched—the two meals were generally merged —for eighteenpence at the Italian restaurant in Tottenham Court Road, where he was becoming a well-known if not too profitable customer.

He had no experience of society in England, and he was not quite sure at what hour calls were generally paid, but he judged that it could scarcely be amiss if he presented himself at four. As it was still early, he took an omnibus to Hyde Park, where he intended to kill some time.

Near to the entrance of the Marble Arch, where he alighted, he noticed several little crowds at a short distance from each other, and as his curiosity was piqued, he stopped to see what was taking place. In the first group a man, bareheaded, with a shaven upper lip and a dark beard, was preaching Christianity as a panacea against the evil consequences of sin. With great vehemence, though in faulty speech, he was flagellating those whose peccant natures kept them in the bondage of the evil one, and quoting text on text to prove the value of repentance. Close to him in the next group, so close that their voices sometimes mingled, an old man, with long white locks and an emaciated face, who seemed to have one foot in his grave, was preaching atheism, denying with as much warmth as his neighbour had asserted it the truth of supernatural belief, and acknowledging alone the evidence of sense. Johns listened to him for a few moments, but finding him no less fanatical than the evangelist, he passed on to a third. This was a negro, out of whose wide mouth poured excited words of Messianic praise, delivered with great gusto. He was listened to with marked attention by his audience, who laughed heartily every now and then at his jokes at the expense of Satan.

A little further on, a socialistic artizan was denouncing capital and monarchies, the misdeeds of the rich, the cruelties inflicted on the poor, and the tyranny of the employer; while almost back to back, yet a little further down the walk, a man in clerical attire was preaching the doctrine of the Trinity, next to a working man who had read Comte and Kant and Hegel, and who cried, "The man who says as what there *is* a God is as big a fool as the man who says there ain't."

A strange discordance caused Johns to turn his head in the direction of the groups he had first seen. The negro's followers and those of the evangelist had each struck up a different hymn, and the socialistic orator was shouting at the top of a stentorian voice, trying to be heard amid the discord. The audiences appeared to find the whole thing natural.

Johns, as he moved along across the park, reflected, "How they listen to any man who preaches! It doesn't matter what he says as long as he speaks loudly. And I'll bet they're the same in other spheres." He walked along slowly till he reached the Row, where he took a seat for a few moments to watch the promenaders, after which he pursued his way to Princes Gate.

As he came in sight of the imposing row of houses, with their high façades and ornamented windows, he cast a look at his attire, which somehow pleased him less than a few hours previously. Such as it was, however, it must suffice.

A man in livery opened the door and glanced at Johns somewhat suspiciously. "He did not know if Mrs. Dawson was at home. He would enquire. If so, what name should he announce?"

"Say Mr. Johns."

Requested to enter, Johns waited in a spacious hall. Presently the man returned, and, with more consideration than he had shown at first, conducted him to the drawing-room, up a monumental staircase with bronze statues in the niches of the wall. The wife of the proprietor of the *Planet* was seated before a tea-table in a corner of a large, square room, which seemed to Johns sumptuously furnished. She was surrounded by a little ring of visitors, one or two of whom Johns recognised as frequent callers at the office.

With the air of grave importance which he knew how to assume at times, holding his gloves in his left hand, he advanced leisurely into the room as soon as he had been announced.

Mrs. Dawson received him cordially, and pointed to a seat not far from hers. Then, turning to a thin, young man, with longish hair and a shaven face, she said, "You can continue, Mr. Stevenson."

"The place of woman in our social system," the young man said, "is growing more and more defined. She is no longer an eleemosynary, fettered to the will of man, but a free agent in the disposal of her person and in the employment of her intellect. Under the new conditions which are rapidly extending, the whole fabric of conjugal ethics will be changed. Woman will be man's equal instead of his inferior. She will bring into the life of the family a co-operation hitherto unknown. She will be a second pillar of the household, supporting the same burdens as her husband. In this way there will be a double capital of will and intellect, and the children of such marriages must be the men and women who will guide the world. Does it not stand to reason that, as the true province of woman is to guard and to protect the race, she cannot do so properly unless she has the free exercise of all her faculties? The Mahommedans have centred the seat of understanding in the male, and have assigned a purely utilitarian place to women. In that they are consistent; but we, who have throughout our system allowed her to have a share with us, are we justified in limiting that share? No; depend upon it, justice will not be done until we have given her an equal share with us."

There was a murmur of approbation as the young man finished his defence of the woman's cause, and he leaned back in his chair with an air of satisfaction. The ladies present, all fashionably dressed and mostly young, looked puzzled, as if they were not quite convinced.

"For my part," said an older man, who looked like a professor, "I think that Mr. Stevenson's remarks are just. It seems to me that the complete enfranchisement of women is naturally predestined by the developmental principle. The position of women must inevitably alter as her capacities are recognised. How long she may have to wait, however, it is difficult to say."

"I don't fancy *I* mind waiting," said a lady with an olive-tinted skin and dark eyes and hair, and the other ladies laughed.

But Mrs. Dawson asked, "And what is *your* opinion, Mr Johns, of our province?"

Johns had been listening attentively to what was being said. Mentally he had voted the thin young champion of the woman's cause a fool, and the man with the professional air a pedant. He had made up his mind that, if his views were asked, he would preach another kind of doctrine.

So he said, "The province of woman is above all things to charm. She is the first incentive to our acts. Since man is man, we have hoped and feared and fought for her. Her beauty is the salt without which we could not live. Her grace and charm are the perfumes which give zest to life and keep us from *ennui*. No one has imagined anything more beautiful than woman's beauty, because nature has none greater, and that beauty is preserved to us by giving woman an exceptional position, by relieving her from the drudgery we do, by affording her the ease and comfort in which to cultivate her charms, by allowing her to rest while we are working, by placing her upon a pedestal, and by contemplating her delightfully upon it. I do not know what woman's brains can do, but I *do* know that if she uses them as we do ours, she will lose a large share of the beauty which we love. There will be lines upon her countenance; the oval of her face will be impaired. We shall grow cold towards her, and then—why, then, we shall retrograde, because the divine spirit of enchantment will have passed away from us. The poetry which decked our lives will have vanished from them. The poets, if there be any left, will only sing of wisdom, *and we shall come to hate that word!* Ah no, the province of a woman is to bring joy into the life of man, and you may depend upon it she will be well employed in doing so."

Before Johns had finished speaking, all eyes were turned upon him. His deep voice, the earnest expression of his face, and his unexpected views, had created an impression.

The ladies, whom he had rightly judged, from their appearance, to be contented with the present state of marriage, clapped their hands, while the thin young man and the professor endeavoured to look sceptical.

"How charming of you, Mr. Johns," the hostess said, " to defend our indolence!"

"And how good of you to place us on a pedestal!" the dark-eyed lady added.

Johns answered, asking, "Was I not especially inspired to do that this afternoon?"

"Let me introduce you," Mrs. Dawson said, "to my friend Mrs. Weber," and John bowed to the dark lady, who was smiling at the compliment conveyed by his last words.

But the thin young man returned to his guns, to the evident regret of everyone.

He said, "We know this cult of beauty well. It softened the Greeks and killed the Romans. It has permanently demoralized the French. Fortunately, in England we have known how to give it the place it merits. The future of society depends upon the raising of the state of woman."

"It seems to me," said Johns, "that the future of society depends upon the maintenance of love."

"And do you say that love will disappear?"

"I say that it will freeze—freeze, sir, in your refrigerator."

Again the ladies laughed approvingly, and the champion of their cause, perceiving that their suffrages by this time were with Johns, gave up the discussion, and went on speaking to the professor.

Johns was now introduced to the other ladies by Mrs. Dawson, and as she explained that he had lived for some time in Australia, they asked him questions about the life and manners there, which he was naturally well able to reply to.

"Australia," he said, "is a land of adventurous romance. A man out there is rated for his strength and pluck, and though he may sometimes have to rough it, he always finds a friend in need when his luck's bad. Ah, one has a fine sense of the intensity, the vigour, the masterfulness of life when one's in the saddle from morning until night, in the thin, pure air. Sometimes I have almost wished I had been born a native."

Johns had a power of investing what he said with interest. When he was speaking, the expression of his face, the intonation of his voice, and the gestures with which he accompanied his speech, conspired to produce an effect upon the hearer which was indefinable, but real.

As he finished his last phrases, he looked towards the window at the London clouds, as if he almost hoped to find in them a reminiscence of Australian skies.

"How I should like to go there!" said the young lady, sighing.

"But it isn't always paradise," continued Johns, "for those who come from England. I remember once in Queensland a young couple came into a little town where I was staying. He was a handsome boy of twenty, with a frank and manly face, and she, a pretty little bright-eyed girl, perhaps a twelvemonth younger. And they had loved each other in an English country town, and married, and had come to seek their fortune in Australia. He was a tax-collector's son, and she, the daughter of a miller. And they had both a little education and some pride. And he had spent a month in Melbourne trying to get work in offices, and failed. And they had spent all their money. And they would not beg, and they found no work to do. Suddenly they disappeared and were forgotten, till, one day, a boy found a couple tied together drowned in a pool on the Burnett river. Poor little English lovers!"

"Poor things!" the ladies said, compassionately and in chorus.

While Johns had been speaking, he noticed that the eyes of the dark lady had been fixed upon him with that meditative look which women have when they are weighing in their minds a man's attractiveness, so he preserved his air of quiet pathos, finding it had been well received that afternoon. Mentally he compared the hostess and her friend, coming to the conclusion that both were interesting.

But other callers came, and the physiognomy of the drawing-room changed. Johns thought it time to retire upon the good impression he had made.

When he rose to leave, however, Mrs. Dawson asked—

"Wouldn't you like to see my husband?"

"I would, assuredly."

"Then stay. I am expecting him home from the club soon."

Thus invited, Johns asked no better than to remain, especially as he wanted very much to see the proprietor in person.

Gradually the room emptied. Mrs. Weber, as she left, gave Johns her hand, remarking—

"We shall meet again, perhaps."

"I trust so, most sincerely."

Johns was left alone with Mrs. Dawson, who said presently—

"I can't think what keeps my husband. He is generally back before."

"As long as his absence procures me a chat with *you*, Mrs. Dawson, I shall not be impatient."

She gave a little laugh.

"Do you know," she said, "you spoke well this afternoon, and I fancy you made an impression on Mrs. Weber. I was quite of your opinion. I'm sure, for my part, I think our lot delightful."

"Delightful," Johns repeated, as he was fond of doing when he wished to mark his appreciation, "delightful!"

While she had been speaking, he was saying to himself, "Thirty, and not bad looking. A little coquetterie, and an old husband. Apparently no children.

"And do you still like the *Planet?*" she asked presently, as if to show that she took an interest in his career.

Here, he thought, was his opportunity. Bending forward in his chair, he said, "Mrs. Dawson, it is in your power to do me a great service. My position on the paper is untenable. I am relegated to the reporters' room and kept there almost unemployed. Now, I didn't come over from Australia for this. I must have a better place or leave. And I should be sorry to leave, very sorry, after this afternoon, when I have had so charming an opportunity of knowing and esteeming you. I have not been able to see Mr. Dawson, and I don't think he knows how I am being treated. May I not count on your support?"

"Of course you may; I'll speak to my husband this very evening."

"*Will* you do that for me? *Will* you *really?*" and he laid a stress of admiration on the "will" and "really."

"Certainly."

"*How* good of you!"

"Not at all. I know how Mr. Boyd is fond of treating people."

"What sort of a man is Mr. Boyd?"

"I mustn't say; but he isn't to my taste."

Johns hazarded—

"His face is rather red."

"Yes," she said, significantly—"*very.*"

"But how shall I thank you," he continued, returning to his theme; "how shall I express my gratitude?" and he looked at her with almost tearful sympathy.

She answered, laughing, "By coming to see me on Sunday afternoons."

"There could not be a more delightful way."

They were silent for a moment, until they heard the noise of a cab driving up to the front door.

She rose and went over to the window.

"Yes, it's he; I'm going to meet him in the hall. Stay where you are."

Johns, left alone in the drawing-room, looked about him at the heavy hangings on the doors and windows, at the sumptuous chairs and lounges, at the bronzes and the nicknacks on the shelves and in the niches. He thought how pleasant it must be to be the owner of such things, and to live one's life amid such beautiful surroundings! A little patience, and perhaps ——

It was several moments before the husband and wife appeared. Dawson shook hands with Johns heartily.

"I read your article the other day," he said, "and found it good."

Johns expressed his satisfaction. "I am only sorry," he said, "that it has not been the means of bringing me more work. I'm not given any work worth mentioning."

Dawson reflected for a moment. Then he said, "Come and see me to-morrow morning, and I'll try to put that right for you."

"Thanks," Johns said, "I will."

And then, as it was growing late, and Mrs. Dawson looked as if she were waiting for him to go, he took leave of them, expressing his thanks to her by a look as he shook hands.

When he reached the hall, where the man handed him his hat, there was a strong odour of good cooking, and he thought, "Why couldn't the old devil have invited me to dinner?"

Still, as he walked along towards Hyde Park Corner for the second time, he fancied he had done pretty well for himself that afternoon. He was delighted to have an ally in Mrs. Dawson. Go to her "at homes" on Sunday? Of course he would. He would like to confront a dozen pale young men with theories about the enfranchisement of women. "The fool," he said, "as if any but ugly women trouble about their rights! But I suppose it suits his game to talk like that. It suited mine, at anyrate, to contradict him."

It was dusk when he reached the Corner, and rain was beginning to fall heavily. This annoyed him, for his umbrella was very full of holes, and he had left his overcoat at home. There was a quickening of the traffic and a rush for cabs and omnibuses, and he stood in the midst of it, asking himself what he should do next.

Evidently he must restore his inner man, so, after a great deal of elbowing, he succeeded in conquering a place in an eastward-going 'bus, which conveyed him to the corner of New Oxford Street. Alighting there, he took a sandwich and a "bock" at the bar of a hotel in the vicinity by way of dinner; and then, as the downpour had abated, he walked slowly home.

As he entered his lodgings, he saw a light in the room of the lady who occupied the ground floor, and as he passed her door he paused. He had made her acquaintance on the stairs a few days previously, and he thought this might be an opportunity of improving it.

As he heard no sound, and the door was ajar, he knocked. A woman's voice replied, "Come in."

A fair-haired girl was sitting at a table in a little parlour divided from a bedroom by folding doors. She was reading by the pale light of a jet of gas.

"Oh, it's you," she said, "Come in."

He looked at her in the faint light. Her face was still fresh and almost pretty. She seemed to be scarcely twenty.

"I'm glad you've come," she said. "I was feeling lonely by myself to-night."

"So was I," he said, taking a seat beside her, "very."

"Then we can console each other," she said, smiling. "I'm going to have supper, and if you like to join me ——"

He said, "I'd better tell you I'm down on my luck just now, and so it must be all for love. But I'll make up for it later."

She looked at him inquiringly as if trying to guess if he spoke the truth; but he had assumed his earnest air, and, apparently convinced, she said, "So many gentlemen are like that! But it doesn't matter if you like to stay."

He supped with her, and it was daylight before he left.

CHAPTER THIRD

WHEN Johns asked to see Dawson the next morning at the office, he was admitted almost instantly to the private room, and the proprietor received him much more cordially than on his former visit.

"So you want to push on, I hear," he said, scrutinizing him as if he had not seen him properly before.

"That is my wish, most certainly."

"Well, you can easily understand that we can't give you leaders to do every day, whether you are able or not to do them. There are other men to be considered. But, if you care to stick to the reporting for the present, I'll see that you get more of it in future. I've already spoken to Mr. Boyd about you."

"My dear sir, I'm ready to do anything on earth. I'll *do* the reporting, and I prophesy that you'll soon find it to your advantage to give me better work."

"Good," said Dawson; "we shall see."

Johns now entered the reporters' room with a different feeling to that which he had hitherto experienced, and he said to Maskelyne carelessly, in the hearing of the others, "It's all right now, I've just seen Dawson."

And the work was not long coming, for the same morning Tarte, in apportioning the tasks by the editor's instructions, told Johns he was to interview a French exiled politician. Johns, who was a good French scholar, managed, by applying the hints he had obtained from Maskelyne, and by exercising ingenuity, to obtain an interview, and to write an account of his conversation which was fairly creditable, although it contained one or two errors of inexperience, which Boyd corrected with something like an oath when Johns handed him the "copy."

THE ADVENTURES OF JOHN JOHNS 35

A few mornings afterwards, when he reached the office, a letter was awaiting him. On opening it, he found that it was an invitation from Mrs. Dawson to dinner for the next evening.

At first, the sight of the card containing a few words in a large handwriting in which the wife of the proprietor "hoped he would be able to come," filled him with delight; but when he reflected a moment afterwards that he would have to find a suit of clothes for the occasion, his joy was somewhat marred. He could not go to the Strand tailors again, and to buy all the articles he wanted outright was impossible, seeing that he would not be paid for a week or more, and that Dawson never allowed advances. Well, he would get out of that difficulty, he supposed, somehow, and if it came to the worst, he would have to hire the apparel for the evening.

He found Maskelyne in the reporters' room, and handed him the note he had just received. When Maskelyne read it, he exclaimed, "lucky person," and turning to the reporters, said, "Here's a man who hasn't been on the paper a month, and he's invited to dine with the Dawsons." The two scribes who were in the room glanced at Johns with a half indifferent, half antagonistic look—one of those looks which drudges have for those who rise above them.

"I wonder," thought Johns, "if Maskelyne possesses a dress suit. Yes, he must, else how could he report banquets?" But when he measured him with a rapid glance, he soon decided that the reporter not only was too tall, but also much too thin for there to be any likelihood of his clothes fitting him. Besides, to have borrowed from him would have exposed the bareness of the land, and he thought that it was unwise to be too frank about one's means. Another combination must be found, and he resolved to seek it.

The next morning, having discovered no solution to the problem, he explored the shops in the vicinity of Covent Garden until he found a costumier who, for the deposit of a pound—the last he had left—supplied him with a complete outfit, exclusive of a shirt, which he was forced to buy at a hosier's in the Strand, thus reducing his resources to a perilously low ebb. He was slightly comforted, however, by the reflection that he was owed a little money by the paper: he must manage to hold out on half rations until it became due. In the evening, after his work was over, he called for his parcels and carried them to Grafton Street.

Many times after he had dressed that evening, he surveyed himself in the little looking-glass which had lost a portion of its plating. The coat shone, and was rather tight in several places, but rub the shoes as he might, he could not make the patent leather shine, and yet, the general effect, he thought, was good. By gas-light it might pass muster. He deemed himself presentable.

It was the first time he had put on a dress coat, and he flattered himself that no one could ever have guessed the fact. "I shall be taken for a rich man indifferent about his dress," he thought. "As to the women, I don't believe they care a fig how a man dresses—if he pleases them."

By a succession of omnibus routes, which he was obliged to take to avoid soiling his shoes, he arrived at Princes Gate at a little before eight, and was shown at once into the drawing-room.

The hostess, in black satin, received him almost as an old acquaintance.

There were few people in the room, and she was speaking to Boyd, who appeared surprised when he saw Johns.

She said, "Mr. Boyd, I need not introduce Mr. Johns to you. By this time, I am quite sure, he is not only a colleague but a friend."

Boyd tried to smile, and said, with some consideration, "Good evening, Mr. Johns. We meet again."

Johns thought, "To your disgust, my friend," but he said, glancing at Mrs. Dawson, "Yes, and under charming auspices."

Dawson himself came up at this juncture, and Johns shook hands with him.

Then, as the hostess was busy receiving fresh arrivals, he crossed to the other side of the room, where he had noticed Mrs. Weber sitting.

"I was wondering," she said, "if you would remember me."

"My memory would have been abominable if I had not," he answered.

"Do you know many of the people here?" she asked.

"Scarcely any of them; pray tell me who they are."

"Well, there is a rather curious medley of letters and finance, and law and politics. Mrs. Dawson likes to have her dinner-table well divided. And I think she's right. One element tones the other down. Do you see that couple coming in?"

"Yes."

"That's the member for North Aldgate and his wife, née the Honourable Sophia Curton. I never understood how they settle their politics, but they manage to get along very well apparently. He's a great man among the radicals."

Johns said, "I'll make a point of speaking to them. I've written about that gentleman; his name is Parker."

"Then, that little man yonder who looks contented with himself is a socialist—not of the desperate type, you know—an artistic and luxurious socialist. Another contradiction as you see. Then, the thin lady in green velvet is a journalist or a literary lady of some sort. Do you like literary ladies?"

"Are you literary?"

"No, of course not."

"Then, I don't mind confessing that I cannot bear them."

Mrs. Weber laughed, showing a set of pearly teeth.

"Near them on the right," she said, "is Mr. Stevenson, the young man whom you rather sat upon the other day. He's the editor of a paper called *The Woman's Cause*, and is considered clever in his way, although you mayn't think so."

"I do, I do, exceedingly."

"Sarcastic?"

"Never."

The dinner was announced.

She said, "It's your duty to take me down. Lucy told me so."

He answered, offering his arm, "How shall I thank her for that privilege?"

In the long picture-gallery dining-room they were seated near the end at which Mrs. Dawson was presiding. Opposite to them, the member for North Aldgate was seated next the lady journalist. On the right of the hostess was the socialist-capitalist, and on her left a gentleman whom Mrs. Weber whispered was a magnate in the city.

Johns calculated rapidly the advantages he might derive from his environment, while he surveyed his neighbour's charms, which seemed to him seductive. He looked also at the *menu*, which was a lengthy one, and he judged that the dinner would last long. All the more chance of an opportunity arriving of making himself heard. In the meantime he would devote himself to Mrs. Weber, who was listening, with evident ennui, to the desultory remarks of a young man on her left.

"It seems to me," he said to her, almost in an undertone, "that I have known you so long, so very long, and yet it's only a few days! You struck me as being a woman who took a sympathetic interest in life, and I told myself that you possessed one of those rich, warm natures of which there are too few."

"Indeed? And is your nature like the one you give me?"

"It is a sister nature, surely."

"Are you often serious, Mr. Johns?"

"I never was more serious. Ah! Mrs. Weber, when you come to know me better, you will find that I can be deeply earnest."

She said, "You must be interesting so; indeed, I'm not sure that you're not interesting now."

He looked at the well-moulded arms and at the fingers which, in the soft light from the electric lamps, took a golden colouring, then at the faultless curve of the neck and shoulders, and he thought for the second time, "delicious."

He said, "How well you heal the wounds which you inflict!"

She answered, "How prettily you dress your compliments."

Presently he asked, "Which of the guests is that fortunate man, your husband?"

She looked down gravely at her plate.

"My husband died two years ago."

He had asked the question to elicit a piece of information, and he said, "I beg your pardon, I did not know. I cannot forgive myself for making you look sad."

She answered, "Yes, you should have ascertained before you spoke."

He thought, "She's a little woman liable to turn round on one," and he gave a sympathetic glance in the direction of the hostess, lest she should think he had forgotten her.

But the member opposite was having a discussion with the lady journalist upon the subject of education, and Johns at once listened.

"Your bill," the lady said, "is too ambitious, too gigantic. What you want to do in one reform will require half a dozen, and I'm not quite sure that it ever will be done at all. A century hence perhaps it may."

She punctuated the enunciation of her opinions with a short nod, which gave her the air of a marionette.

"But, my dear Miss Noakes, my bill is above all things practical. There is not a single clause in it which cannot be applied in the present day, at the present hour. It is meant to suppress the abuses of the present system, and at the same time to extend the scope of education. In the *Planet* there was an article a little while ago which put the case for higher education better than I have ever seen it put before. It said that the state of public education was the barometer of the nation's progress, and that to prevent the mercury from rising was to defy a law of nature. I must ask Mr. Dawson who wrote that article."

Johns thought this was his opportunity.

"That article was mine."

"Indeed," said the politician, looking at Johns through his glasses, "then I congratulate you, sincerely."

And as it happened there was a lull in the conversation at that moment, the congratulation was heard by everybody, even by Dawson at the other end of the table.

Wishing to make use of so good a chance of being heard, Johns continued—

"Public education, as your admirable bill regards it, and as I, too, conceive it, should not mean the teaching of mere elements. It should be, to use a metaphor, the sowing of the finest seed broadcast. It is from the lower strata of society that those great rude minds have sprung which have left their stamp indelibly on history. There is a vigour in the minds of children whose parents have led lives of toil. Their constitution is robust and their brains are virgin soil, often of the richest quality. In the higher ranks, where education has exhausted itself for generations, the soil is weakened and impoverished, the vital force is failing. If you wish to bring forth *all* that the English brain can yield, you must open the gates of higher education to the democracy. Then you will be certain that no capacities are lost, that the best brains among the forty millions of inhabitants will come to the front to advance the work of progress. That principle is unassailable. It is natural. It cannot long be stifled by the egotism of conservative opinion."

This little speech, pronounced in Johns' penetrating voice, produced a considerable effect, and he fancied that he heard "who's that?" whispered in several quarters.

Dawson at anyrate smiled appreciatively from the bottom of the table.

The member said, "Your ideas exactly coincide with mine. I'm glad to have had an opportunity of meeting you."

But the lady journalist, who was of another way of thinking, said, in her nasal voice, "Your theory is quite against statistics. It has been shown conclusively that the children of the working classes give very poor results for the money which is spent in educating them—very poor results indeed."

But Johns, having obtained the effect he wanted, and seeing that no one took much notice of the thin lady in peacock green, contented himself with smiling and not answering.

Presently, however, when Mrs. Dawson said, "You are quite an authority on education, Mr. Johns," he thought that a little show of modesty would not now be out of place. So he replied, "Oh! my contributions to the subject have hitherto been slight."

"But I hope," interposed the member, "that in future they will be more numerous."

"That depends more upon others than upon myself," Johns said, glancing in the direction of Boyd, who was sipping his champagne discontentedly at the other end of the long table.

Mrs. Weber, who had been listening to the discussion with a smile, said to Johns as soon as the conversation became general again, "And do you really believe all those fine things about the democratic intellect?"

"Oh, absolutely."

"Yes, but really, truly? You needn't be afraid to tell me. No one's listening."

Johns thought, "Smart little woman," but repeated gravely, "Absolutely."

"I don't believe you."

"Oh, how incredulous!"

"Yes, I own I am as incredulous as you are discreet."

Johns smiled enigmatically, and looked at the roses which decked the table, saying to himself, "Perhaps she's met my type before," and he could not help admitting that the widow was rather puzzling.

"You're very silent," she said presently.

"I was thinking," he replied, "that you remind me of one of those figures in the Table of Cebes which no one could identify at first sight, but which represented an allegory. I wonder what you represent?"

"You must study me, and find out for yourself."

But, as Johns anticipated, the dinner, which he found excellent, lasted a long time, and he began to regret that no other opportunity had come to him of making himself heard. He wished he had spoken longer while he had the ear of the whole table. Still, perhaps he should not grumble. He had astonished Boyd, of that he was quite sure. His attention, however, was diverted from these considerations by a discussion between the socialist and the financial baron.

The baron said, "If your theories had been applied yesterday, you would not be sitting here this evening, you would not have had an extra suit to come in, you would be taking soup in the free larder of the State."

"My dear sir," the socialist replied, commiseratingly, "you have ideas of socialism of fifty years ago, when it was thought we wanted to divide all property among the population. Of course, that's nonsense, and you might credit us with a little more intelligence. No, what we want to do is in the direction of reform. We want to abolish all extravagance in government. We want to reduce high salaries. We want to clip your wings."

The baron looked around the table.

"Is there any one here," he asked, "who wants to have his income reduced by Mr. Brewer's method?"

There was a laugh, and a general murmur of dissent.

Addressing the socialist, Johns said, "In your theories, which I know well, you underrate the worth of that little quality of brain which happens to be a gift of nature. Of course, we, as good radicals, are desirous that the democracy should have all possible advantages, but if you limit the rewards for the best brains, you prevent them from making their best efforts."

"Quite so," said the baron; "that is exactly what I think—what we all think, really."

"Comfort yourselves, then, with that thought," said the socialist, "and go on living in your paradise of misconceptions. This is not the place for me to refute you, as I could; but I will send you both a copy of my book, although I know that there is no remedy for egoism."

"Thank you," said Johns; "I will read it with avidity."

The socialist smiled feebly, and went on speaking to the hostess.

"I don't think you're likely to be convinced," said Mrs. Weber.

Johns answered in a low tone, "I don't fancy there's much chance of it," and they exchanged a look of quick intelligence, a look which meant, "We understand each other."

As soon as the dessert had been discussed, Mrs. Dawson rose, and the ladies left in the solemn Indian file peculiar to English dinner parties.

Johns, as soon as they had left, moved round to where Boyd was sitting, thinking that he would lose nothing by endeavouring to propitiate the chief.

"Mr. Boyd," he ventured, "I am delighted to meet you here. In the office our interviews are necessarily short, and we have no opportunity of getting to know each other."

Boyd, who was unprepared for this, and whose face denoted that he had done justice to his host's vintages, looked embarrassed, thinking, no doubt, that in the house of the proprietor he was bound to treat Johns with some consideration. He hesitated for a moment, then he said, awkwardly, "Oh, yes. Thanks."

But Dawson, who had been listening, struck in, "All right, Mr. Johns. We won't make you hide your light, you may depend upon it."

This was all that Johns could wish. He thanked Dawson, and, without troubling more about Boyd, listened to a renewed discussion between the socialist and the financier without joining in it, for he preferred to speak when there were ladies present, finding that he succeeded better then.

As soon as he reached the drawing-room, shortly afterwards, Johns said, regretfully, to Mrs. Dawson, who was standing near the door—

"You were so far away at dinner that I could not speak to you."

She answered, "I don't think you minded much — you seemed to be quite happily engaged."

"But happiness is apt to be so relative!"

She laughed and hurried off.

Johns now surveyed the room. The lady journalist was looking engagingly in his direction, but as she belonged to a category for whom he had no taste, who didn't enter into his combinations, and who seemed to him unprofitable, he decided that he would waste no time in speaking to her.

As he was looking round, he suddenly perceived that the lady whom he had met before—the bejewelled lady of the Berkeley—was making a sign to him to come to her.

She was talking to three other ladies, and her daughter was by her side.

"We want to beg of you," she said, "to give us another of those pretty little stories about Australia like the one you told us here the other day. I'm quite sure you must know some more."

"Nothing would give me greater pleasure," Johns answered, and he told them a fresh tale. He told it with humour and a little pathos, and when he finished he was thanked enthusiastically. A little circle had gathered round him, and he told them another story, and yet another, until he declared that he could tell no more that evening.

Then, as he perceived Mrs. Weber sipping tea at the further end of the room, and as he thought he had produced a sufficiently good effect, he excused himself and crossed to where the widow sat.

"So you felt no curiosity to hear my little stories?"

"I heard them quite well from here. What curious experiences you must have had!"

"But I did not say they were mine."

"No, but I guessed they were."

Johns was taken aback, and for a moment almost disconcerted. The way in which this little woman seemed to penetrate his motives gave him a feeling of insecurity he scarcely liked.

"Even to please *you*," he said, "I could not father them!"

"No?—Oh, you will some day. When are you coming to see me at Carsdale Mansions?"

"Not later than to-morrow, if you will be at home."

"Yes, after four."

"I'll come."

Their talk was interrupted after this by a succession of duets played by two "professionals" who had appeared suddenly upon the scene, and Johns had no other opportunity of saying much to Mrs. Weber; but twice, when their eyes met, he noticed that she looked down quickly—once with a little smile. Johns thought, "She's the prettiest woman in the room. I'll call at Carsdale Mansions."

When the party broke up, shortly before midnight, Johns waited till the hostess, having taken leave of most of her guests, was standing on the landing outside the drawing-room door. Seeing his opportunity, he glided quickly up to her and asked, "When can I come and have a chat with you? I would so much like to come some day when you are free—I mean, when you are not receiving."

He fancied that the colour of her face heightened as she answered—

"Come and lunch with me, then, to-morrow."

"How kind of you!"

He pressed her hand warmly as he parted with her to express his gratitude, and descended the staircase thinking that his evening had not been spent in vain.

As he was leaving the house, a lady in a hansom, which was just starting, gave him a little nod, and recognising Mrs. Weber, though her face was partly hidden by a lace mantilla, he made her a profound bow.

"Yes," he said, as he started on his walk home, "it's been a good evening, and if I don't turn it to account, it won't be *my* fault."

An hour's walk through the moonlit streets, still somewhat animated, brought him home again; and as he entered his abode, he noticed that there was no light in Maggie's room.

"Still out, I suppose," he said; "bad trade that—deuced bad;" and he climbed the three flights quickly to his room.

As he undressed he folded the dress clothes as carefully as

if they had been his own, for he attributed a share of his success that evening to them. They, he thought, had made him acceptable and he them. In bed he remained awake for some time, thinking of the two women to whom he had spoken most, and forming a plan of action for the morrow. He must make an ally of Mrs. Dawson, no matter by what means, and as for her friend, the widow, he must find out exactly who she was, and shape his course accordingly. At all events she was the smartest and the prettiest woman in the room, and he went to sleep with that conviction in his mind.

The next morning he walked into the office with a loftier air than he had assumed before, and instead of mounting to the reporters' room, he sought that of Tarte.

"Good morning, Mr. Tarte," he said, "since yesterday my position has considerably changed. I was dining last night at the Dawsons', and I had a talk with Dawson and with Boyd. It was understood that my present place upon the paper was only to be temporary. Now, while it is being decided what I am to do, I want you to let me sit here at your table. There's room enough for two, and as I told you before, you'll not regret it if you do me a good turn!"

Tarte answered, "When Napoleon wished the State to give him anything, he thought it best to take it first. In journalism that is an admirable system, and it ought to lead you far. Had I adopted it I should now perhaps be editing the *Times;* but it was not in my nature. You, young man, seem to me possessed of the spirit which I, alas, did not inherit. I thought, when I was young, of such abstract things as philanthropy, simplicity, sobriety, while you, my friend, are wiser, and only trouble about Johns. Yes, you can sit here; I want to watch you."

"Rum old chap," thought Johns, as he divested a chair of its pile of papers and installed himself at Tarte's writing-table; "at all events he's useful."

"You won't see Dawson to-day," said Tarte; "he's going to Manchester this morning, and Boyd has come to the office in a demoniacal temper. He's already vented some of it on me; but I'm old and tough, and it fell like water on a duck's back. His dinner last night doesn't seem to have agreed with him."

Johns, resisting the temptation of seeking Maskelyne to give him an account of the Dawsons' dinner party because he thought that to do so would be trivial, passed the morning in Tarte's room, preparing a fresh article on education, which was to be an impeachment of the prevailing system.

Then, when the time arrived, he left for Princes Gate by 'bus.

The first words which Mrs. Dawson said to him, as he came into the room, were—

"I've been terribly disappointed. I had asked one of those young ladies whom you met last night, and only five minutes ago I had a telegram from her to tell me that she could not come."

Johns thought, "I wonder if that's true," and he said, "How gladly I can dispense with any other company!"

"Yes, but in this way I am receiving you alone."

"And is that so very wrong?"

"I don't know. I'm almost afraid it is."

Again Johns thought, "I wonder if that's true."

He said, "I would be very loath to forego the pleasure; but, of course, if you really think that ——"

"Oh, no. It's not so bad as that. Now you have come so far, you certainly must stay."

Johns bowed.

"Come and look at my canaries," she said after a moment, and, leaving the drawing-room, she led him to the recess upon the landing, in the centre of which stood a large cage filled with little golden-feathered birds who were chirping merrily while basking in the ray of sunshine that streamed through the high staircase window.

"Are they not sweet?" she said, in a girlish tone, which scarcely seemed to suit her. "Unfortunately the mortality among them is quite dreadful, and I am constantly finding, when I come down in the morning, one of the little dears at the bottom of the cage upon his back. It makes me feel quite sad."

"Ah yes," said Johns, "we must always suffer for our feelings! The people who are happiest are those who have those flinty hearts so common nowadays."

"You are not one of them, I hope."

"Can you ask that question?" and he assumed a look which was so sorrowful and earnest that Mrs. Dawson expressed herself convinced.

Presently a servant came to announce the lunch, and Johns led his hostess to the dining-room.

"You see what it is to have no family," she said, as they were sitting down, "when my husband is away I'm quite alone."

Johns answered sympathetically, "And have you then no family?"

"No, none."

During the lunch, as the presence of the servants somewhat disconcerted him, and as Mrs. Dawson seemed to wish it, Johns spoke chiefly of passing topics. He felt relieved when the meal was over and they went back to the drawing-room.

She took a seat on a long divan-like sofa, and Johns, without waiting to be asked, sat next to her.

"Do you know," she said at once, "I've already spoken to my husband about you?"

"Yes, I knew from what he said to me the other day that my good angel had interceded for me. Will you allow me to call you my good angel?"

Mrs. Dawson laughed, and Johns continued—

"And now I feel that I don't know how to thank you!"

"I don't want any thanks. I consider it a duty to defend any one against Mr. Boyd."

"What a curious individual he is! Pray tell me what you know about him."

"I don't suppose I know more than you, only I'm quite sure that I don't like tyrants. Besides, a man who's seldom sober does not seem fit to be an editor. I tell my husband so, but he's afraid to part with him, lest the circulation should diminish."

"He'll have to go some day," said Johns; "it's only a question of time;" and he thought, "If *I* could get his place!"

There was a short pause, during which Mrs. Dawson, finding that there was too much light, rose and drew down a blind.

"You haven't told me," she said, as she resumed her seat, "what you think of Mrs. Weber."

Johns answered, with the air of a man who has not quite made up his mind—

"Oh, no doubt Mrs. Weber's interesting, and on the whole, I fancy, not bad looking."

"You're rather lukewarm in your praise, and yet I thought you seemed impressed."

"Scarcely that," he answered, adding carelessly, "who is Mrs. Weber, by the way?"

"Mrs. Weber is the widow of a German military attaché who died a few years ago, without, I'm afraid, leaving her very well provided for. She lives in a little flat in Westminster."

"Ah yes," Johns said, as if he had received a piece of information which was of dubious interest, "it's unfortunate."

Then, suddenly turning round and facing her as if he were moved by a sudden impulse, he exclaimed, "Do you know, dear Mrs. Dawson, the first time I saw you at the hotel I was reminded of those lines from Haidee :—

> " Her brow was white and low, her cheeks' pure dye
> Like twilights rosy still with the set sun ;
> Short upper lip—sweet lips ! that make us sigh
> Ever to have seen such ; for she was one
> Fit for the model of a statuary."

They were lines which he had used successfully many a time before to farmers' daughters in Australia, and as he thought humanity very much the same in all latitudes, he ventured to use them now, and with a practised intonation.

Mrs. Dawson, taken by surprise at first, blushed deeply, and then exclaimed in a severe tone, " Mr. Johns ! "

He thought, " I've gone too quick," and he said at once, " Don't be offended, dear Mrs. Dawson. It's in my nature to be frank and to express my feelings. I only recited the lines of a great poet which came into my head that night. They occurred to me because it was so natural they should. Do not scold me for them ! They are as harmless as they are true ! "

Partly restored to confidence, she said, " I'm afraid, Mr. Johns, you're a great flatterer."

He answered, " It is not flattery to speak the truth," and he gazed into her face so searchingly that she moved a little from him, looking down. Then he continued, " Where there is sympathy it cannot be restrained. One nature is drawn towards another as the needle to the pole, and it is beyond the power of either to resist. Ah, Mrs. Dawson, do not try to check that precious sentiment which exists between us, for it is all too rare in life ! Promise me that we shall be always friends." And, as he said this, he stretched out his arms with an imploring gesture. In doing so, his hand touched hers.

She drew back quickly, and he resumed, " How can I teach you to see in me the sincerest of your admirers, the most devoted of your friends ? "

" Really, Mr. Johns," she said at length, " I'm quite ready to believe you as long as you talk as a friend should."

He said, " It's very hard, but I promise that I will."

" Why should it be hard ? " she asked.

The question almost made him smile, for he attached great weight to women's questions, thinking them the key to their inner thoughts.

He answered, " If I were to tell you that, I would break my promise. Will you let me break it ? "

" No, no," she said, " in that case, please don't answer me."

But he considered now that he had gone far enough that day. "Dear Mrs. Dawson," he said, "let us not quarrel. I will submit to a hard fate."

There was a pause, and presently he began to tell her a story of two lovers in Victoria, a pathetic little story describing what he called "a great immeasurable love," such a love as only earnest natures could experience, an invincible absorbing love, which neither calumny nor age could quell, a love which only grew in its intensity when one of the two lovers was disfigured by an accident for life.

"Ah," he said, as he concluded, "that is the ideal for which life should be lived."

With a shade of sadness in her voice, she answered, "Yes, but it's not given to every one to reach it."

He thought, "You can't have reached it with old Dawson," and he answered, "Alas! no," after which there was a silence.

A little later, when he rose to leave, he said, "I trust I am forgiven?"

"Yes," she answered, "but another time you must not be so frank."

"Have I not promised to dissimulate in future?"

"Come and see me again soon," she said.

He left the house with a light heart, humming a tune as he walked along, and thinking, "She's not the smartest woman I ever met, but she may be the most useful."

The afternoon was advancing, and as he had told Tarte he would not return to the Strand that day, he set out on foot for Westminster to pay his visit to Mrs. Weber, saying to himself, like the porter in the Eastern tale, "Oh, what a blessed day this is!" For he looked forward with a keen sense of anticipation to his meeting with the widow.

Carsdale Mansions stood, he found, behind Victoria Street, and Mrs. Weber's flat, the porter told him, was on the fourth floor.

He refused the lift because lifts sometimes broke, and he did not want to run the risk, however slight, of ending or impeding his career. But he mounted the four flights nimbly.

A maid opened the door to him almost as soon as he had pressed the knob.

Mrs. Weber was at home, she said, and she conducted him along a narrow hall to the drawing-room at the extreme end. At once he surveyed the room — a square room furnished modestly but tastefully, as if the owner had more taste than means. Here and there an ornament, a piece of tapestry, or a work of art seemed to be meant for richer surroundings, and there was a fine Sèvres vase in a corner of the room, which seemed out of keeping with the cheap upholstery.

Johns had scarcely finished making these observations when the door opened and Mrs. Weber entered.

"So you've kept your word," she said, as she gave her hand.

"What human power could have made me break it?"

"Oh," she said, with a little laugh, "one never knows."

"You seem to have little confidence in our sex."

"Only a very little."

"Your experience has not been bad, I hope."

"Not worse, I suppose, than most women's."

He had taken a seat opposite to her in a low chair, and he was admiring the lines of her faultless figure draped in the folds of a soft woollen dress.

"Mrs. Weber," he said, "I have been thinking of you very often since last night. The first moment I saw you my attention was arrested. I was impressed. You seemed to me to be one of those rare women who embody in themselves all the qualities which we men prize, as well as an indefinable distinctiveness which I had not met before. And now as I see you this afternoon in this charming nook, and I hear you speak in an accent almost of disenchantment, I ask myself—why is this?"

"I'm afraid you're asking a question to which there is no answer. And if you please, I don't want to be made out to be peculiar. No, I accept things as they are, and take them at their value."

"How well I understand you," he exclaimed. "That is just my philosophy!"

"Yes," she answered, smiling, "I should think we ought to understand each other."

"I'm convinced of it."

He was in reality perplexed. Never having met a woman who resembled her, he felt undecided what method of behaviour to adopt.

"And so you live alone in this retreat," he said, in order to say something.

"Quite. I suppose you, also, live alone?"

"Yes, and that's another point of similarity between us. We neither of us have chains."

"Except those which society imposes on us, and those which we forge ourselves."

"Oh, those are easily undone."

Without noticing his remark, she asked—

"Are you going to make a stir in journalism? I like men who make a stir in something."

E

Johns thought he now possessed a clue.

"Certainly," he answered, resolutely, "I mean to try to make a very big stir indeed."

"That's right. I fancy you'll succeed."

"Ah, Mrs. Weber, you don't know how much it depends on you!"

"On *me?*"

"Yes, on you. To conquer, I need sympathy, encouragement, and friendship. I need to think, while I am fighting, that there is a woman of surpassing charm who understands me, in whom I can confide, in the sunshine of whose beauty I can sometimes bask. And I felt from the moment I beheld you that you were that woman! Do not say that I was wrong."

He leaned forward in his chair, and the expression of his face was as eager as if his life had depended on her answer. He was watching her every gesture, to see if she were touched.

"Of course, I'll promise you my sympathy," she said, "if that is of any use to you."

"It's everything," he said, triumphantly. "*How* shall I thank you?"

"By being less enthusiastic."

"Ah, Mrs. Weber, Mrs. Weber, you little know the ravage you have made! You don't suspect that I have not said a tithe of what was in my thoughts. You cannot guess, you cannot guess."

"Really, Mr. Johns!"

"You reminded me last night, when you were sitting in that corner, with the velvet curtain for a background, of one of those portraits of the divine Rembrandt which, once seen, can never be forgotten. If those duettists prevented me from speaking to you, my eyes, I fancy, spoke."

"They are saying too much now, it seems to me; too much for sincerity."

"How cruel you can be. I will swear to my sincerity."

"Don't," she said. "In these days there's nothing left to swear by."

A servant entered with a tea table, and she did the honours.

"At all events," he resumed presently, "I hold you to your promise of sympathy, and, I hope, companionship."

When he rose to leave, as he wanted to make a supreme demonstration of his sentiments, he held her hand in his a moment, and raised it quickly to his lips before she was able to prevent him.

Then he withdrew without another word.

CHAPTER FOURTH

JOHNS was not long mastering the art of interviewing. He had shown a certain talent in questioning the reticent, in worming from them the information which the public wanted, and there was something in his presence, in the intonation of his voice, in the expressiveness of his physiognomy which often opened doors to him that were shut even to experienced men like Maskelyne. He had a commanding way of saying "Mr. Johns," in sending in his name, which impressed janitors and clerks. His knowledge of the world, too, stood him in good stead. He possessed the scent, the instinct, which places the journalist on the track of news.

Still, although his finances were somewhat better since he had received payment from the paper, they were by no means good. For the interviews were far from numerous, and Boyd gave him no other work to do. He had, also, been obliged to buy an evening suit, which he obtained on credit from Townsend Brothers after paying the remainder of his bill. But he made the best of circumstances, and, in his leisure moments, he amused himself by writing articles which he tore up after he had read them out to the approving Tarte, who, to his surprise, seemed to take an interest in his career. "Some men are born," he thought, "to pave the way for others, and certainly he's one of them." In the meanwhile, fact by fact, he collected all the information he could gather about Boyd—his disposition, character, propensities—and he stored these in his memory, hoping to find use for them later on.

During Dawson's prolonged absence Johns received no more invitations from his wife. When he called on her on the Sunday following, although she received him cordially, she was reserved, and she glanced down when she spoke to him, seeming anxious to avoid looking at him in the face. Prudery or timidity, whichever it might be, he thought it a good sign; though he was a little disappointed that at parting she had not asked him to return soon. Probably the room full of guests prevented her, or she had been reflecting, and he was always distrustful of feminine reflections.

Might the widow have related his visit to her? But no, he thought he knew women well enough to know that, where men were concerned, there were certain confidences they preferred avoiding. As he did not find that he was being made much of that afternoon, and as the widow was not there, he did not remain long.

For a few days after this, however, he was restless and unsettled at the office, beginning to think that, after all, things weren't going so well as he expected, and asking himself what he could do to accelerate their progress, when one morning, as he was sitting at Tarte's table, a clerk brought him a letter addressed in a woman's hand. He opened it and read, "Come and dine with me to-morrow. Shall expect you. Yours, Ellen Weber."

After reading these few words several times, he seemed so pleased that Tarte looked up enquiringly. But Johns, thrusting the note into his pocket, said calmly, "It's only a lady who's come back to her senses."

"Ah," said Tarte, "of women I know nothing. For three and seventy years I have kept my body chaste; and chaste, one of these days, I mean to die."

"What?" said Johns, looking at Tarte with open-mouthed astonishment; "you don't mean to say that ——"

Tarte interrupted with "Yes, sir; I do."

"Extraordinary!" and Johns contemplated Tarte, feeling more convinced than ever that the man was indeed an oddity. He had thought often of the pretty widow since his visit, and always with increased pleasure. She seemed so self-possessed and so attractive in the reserve which she maintained. He would have called on her again had he not been restrained by a wish to wait until she asked him. Now, she was inviting him to dine with her—no doubt alone—and nothing could possibly be more propitious.

The next day, at the office, he was afraid lest he might be given some duty which would prevent him reaching Carsdale Mansions in time for dinner; but the day passed uneventfully, Boyd refusing to see anyone, and mysteriously shutting himself up in his room, as he was wont to do, after the paper had gone to press.

At home that evening, as he was putting on his suit, reviling Townsend Brothers for the faults he detected in its fit, he was troubled by one consideration. Should he put on a white tie or a black? He was anxious to do what was strictly right, but his experience was so limited that he did not know which would be most proper for the occasion, and, in spite of his assurance, he had a great dread of ridicule.

After much wavering, he decided for the white. It would be better to err on the side of too much ceremony than on that of not enough.

When he had given the last touch to his toilet, he left by omnibus for Westminster.

He found Mrs. Weber in the drawing-room alone. She received him with familiarity, as if he had been an old acquaintance, and she seemed to him to be less reserved than previously. She gave him her hand with a frank, free gesture.

"So you have let all that time elapse without even caring to know if I was alive."

"Only two little weeks!"

"Three."

"Two only by the calendar, and two weeks of happy recollections for me, spoilt only by the petty duties which kept me away from here."

He looked at her intently, then he asked, "May I be allowed to say what I am thinking at the present moment?"

"Yes, if it's nothing too extravagant."

"Well, then, I was thinking that each time I see you I discover some new charm."

"Let us lay aside compliments and talk seriously."

"Very well. Are you alone this evening?"

"Yes; a friend has disappointed me."

Johns said, "I've no grudge against that friend."

Then, as she only smiled, he added, "I almost wish that your friend would always disappoint you when I am coming."

"Do you know," she said, without noticing his remark, "I've been hearing something about you."

"Indeed," he answered doubtfully, a little apprehensive lest the "something" might relate to his Australian career.

"Yes, Mrs. Dawson was here this afternoon, and she said her husband thought a lot of you, and that you were certain to get on."

"Oh, she said that, did she? When Dawson returns, I must make him provide the means."

"Yes, do. And now what do you think of Mrs. Dawson? Do you think her pretty?"

Johns answered with indifference, "There are so many ways of being pretty."

The dinner was served in a little plainly-furnished room, in which the most conspicuous object was a full-length painting of a German officer in uniform. Johns, on the right of Mrs. Weber, faced this portrait, and the officer's head was turned in such a way that he seemed to be scrutinising him. And Johns, who had a peculiar dislike for soldiers, said to himself, "She makes one dine with the departed!"

"This, you see," she said, "is my modest little home;" and she looked round at the two maids who were serving them, as if to say, "You see, I'm served by women," while he was thinking, "She's asked me here alone, for, of course, no one else was coming," and he concluded that there must be some significance in the invitation.

But the dinner had a surprise in store for him. Mrs. Weber, who had hitherto, when he had met her, been somewhat taciturn or rather economical of words, now showed a vivacity, a charm in speaking, which he had not expected. She chatted gaily about the theatres she had been to, the pictures she had seen, and the music she had heard, with taste, giving reasons for her preferences which were always clear and sometimes clever. As she became animated and her cheeks flushed, her ripe beauty was heightened in intensity, and Johns looked at her with unfeigned admiration, wondering for a moment how he had had the boldness, or the simplicity perhaps, to use his ordinary tactics upon such a woman. But he soon told himself that, after all, with a little more, or a little less, intelligence, all women were alike by nature. He hadn't up to then succeeded badly, or he would not have been dining with her at that moment.

The dinner did not consist of many courses, and Johns was too much engrossed in studying his companion to notice what they were. Throughout he listened to her with the expression of intense interest and sympathy which made him so good a listener.

At dessert, giving expression to a thought which struck him suddenly, he inquired, "Are you English, may I ask?"

"Only half. My father was Italian."

"Ah, *now* I understand those large dark eyes, and that olive tint which I so much admire."

"Hush," she said, "you mustn't say those things when my servants are in hearing."

He bent forward towards her, and said in a low, half-supplicating tone, "But may I presently?"

She shook her head.

"But I must," he said, "I must."

"Will you take some grapes?" she asked.

But he refused, and there was a silence, during which their eyes met frequently.

At length, pushing her chair from her hastily, she rose.

"Come," she said, "let us go back to the drawing-room. You can smoke there if you like."

They passed again into the drawing-room, and sat together on the sofa.

"Now," she said, "what is it you have to say to me?"

Johns thought, "This time I must try my best," and he broke out, passionately, "That not one day, not one hour since I saw you first, have I ceased to long for you, to dream of you, to know that no woman I have ever met has realised so perfectly, so sweetly, the ideal I had formed. I scarcely hoped to see that creature of my dreams. She seemed to me too rare to be discovered in a single lifetime. And suddenly one afternoon I met you! Ah, if you knew how often, since I saw you last, I have been on the point of coming here to tell you how I loved you, how I cursed the slavery that kept me from you! And now, this evening, you have made me hope that you are not quite insensible to the flame which tortures me. Oh, if I had been mistaken when I thought I read just now a spark of tenderness in those lovely eyes, I would have nothing left to hope for or to live for—nothing! You have filled me, overwhelmed me, with a profound passion!"

Without waiting for an answer, and suiting his action to his words, he seized her in his arms and kissed her twice upon her cheek.

She disengaged herself, and said, with a slight frown, "I wonder what you think of me, to act like this."

But he knelt beside her and clasped her round the waist, looking up into her face with an expression of deep earnestness, of intense longing.

"I think," he said, "that you are a woman destined by all the laws of nature to be the solace of a man who loves you, who adores you, and who finds you living in a cruel solitude, and I think, I think, you love me."

She did not answer, but her hand played with the lock of hair which fell upon his forehead.

"You do! you do!" he cried triumphantly, and as she was still silent, he rose and took her in his arms again. This time she returned his kisses.

Then, disengaging herself again, she said, "What a subtle

man you are to have made me be so weak. I would not have thought it possible! But, remember, if I am to be anything to you, it cannot be your mistress."

"My wife? You would consent to be my wife?"

"Perhaps."

"Ah," he said, covering her hand with kisses, "if that could only be, I would be the happiest man on earth; but, alas! at present, I am without means."

She said, interrupting him, "I know; and as I myself am barely comfortable, we could not think of marriage yet; but later, when you have made your way ——"

"Ah, then, how gladly!"

But he drew her near to him again, and whispered in her ear, "Ellen, my sweetest Ellen, nothing shall prevent our union, but have pity on my suffering. Think of me day by day for perhaps a year longing for you, sighing for you, and remember mine is not a cold, patient love, which lets the weeks and months go by with small regret, but a great absorbing passion beyond control, a passion which has taken hold of me for good. Ellen, I implore you to be kind, to have compassion on a man who loves you to distraction."

She remained silent, turning her head away from him and breathing fast.

"Ellen, my little Ellen," he continued, "listen to me. We will love each other so delightfully, supremely, and the world shall never know until the time arrives. And we shall not have lost a precious year of our lives in anxious waiting, tearing our hearts to pieces and leading an existence of privation. Ellen! that could not be. It would be beyond nature. I can answer for myself—it would be beyond my powers of endurance."

For a few moments she reflected. Then, in a low voice, she asked, "But how is it possible? My reputation and the servants ——"

"We will be prudent, intensely prudent. I will guard your reputation jealously, so that not a living soul shall know. We will lead a life which will be full of joy, which will be all the sweeter for the need of secrecy."

She remained silent, thinking. At length she said, "You are a dangerous man, a very dangerous man. Where do you live?"

Johns thought of his third-floor room, with its dirty carpet and its musty furniture, and for a moment he felt embarrassed.

"In Grafton Street," he said, finding no better answer.

"That's close to my dressmaker!"

He thought it useless to tell her which Grafton Street it was, and he said sorrowfully, "Yes, but I have only a very little box, right up in the skies, and, what is more, the rules of the house are Spartan as to ladies."

"You see," she said, growing very serious, "that there are all kinds of obstacles. We must wait, we really must."

But he vowed that he could not live without her; that if obstacles existed, they must be surmounted; that if they wished, they could find a way to conquer them.

"Here," she said, "it is impossible."

As he appeared to wonder why it was impossible, she added—

"It would get known, and you know what Society is in England."

He said, still looking at her longingly, "How then?"

"Listen," she said, placing her hand upon his shoulder, "if you are very good, we will take a trip into the country now and then."

"Alas! I cannot leave the office."

"But on Sundays."

"Oh, then, of course!"

"Very well, then, let us go next Sunday, say to Seven Oaks. It's quite unfashionable, and we shall meet no one there we know. I've heard there's a delightful little inn, with an old English garden, which is a perfect Eden."

For financial reasons, this arrangement was far from pleasing Johns, but he said enthusiastically, "How good you are! How happy you have made me! Yes, we will go to that little Eden. I will dream of Sunday."

"And now," she said, "will you please sit on that chair opposite. We might be surprised at any moment. Don't be afraid of losing me. I'm fonder of you than you fancy. I liked you at once that afternoon at Mrs. Dawson's, though I didn't think I should have given way to you so soon."

"You will never regret it, never!"

The rest of the evening was spent in making plans, in chatting, and in smoking cigarettes, which Mrs. Weber did gracefully, and without pose.

When Johns rose to leave, she allowed him to embrace her, saying, "Be punctual at Victoria at half-past one."

When Johns found himself in the street again, walking up Grosvenor Place, he broke out into a laugh. "By God," he said, "I didn't think it was so easy, with such a woman too!"

For he reflected that he was now embarked on an adventure which could only turn out to his advantage, and with a woman of whose beauty any man might feel legitimately proud. He fancied himself lifted into another sphere, protected, in some measure, from the risks and pitfalls of existence. One thing, however, troubled him. This trip into the country could not be made for nothing, and how was he to find the money for it? That was indeed a problem. But then, had he not already solved that of the two suits? He would solve this one also!

The next morning at the office he consulted the clerk who kept the books as to the possibility of obtaining an advance, but he was at once informed that such a thing was entirely against the rules.

"Damn the rules," he muttered, as he made for Tarte's room. But as he reached the door a thought struck him. Why not ask old Tarte?

"Mr. Tarte," he said, as he took his seat as usual, "I want money. What's the largest sum you can advance me on my month's payment?"

The old man, who was employed at a fixed salary, was the only person in the office, except the clerks, who was paid weekly, and Johns, for this reason, thought him the most likely to be in funds.

But Tarte drew a purse from his pocket, the leather of which was greasily dimmed from wear. He opened it, took out its contents, six shillings and a few pence, and placed them in a row upon the table.

"That," he said, "is what I have to take me on to Saturday, and to-day's Wednesday. And that represents my total funds on earth. Judge for yourself whether I can lend you any."

"Incumbrances?" asked Johns.

"A little orphan girl, the fruit of irresponsibility. Ah, my friend, if ever you get into Parliament, for God's sake make a law to prevent the marriage of incapables."

"Good," said Johns, "I will."

Evidently there was nothing to be obtained from Tarte, and as to Maskelyne, he had confessed, a few days previously, that he was extraordinarily embarrassed, his wife having recently presented him with twins.

Altogether the prospects of obtaining the required sum by the week's end were extremely vague. His luck, this time, seemed to be growing dim.

But chance arranged the difficulty by the return of Dawson on the Friday morning. As soon as Johns heard he had arrived, he went to his room and knocked loudly at his door. Dawson received him almost as a friend, and asked him, in a tone of consideration, what he could do for him.

"Mr. Dawson," he said, with gravity, "you can do me a great

favour. An old friend of mine in Wales, an unfortunate man who married a girl under the blind influence of profound love, is ill and penniless, and he has appealed to me, in a letter of intense despair, imploring me to help him. I can only do this, sir, if you will consent to give me an advance on my current work. It is only a matter of a few pounds, and I hope you will oblige me."

Although he used this pretext, Johns knew quite well that Dawson was not a man to be affected by a story of distress, and that if he gave him what he asked, it would only be because of the value he had set upon him journalistically. He was doubly pleased, therefore, when Dawson said—

"Certainly, Mr. Johns, tell the cashier, as from me, to give you what you want."

Johns thanked him warmly, and Dawson asked, "Have you been doing much for us during my absence?"

"Much less than I should like."

"Very well, I will see to that. Mr. Boyd is fond of nursing his dislikes."

Johns left with a feeling that he had not done badly for himself. He descended the stairs again, and requested the cashier, in the name of the proprietor, to hand him a five-pound note. This the man did, after sending up to know if he was really authorised to give it.

Thus armed, on the Sunday Johns left his lodgings in a hansom for the station. It was a fine summer morning, and the bright sunshine did its best to enliven the empty streets, and the dulness of the closed shops. Johns had been thinking of the widow since he left her four days before, and his pulse beat faster as he alighted at Victoria and gave his black portmanteau to a porter. The station clock, when he arrived beneath it, after having bought a ticket, pointed to a quarter after one, and the train started at half-past.

He looked around, but saw no signs of Mrs. Weber. If, after all, she had repented, and were going to disappoint him! But no, it was still early, and women were always late. He lit a cigar, and began to pace up and down, close to his portmanteau, scrutinizing every woman who came into the station. For although it had been agreed that they should travel, at least as far as the first station, in separate carriages to avoid suspicion, he wanted to see that she was in the train before he started.

The hands of the clock moved steadily on towards the half-hour, and still she did not come. He was beginning to be uneasy.

A lady in a travelling cloak and a thick spotted veil appeared, and Johns thought she was the widow. When she came nearer to him, he saw that he was mistaken.

At last, when three minutes only were wanting to the half-hour, and Johns was beginning to despair, he suddenly saw a lady in a tweed costume issue from the doorway and cross the platform hurriedly, followed by a porter with her luggage. This time there was no mistake. It was Mrs. Weber.

She did not appear to see him; but he followed her to the train at once, and took a seat in the carriage next to hers, after making a sign to her as he was entering.

"Ha," he said, as the train moved off, "it's all right *this* time."

At the first station he alighted, and, as she nodded to him to let him know that he might enter, he jumped into her carriage quickly, after the only other passenger alighted.

"Ellen, my little Ellen, how good, how kind, how sweet of you to keep your promise! If you knew the moments of suspense I passed when I thought you weren't coming, when I feared you might have changed your mind, or been prevented, or I don't know what."

"What would you have done if I hadn't come?"

"I would have gone home and shot myself."

She laughed and said, "You know very well you wouldn't."

But he vowed he would, while he kissed her beneath her veil.

An hour's ride through the rich Kentish country brought them to Seven Oaks, and, as Johns had telegraphed for rooms the day before, a trap, which was waiting for them at the station, soon brought them to the hotel. They were shown into a little parlour on the first floor, looking out upon the gardens and communicating with the bedroom. Through the open window came a perfume from the large roses which climbed upon the wall outside, and there was a bright sunny view of lawns and trees and hills.

"At last!" he said, as soon as they were alone, drawing near to her and assisting her to take off her hat. But she asked, moving a little from him, "What name did you give downstairs?"

"Sir John and Lady Johnson."

"Capital. And now, Sir John, please go and wait for me in the garden."

"But, Ellen ——"

"You really must let me manage things in my own way. You'll have nothing to regret by waiting."

Johns had been looking forward the whole time in the train

to the moment when they should be alone, the moment which must, he had calculated, follow their arrival, and he was disappointed. But he suspected that some feminine consideration, some scruple of declining virtue, had prompted her to impose upon him this condition, and he thought that it would be more delicate on his part to accede docilely to her wishes. One could not quite behave in the same way towards the widow of a diplomat as to the daughter of a cattle dealer. No, he must be discreet.

He asked, "And must I really go?"

"You must really. I'm quite in earnest."

He took up his hat again, and after a look in which he endeavoured to express his longing, he left and went down to the garden.

Then, as he walked up and down the gravel paths, between the grass-plots gay with flower-beds, he muttered, "I wonder what this means. She can't be going to play modesty!" and he reflected on the subtleties of the female conscience.

A gardener in shirt-sleeves was showering fine spray from a long hose upon the grass which glistened in the sunshine, and the air was cool and fragrant.

Johns looked about him. The high laurel hedges, which divided the garden from the fields beyond, had deep cut-out recesses furnished with wooden benches, and as he explored further, he saw some secluded arbours formed of trees and bushes, one of which was already occupied by a couple who, he concluded from the peep he caught of them, were lovers.

"It's curious," he reflected, "that she should have known of the existence of this dove-cot."

When he had reached the end of the paths, he turned and retraced his steps, walking leisurely along towards the house. As he was reaching it, Mrs. Weber was coming from it.

"Have you been reflecting on my cruelty?" she asked, as they met on the gravel path.

"I have been thinking of the rewards which my obedience certainly will merit."

They made, as by a tacit understanding, for the last arbour at the extremity of the garden walks—one that had the double advantage of being more shut in than the remainder, and of commanding a fine view of the hills, which rose in a long ridge of purple from a wide stretch of fields and meadows in the foreground.

In her close-fitting costume, and the light straw hat which rested prettily upon her dark hair, Johns, as they sat down, thought his companion exquisite. He was, therefore, perfectly sincere when he exclaimed enthusiastically, "You are a perfect Hebe!"

She answered, smiling, "I'm going to lecture you. You achieved much too easy a victory the other night, and I'm still wondering how you did it, and how you contrived to make me like you. But now I must ask you to remember that I am not a woman to be trifled with."

Johns made a sign of protestation.

"Or to submit to be cast aside lightly if the fancy of my lord should change. So I want you to reflect before you—love. Because, you know, there are plenty trains to town this afternoon, if you feel fickle."

But Johns, who at that moment would have sworn fidelity by every god he knew, said quickly, "Child of little faith! How often shall I tell you that I am an anchor of fidelity!"

"If you really are, I warn you I will fix a very strong chain upon that anchor."

"The stronger it is the better it will please me."

"Are you quite sure of that?"

"As certain as I am that those birds over yonder are flying in the sky."

As he said this he thought, "I was too quick the other night; she's drawing back a bit."

"Very well. But remember that I can be much more troublesome than you may think if I am played with."

But he was growing impatient of her warnings, and to put an end to them, he seized her suddenly—almost savagely—and kissed her.

His sudden act had the effect he wished, for, flushed and evidently pleased, she said, "I want to trust you, and I suppose I must."

A light breeze was blowing from the hills, and the air, which in London had been warm and heavy, was delightfully refreshing. The spot was full of stillness and repose.

He said, after a few minutes, "What a charming place this is! How did you know of it?"

She answered, "I was told of it by a pair of little lovers who come here sometimes."

He thought, "I wonder if that's true."

"Yes," she continued; "I feel invigorated already. Is it the air or your society?"

He whispered something in her ear which made her give a little laugh, and then presently, as he felt a need for speaking of himself to women, he told her of his doings at the *Planet*, describing the people he had interviewed, the types whom he had met with in the ante-room, the bearishness of Boyd and the eccentricity of Tarte, keeping her amused and interested.

"And you," she said, looking into his face when he had finished, "are you going to outstrip them all?"

"I mean to try," he answered resolutely.

And she glanced at him again with an expression of half-deferential admiration.

"How I shall love you if you do."

"And only if I do?"

She answered, with a smile, "No, whether you do or not."

They remained there till the sun was beginning to decline, and the purple of the distant hills was darkening.

Then he asked her, in a plaintive tone, "Is my probation nearly ended?"

She replied, "*Now* we're going to have dinner."

They returned to the hotel, and Johns, after a consultation with the proprietor as to the resources of his larder, ordered the best meal the place could give. For he felt that his five sovereigns were equal to the occasion.

While he was doing this, she had gone up to her room, and returned quickly before he had time to join her.

So they dined at a little table before an open window looking on the lawn, in a long dining-room in which three other couples were being served. They both were somewhat silent, though their eyes were eloquent, and the brilliancy of hers increased as she sipped the Rœderer with which he filled her glass repeatedly. Her beauty was intensified as the crimson flushes mounted to her cheeks, and they did so much justice to the Rœderer, indeed, that when they rose from the table to take a stroll upon the lawn, they were in that state of triumphant calm which a good vintage, indulged in freely, brings about.

After strolling arm in arm for a few minutes, they decided that it was time to enter, and they went up to their rooms at once. As soon as the door of the little parlour was closed, Johns took his companion in his arms.

"Ah, Ellen, cruel Ellen," he exclaimed, "at last my trial is over! If you knew how I have pined in bondage all the afternoon, how I have counted every moment while we were over yonder in the garden, when I could only gaze upon your beauty and not taste its sweetness! And now that you have softened and become humane, now that I see you in my arms in all your splendour, I feel that no one happier than I exists. It seems to me as if I were beginning a new chapter in my life, the true, the only chapter. How often in Australia on the long rides through territories where a horseman is a solitary speck on a vast track, how often did I dream of meeting, some day in my career, a woman who should resemble you! I gave her then your eyes, your hair, your features and your form. That was my ideal, and you have incarnated it."

They moved to the open window, and he drew her to him on the sofa till she sank upon his knee.

"Ah," she murmured, in a voice which now betrayed emotion, "you make love well!"

* * * * * *

The next morning, before breakfast, Johns was walking on the lawn smoking a cigar and indulging in reflections.

As he paced to and fro alertly with the step of a man who has succeeded in an enterprise, and who is on good terms with himself, he could not help admitting that his expectations had been fully realized, and that Mrs. Weber, by the passion which she had evinced for him, had made amends for the coquetry which she had shown at first. This was his first experience of the kind, and it had been so incontestably superior to anything he had known before, that he almost wondered he had ever found it possible to interest himself, even in the most remote degree, in the plebeian lasses who had crossed his path. While there were delightful women to be conquered in what was known as good society, why waste one's time in humble wooing? And he reflected with a feeling of self-congratulation that, unless he was mistaken, he had ignited a considerable flame in the heart of the pretty widow. Of course, there might be a drawback to this some day; but for the present he was happy, and he was not given to troubling over much about the future.

Thinking in this way, he continued strolling until at length the noise of a window being opened made him stop and look up at the house. Mrs. Weber was leaning out of the French window, around which the rosebuds formed a kind of garland.

He kissed his hand to her, and then, contemplating her, exclaimed, "A perfect idyll!"

Shortly afterwards they returned by an early train.

CHAPTER FIFTH

WITH the return of Dawson, Johns' position mended. Not only was he kept more continuously employed with minor tasks of news-collecting in the intervals when there was a dearth of interviews, but another article of his was published in the paper, by order of the proprietor, at the instance of the member for North Aldgate. The enmity of Boyd had become unrelenting, although the chief was forced to make some show of hiding it, since Johns enjoyed the protection of the Dawsons. And Johns, accepting this antagonism, did nothing to conciliate the editor, thinking that as long as he was in favour with the controlling power he had not much to fear. Besides, this attitude of Boyd's gave him more liberty of action.

On the other hand, although he was receiving larger pay, he was still embarrassed, owing to his intimacy with Mrs. Weber.

He had succeeded in convincing her that it was absolutely necessary that he should be in London on the Sundays, so that he might pay visits to the Dawsons and to others who received on that especial day; but she had at once discovered a variety of ways of meeting, now in a hotel at Sydenham or Richmond, now in one of the great caravanserais of the metropolis, where they arrived in the evening and left again early the next day. Each of these little escapades, however, made a call on Johns' slender purse, and he soon went into debt with his landlady in Grafton Street for the modest rent he owed her.

Then, on the days when he was most straitened, he would arrive at the place of meeting (generally a railway station) vexed and irritable, vowing he would break with her unless

F

she let him visit her at home. But she attributed his peevishness to his worries at the office, and increased in tenderness, in graceful little ways which flattered him and soon drove his ill-humour away.

He soon discovered, also, to his surprise, that she possessed a head far more resourceful and capable of good reasoning than he had at first suspected, and that he could find in her an intelligent and patient hearer whenever he wished to speak about his affairs, as he generally did on the Wednesday evenings, when he dined with her alone at Carsdale Mansions.

On one of these evenings, a few weeks after the flight to Seven Oaks, they were sitting in the drawing-room after dinner, talking of the resignation of the Ministry which had surprised all London the day before. The Government had been defeated by a vote of want of confidence, just on the eve of a general election, and there was joy in the ranks of the radicals, who thought their prospects of obtaining a majority in the next Parliament exceptionally good.

"John," she said, "I've been thinking over it, and I've come to the conclusion that you ought to take some part in the election. Why not offer to help Parker?"

"But I can't. I haven't time enough."

"Why not address meetings of an evening, you who speak so well?"

Johns, who had been looking at the floor reflectively, glanced up at her.

"By God," he said, "that's not a bad idea!" and he resolved that, if it were at all possible, he would put it into execution.

"You see," she said, "I can be of some use sometimes."

He answered, "Dear little Ellen, of course you can; you're the most delightful, precious little woman that was ever born the most admirable companion any man was ever blessed with." But he thought, "You would be if you didn't cost so much."

She asked, "Will you adopt my plan?"

"Certainly, if it's at all feasible."

"I know Parker pretty well," she added; "if you like I'll write to him to tell him he must let you help him."

But Johns did not fall in with this proposal. He did not want to be so openly patronized or aided by a woman.

"No, thank you, Ellen, he might then suspect something. I'll go to him myself."

"Just as you like," she said, with a little disappointment.

"I didn't know that you knew Parker," he pursued.

She answered carelessly, "Oh yes, all the Dawsons' friends." A little later, as he was leaving, she whispered in his ear, To-morrow evening at St. Pancras."

She had spoken of this meeting once before that evening, but nothing had been fixed, and Johns had tried to avoid the subject. Now, however, when she returned to it, and wanted him to promise, while he knew he hadn't a sovereign in his purse, he said, "No, not to-morrow, I may have to work too late."

"You didn't say that before," she answered quickly.

"Probably because I didn't think of it."

"You were not so forgetful a few weeks ago."

He thought, "She's showing her claws already," and, as he frowned, she added, putting her arm around his neck—

"No, John, I didn't mean to be unkind. We'll meet when you are able."

But as he saw no prospect of an improvement in his finances for some time to come, it seemed to him that the best thing he could do would be to make a clean confession.

"Ellen, I may as well be frank with you. The truth is, I can't afford it. I didn't want to tell you, but you've forced me to. I'm simply what is called hard up."

But now she drew him towards her eagerly, exclaiming—

"Poor little Johnnie! How could I have been so stupid as not to think of that. How silly, how clumsy of me! Forgive me, Johnnie, won't you?"

He kissed her without answering. He was curious to know if she had something to propose.

"But what is to be done?" she asked, despondently.

"Ah! what?"

She reflected for a moment.

"In a little flat like this it's impossible to avoid the vigilance of servants. But listen, I've thought of something ——"

She hesitated, glancing at him sideways, as if afraid to express her thought. Then she whispered, "You must let *me* pay the bills."

But Johns recoiled from her.

"Never!" he said, in a tone of wounded pride.

"But, Johnnie, listen to me. It will only be for a little while, only until you are better off. And since we are going to marry, what *can* it matter?"

But Johns was obdurate. In refusing, he considered he was acting a remarkably fine part—a part which he remembered having once seen acted on the stage—and he had no intention of spoiling his effect by giving way.

"No," he said firmly, "that is impossible. What would you think of me if I agreed to that? What would I think of myself? Never!"

"Perhaps you're right," she said, sighing and drawing near to him again. "How chivalrous you are!"

He answered, "We must have patience. In any case, if I take up this election work, I shall be very busy."

They spoke no more about it, but later, as he was walking home, he congratulated himself that he had acted prudently. She would be more fond of him than ever now, and for the moment, what more charming mistress could a man have? And who knew? If it came to the worst, she might be useful in other ways. As to the place of meeting, she would have to conquer her fear of the servants (if that were the real obstacle) and receive him in her flat, which, in reality, was what he wanted. He found himself at home there—was at his ease. At all events, he had broken the ice on the question of his means, and that relieved him of a source of much annoyance.

The next day, as he was fond of putting his plans into execution quickly, as soon as he had finished his work at the *Planet*, he set out for Eaton Square, where the member for North Aldgate lived.

Parker was at home, and received him in his library, on the ground floor of a large house with a wide Roman portico.

Without circumlocution, Johns explained the object of his visit. He had come, he said, to offer help in the contest which was to be held shortly, and which promised to be particularly acute, for the Aldgate seat. The Conservative opponent, Parker knew, was popular, and therefore a strong propaganda of radical opinions was essential. He was ready, if Parker wished, to undertake that campaign, and to lay special stress on Education.

"My dear sir," said Parker, "you're the very man I want, and to tell you the truth I had already thought of asking you. As you say, it *is* necessary to preach a great deal to the public this time, and I am infinitely obliged to you. You will assist me when I address my constituency, and if you like to lecture them on other nights, the hall will be at your disposal. I will give instructions to my agent."

Johns said, "Then it's agreed. I prophesy that you'll get in."

"Thanks. Of course, you're used to speaking?"

"In Melbourne I have addressed thousands."

"Quite so. Then it's settled."

They discussed the situation and the prospects of the party

for half an hour, and when Johns left, it was understood that he should speak at the meeting which was to be held in three days' time.

As he walked through the park afterwards, he said to himself, "By God, I wonder if I *can* speak!" for the Melbourne thousands had existed only in his imagination, and he had dived into this business because he could not resist the temptation to make use of an opportunity whenever one was offered. "But," he soliloquised, "how I shall score with Dawson if I pull through!"

During the three days which intervened he worked very hard, devoting every minute he could spare to reading up Parker's speeches in the previous session, saturating himself with the nostrums of extreme radicalism, becoming familiar with the aims and routine of the party, and having meetings with Parker and his agent. He had said nothing about the meeting at the office, but when the day arrived Boyd sent for him.

"You'll be good enough," the editor said, "to go to Aldgate this evening to report the meeting of Parker's constituents."

"I'm sorry, but I shan't be able to. I'm going to speak myself."

"You!" exclaimed Boyd, astounded.

"Yes, I."

As soon as Boyd had realised the situation, he said slowly, "Oh, very well, I'll send Maskelyne." And so it was arranged.

Tarte, when he heard of it, remarked, "My friend, you're climbing the right ladder," and Johns replied, "I hope so."

Still, when he was in the cab with Parker's agent later on, bound for Aldgate, he felt uncomfortable, for he could not help confessing to himself that he was ill-equipped for the task he had undertaken. It was true he had arranged with Maskelyne that, if he halted or became confused, the speech would be "touched up"; but he knew that there were half a dozen reporters of other papers who would make capital of it against him.

After a long drive, partly through the City, they reached a district of sullen slums where Johns wondered that politics, or indeed anything, should have an interest for anyone, and they stopped at a large brick building in what seemed to be the best street of the locality. As Johns and the agent entered, the large bare hall was beginning to fill, although no one as yet was on the platform. Parker arrived a few moments afterwards, and after him several well-known radicals, most of them in frock coats.

There was a short consultation in the ante-room. Then

they mounted to the platform. On the stairs Johns found an opportunity to say to Parker, "If you'll let me speak about your Education Bill *to-night*, I should prefer it."

"That's just as I intended it," the educational reformer answered, and Johns thought he had reason to congratulate himself, as he was well versed in that subject, and knew his telling phrases quite by heart.

From the platform he looked down on the sea of heads beneath him. The audience seemed to be drawn almost entirely from the lower classes—a rough, untidy audience, who diffused about the room an odour of dirty clothes and stale tobacco.

As he was contemplating them, and wondering what words and terms would be most likely to attract them, he suddenly perceived, in a row of chairs immediately below the platform, not only the wife of the member, but, to his astonishment, Mrs. Dawson and Mrs. Weber.

He had not written to Mrs. Weber that the meeting was going to be held, neither had he more than casually mentioned it to Mrs. Dawson. Their presence there among that throng of artizans was certainly remarkable. Whom had they come to listen to? Parker or himself? And had they come together, or had they met there? He would have to find that out.

But at that moment they were both looking in his direction, smiling. He bowed and returned their smiles.

Mrs. Dawson, he noticed, looked away again quickly; but Mrs. Weber kept her eyes fixed upon him so intently that he began to feel annoyed, finding that she was carrying the thing too far, and asking himself why women always ended in exaggeration.

As soon as the seats were filled, and the clatter of thick boots on the deal floor was over, Parker rose from his chair amid applause, and began his speech. He told his audience that they were on the eve of a great struggle, in which the party of pure egoism, of unjust privileges, of undue wealth, was going to war against the friends of industry, against the champions of the artizan. And he urged on them the need of union, of solidarity in the great effort that radical opinions were about to make against the narrow doctrines of conservatism, which never *could* be in the van of progress.

He told them this, and a great deal more, using many of the well-worn phrases which seldom fail to impress the masses, and now and then he was interrupted by applause. Then he alluded to his efforts to give them the inestimable benefits of higher education, and he ended with a promise that he would never relax those efforts until he had achieved his purpose. He spoke fluently, and in a manner calculated to flatter hearers of their class.

But the latter part of his speech fell flat. The gentlemen of North Aldgate did not seem impressed with the educational advantages he wished to offer them, and showed some signs of disapproval. Seeing this, he said, " I hear to my regret some expressions of dissent, and, as it is always difficult to speak in praise of one's own handiwork, I will ask you to listen for a few moments to Mr. Johns, who has made a special study of the subject of higher education, both in this country and in Australia."

But, as Johns was rising, a voice from the middle of the hall cried out, " It's 'igher *wages we* wants," and there was a general murmur of approval, which was extremely awkward at that juncture. The moment was somewhat critical for Parker.

Johns commenced his speech in a voice which was so deep and clear that the hall resounded with it. Standing well forward, with his arms folded, and, looking down upon his audience almost with compassion, he began—

" I have heard with feelings of profound astonishment some gentleman in this hall say that higher wages and not enlightenment were his chief desire, and I have felt sorry for that gentleman, sorry that it should be possible that such a misconception in these times of progress should exist. For, do you know what this grave error means? It means that there is among you—amongst *you*, who represent a section of the gallant toilers who make England great, an extraordinary blindness to your own welfare, a lamentable failure to appreciate the noble efforts which are being made by your enlightened representative in Parliament. And I suppose that, if I were to tell you that the murmur of dissent you made just now was a great and flagrant wrong towards your sons—aye, and towards your daughters—you would be incredulous, you would wonder what I meant, you would think I was romancing. And yet such is the case—the wrong is flagrant, the injustice is extreme. What is it, I would ask, that keeps the best intelligences among you from rising to the rank which is their due? Want of a higher education! What is it that condemns you to be the users of mechanical appliances and rarely the inventors? Want of a higher education! What is it that gives capital so tyrannous a power over you? Want of a higher education! You are paid in proportion to the cunning of your brains, and brains do not come into the world equipped. To equip them in accordance with their strength costs money, and you cannot afford that money because you are working for employers who do not wish you should. But if the State provides your sons, whose interests you have been ignoring, with the means of rising as far as their brains will carry them, can you not see that there will be an end for ever to the supremacy of class, and that every boy you send to school will carry in his satchel a marshal's staff, a judge's gown, or a statesman's wallet? And those are the supreme advantages you would deny your sons in refusing to take interest in the great question!"

Johns paused a moment to gauge his audience, who, in answer to his question, cried "No, no," enthusiastically.

Then, finding that he had gained their confidence, he continued praising Parker's system, and denouncing the shortcomings of the Board, just as he had already done in the columns of the *Planet*. And as he had the subject at his fingers' ends, as he knew the best terms to employ, the most useful adjectives to use, and as he suited his address to the understanding of his hearers without simplifying it too obviously, he was listened to, throughout, with marked attention, and rewarded, when he sat down again, with a prolonged outburst of applause. He had made them think, had interested them. They were satisfied and grateful after their own manner.

A few more speeches after this were made by others on the platform, and a concluding one by Parker, who, this time, was loudly cheered.

When the meeting closed, amid the noise of shuffling feet and shifting chairs, Parker shook hands with Johns.

"I congratulate you on your speech," the member said. "It was timely and well-made, and I am indebted to you greatly for it."

Johns thought, "I should think it about stuck you on your legs again." He merely said, "It was lucky they received it well."

In the ante-room they found the ladies waiting for them.

Johns said, addressing them, "I was not aware we were to have had this honour."

Mrs. Weber answered, "You forgot to tell your friends about the meeting, but Mr. Parker was less neglectful."

Mrs. Dawson said, "We thought you spoke *so* well, Mr. Johns!" while the Hon. Mary Parker acquiesced with, "Admirably, I'm sure."

Johns ventured, "If I said anything worth listening to, I must certainly have been inspired by your presence," and as he said this, he included the three ladies in a single glance. Mrs. Dawson said, "Mr. Johns is *never* at a loss for a speech of any kind," and the rest laughed.

Parker, who had been talking to his agent, now came up and said a few words to his wife and Mrs. Weber.

Mrs. Dawson took advantage of the opportunity to say to Johns, "You should come to see us oftener, Mr. Johns."

He answered, in a tone which could not be overheard by the remainder of the party—

"I'm dying to. If you will tell me when you are at home alone, quite alone you know, I'll come to have a chat."

She hesitated for a moment. Then she said, "Come on Saturday at four."

"Depend upon it," he replied, "I won't fail," and he looked into her eyes with that penetrating look the force of which he had often tested. Parker, put into a good temper by the success of the evening's meeting, now invited them to sup at Willis's, and as they all accepted, they left the hall together to proceed to King Street. But as the Dawsons' brougham could naturally only contain four, the party had to separate, and Parker proposed that Johns should escort his wife and Mrs. Dawson, while he would accompany Mrs. Weber in a cab.

It seemed to Johns that this arrangement was not entirely to Mrs. Parker's taste, but as she made no objection, it was carried out.

During the drive, which was a long one, the two ladies whom Johns accompanied talked together, while he, leaning back in his corner, and thinking over his experience that evening with a warm feeling of satisfaction, kept his eyes fixed on Mrs. Dawson, whose face looked pretty against the dark background of the carriage as the street lights revealed it. Now and then she gave him a rapid glance as if to show that she was conscious he was looking at her, and in this way they reached the Restaurant.

The supper, which consisted of a few delicacies in season, was served them at a round table in the largest of the rooms. Parker and Johns did their best to enliven the repast, but there was a reserve on the ladies' part, the reason of which was not apparent. Mrs. Parker seemed disinclined to speak, and Mrs. Weber was far less talkative than usual. There was a complete absence of expansion, and instead of being solely interested in the conversation, the ladies looked around them frequently, studying the fit of an evening dress displayed at one of the adjacent tables, or watching a famous actress supping with a Jewish banker. Altogether, the spirit of concord was somehow wanting, and no one seemed sorry when an hour afterwards the party ended.

This time Mrs. Dawson went with the Parkers, and Johns, who had offered to see Mrs. Weber home, entered a hansom with her.

For some moments neither said a word, each waiting for the other to speak first.

Presently Johns said, "Ellen, I'm going back with you to-night!"

But she replied, "What were you saying to Mrs. Dawson in the hall?"

"Merely that I would call some day."

"You were saying more than that."

Johns thought, "She's going to be jealous," and he answered, "Ellen, my little Ellen, don't be foolish, I have no other thought but you. *You* are my whole life."

She asked, "Why didn't you let me know that the meeting was coming off?"

"Because I wanted to surprise you, and I thought you wouldn't care to go to such an unwashed gathering."

"You might have guessed I would like to hear you speak."

He kissed her on her ear, whispering, "Ellen, I'm going home with you; I'm going home with you to-night."

Half conquered by his words and the sensation of his lips and breath upon her face, she leaned towards him, saying, "John, it's quite impossible."

He answered, "It's going to be done."

They had reached Victoria Street, and the hansom dashed along the wooden pavement, past the high, gaunt, blackened rows of houses, placid in their sombreness, and in a few minutes it stopped before the door of Carsdale Mansions.

Johns, to avoid delay, thrust the fare through the trap in the roof of the vehicle and hurried in with his companion, taking her arm to assist her quickly up the stairs.

When they reached the door of the flat, she said, "Fortunately I told the servants not to wait if I should be late."

As soon as they were inside, and the door of the drawing-room closed upon them, she threw herself into his arms, exclaiming, "You looked so well when you were speaking that I could not take my eyes away from you for a single instant."

"And you so charming down below there, that I dared not look lest I should get confused."

"Is that the real truth?" she asked.

"Do you doubt me?"

"Oh, no, John dear, I never want to doubt you.'

He led her to a seat, and feeling at his ease in the pleasant room in which he seemed to have suddenly acquired a peculiar right of sojourn, he pulled out his cigar case and offered her a cigarette.

She took one, and they smoked together.

Presently she said, "I little thought this evening when I started that you would make me break my resolution in this way."

He answered, "Your resolution was too cruel. It was destined to be broken."

Then, sending a puff of smoke upward and watching it as it ascended to the ceiling, he exclaimed, "Ah, Ellen, you don't know what I felt when those worthy men applauded me to-night! It seemed to me that I had found the road which was to lead me on to fortune. I fancied I heard in the echo of their applause a note which was particularly sweet. Think what they can do for a man who gets their ear. It doesn't matter what you preach to them as long as you manage to catch their fancy. Then they stick to you for ever. Ah! Ellen, one has only to believe sufficiently in the folly of one's fellows to succeed!"

She said, "I hope you don't apply that principle to me."

He answered, "How often you need to be reassured! Where is the parallel, I should like to know, between a lovely woman and a populace?"

"Forgive me, I was joking. I *know* you will get on. I can see it in everything you do."

He answered, "My best achievement will always be to have won you."

The next morning Johns left Mrs. Weber's flat before the servants were about, and went down the four flights of stairs slowly.

As he was descending the last flight, he perceived that the porter whom he had hoped to avoid was in the hall polishing the mahogany of the kind of sentry-box in which he generally sat.

Johns thought, "Here's a man who must be squared," and as he always liked to remove obstacles as soon as they presented themselves, he dived his hand into his pocket and produced a half sovereign—the last that he had. Armed with this, he approached the porter who was looking at him with a half-perplexed smile. Evidently the man had recognized the cavalier who often called on Mrs. Weber.

"My friend," said Johns, "I shall probably be often leaving this house early in the morning, and I want you to let me make you this litttle present—as an earnest of more of the same kind if you appreciate sufficiently how absolutely unnecessary it is to tell anybody that you've seen me."

The man took the modest offering and said, with a reassuring nod—

"All right, sir, thank you, you needn't trouble. You can trust to me, sir. My motto is, never let your right 'and know what your left 'and doeth."

"An excellent motto," said Johns; "it's one I use myself."

The man smiled, and Johns left Carsdale Mansions.

It was so early that the refreshment room at the station, where he wanted to have breakfast, was not open when he reached it, and he was obliged to stroll about in the vicinity while waiting. It was a fresh, bright morning, however, and the time passed pleasantly as he reflected over his experiences. There was no doubt about it; things had gone extremely well. If this luck could continue thus, he wouldn't grumble, and as he thought of the many more happy moments he would spend in Carsdale Mansions, he said, "John, my boy, you've not been doing badly." Perhaps it would have been pleasanter not to have been turned out at that early hour amid the dust of doorstep sweepings, but that was a mere trifle. How tender she had been when he had left her! How pretty she had looked in the faint light of her room, with her long silk-like hair falling over her neck and shoulders, as she had opened him the door, ever so regretfully! Yes, all that was extremely satisfactory.

When it was nearly eight, he returned to the station and ordered a modest breakfast—being forced to be economical, not knowing how he was to obtain fresh supplies. This want of money, he knew, was the true weakness of his position, and it was always leading him into awkward straits.

While he was eating, he unfolded the packet of morning papers, which he had bought at the bookstall, to see what mention had been made of the meeting of the previous evening. All, with the exception of the *Standard*, contained accounts of the proceedings, and to his delight he saw that, not only had his little speech on education been reported almost verbatim, but one of the chief liberal organs had devoted a leaderette to it. Unfortunately, to mar his joy, the paragraph ended thus: "We have not heard of this Mr. Johns before, but it must be admitted that his views on education, if somewhat too Utopian, are not deficient either in force or clearness." This last sentence he did not like. It annoyed him to be called "this Mr. Johns," and that it should be published to the world that he was an unknown man. He swore that some day they should hear of him till their ears ached. *This* Mr. Johns, indeed! Let them wait till he got a chance!

When he had finished his breakfast it was still early; but he calculated that, if he walked slowly, he would reach the office at a convenient hour, and he would be able to stop at a barber's upon the way in order to be shaved. For it would not do to look disreputable after his success, and a success it was undoubtedly, in spite of the qualified praise of the leaderette. He felt as proud as the day when he had seen his first article in print, and he looked at the people he met, in the face, with the calm demeanour of a man who has done "something big."

And then, after ten minutes spent in a hairdresser's shop in the Strand, he made his way to the office of the paper.

The first to congratulate him was Maskelyne, whom he met upon the stairs.

"You were splendid," he said. "Voice, gesture, and ideas were all admirable."

Johns, to whom praise was as ambrosia, said, "I hit it off pretty well, didn't I?"

"Couldn't have been better! I've written it up for you in to-day's, and if Boyd lets all I've written pass, you won't have cause to grumble."

Johns said, "I'll remember it."

A little higher up the stairs he met Coulston, who said, in a tone which was not free from sarcasm, "So, I hear you made a remarkable oration last night at Aldgate."

Johns answered, "I made a speech which has been remarked; that was all, Coulston."

He had been in the habit of saying "Mr. Coulston" to the sub-editor, but he intentionally dropped the "Mr." to mark familiarity, equality, indifference.

Coulston passed along without answering, and Johns reached Tarte's room.

The old man was looking over manuscripts. He glanced up as Johns entered.

"Demosthenes," he said, "spoke only for his country's good. Did you, last night, do likewise?"

Johns answered, "Did you think so when you read my speech?"

"I haven't read your speech."

"Then I'll answer you when you have." But he added afterwards, "All right, Tarte; we understand each other."

Towards mid-day Dawson sent for Johns, and, when the latter appeared in the private room, the proprietor rose and held out his hand to him."

"My dear Johns," he said, "a thousand congratulations. I hear you were quite brilliant."

"They tell me so," said Johns, coolly.

"I had no idea," the proprietor continued, "you could do that sort of thing."

Johns smiled.

"Do you know, I'm afraid we must really find something better for you to do than mere reporting. I will speak to Boyd about it this very day!"

In the afternoon Johns was called to the editorial room, where he found the two chiefs.

"We have decided," Boyd commenced, "to offer you the preparation of the events column, jointly with Mr. Coulston, who has been for some time endeavouring to do it single-handed In this way you will receive a fixed salary of, let us say, sixteen pounds a month. Will that suit you?"

"It will suit me admirably for the present," Johns replied.

"You see," said Boyd, turning to Dawson, "Mr. Johns is somewhat ambitious."

"Well," said Dawson, "I don't object to that. It's often good for the paper."

Johns asked for a few days to study his new duties, and these were granted, as well as an additional advance of which, he told Dawson, he was much in need. He became so much absorbed studying the files of the paper to make himself familiar with the column to which he was henceforth to devote his energies that, when the Saturday came, he was well-nigh forgetting his appointment with Mrs. Dawson. As soon as he remembered it, however, he took a hansom (he could afford one now) and drove to Princes Gate.

As he approached the house he recalled the few words he had exchanged with the wife of the proprietor after the meeting in the hall at Aldgate, and the look of timid, yet ready acquiescence which he had noticed on her face when she had consented to receive him. He thought that he must be very much mistaken if Mrs. Dawson was not seriously inclined to fall in love with him.

And if so, what could he derive from it? Nothing perhaps directly, but a great deal indirectly. Did he not want to be editor, and wouldn't this woman's love, if he obtained it, be a splendid lever ? He knew by past experience what a woman in love could do for the man she loved, and it would be magnificent if he could get rid of the many obstacles which stood between him and the post he coveted. Besides, Mrs. Dawson was a pretty blonde, and he remembered that he had found her particularly attractive that evening at the hall. And then it was impossible that she should be attached to such an old brute as Dawson—quite impossible. These reflections lasted till his hansom stopped before the house.

The servants knew him now, and had probably, he thought, pardoned the want of orthodoxy in his dress, for he was immediately conducted to the drawing-room, where he found Mrs. Dawson.

She was sitting near the window reading, and her first words were, as she gave her hand—

"I was beginning to think you were not coming."

"Not coming!" he repeated in a tone of sorrowful surprise. "You little know me. You do not know that if Princes Gate had been as difficult of access as the summit of Mont Blanc on a stormy day, I would not have failed to come."

"You are always so enthusiastic!"

"Always—when with you!"

"I hear," she said, "that you are going to do something more suited to your ability at the office. I told my husband after the meeting the other night that it was ridiculous that you should be a reporter when you can speak so well."

"And it is then to you that I owe the sudden offer that they made me! Ah, was I not right a little time ago when I said you were my guardian angel?"

"I'm afraid my share in it was very slight. It was your own merit."

He gazed wistfully into her face.

"And you really think I have some little merit. Ah, if you knew how your words enchant me, how they give me strength to triumph. I feel, when I hear you speak, that there is comfort in the sound of your soft voice, solace in the very movement of your lips, promise in the words they utter."

He paused a moment, for, before diving deeper into sentiment, he wanted to know if the coast was clear. Then he continued, "And when I see your husband this afternoon ——"

But she interrupted with—

"He's gone to Manchester."

"Oh, then it doesn't matter. Mrs. Dawson, shall I make you a confession?"

"If it's not anything I should not hear."

"It is that I am unhappy! You may see no change in me perhaps; I may even laugh at times, but I swear to you that I am unhappy, terribly unhappy."

"May I know the cause?"

"Ah yes, you may. I am hopelessly in love!"

"And may I know with whom?"

"With you, alas! with you!"

Her lips quivered, and she moved in her chair nervously.

"I thought," she said, in a voice which she tried to make severe, "that you had promised not to say such things to me again."

He reflected, "If she didn't expect it, why was she willing to receive me here alone?" and he said—

"There are some promises which are against nature, which are beyond the power of the will to keep. I have done my best. I have wrestled with my longing, tried by every means I knew to silence, to subdue it; but in vain, in vain! Lucy—oh let me call you Lucy—I told you once that you suggested those fine lines from Haidee, but now, as I see you there with those golden tresses and that perfect face, I say that Byron himself never was inspired by such charms. You asked me the other night why I had not been to see you. Could you not guess why I kept away? It was because to see you, to speak with you, and to know that you were the wife of another is torture for me—torture and fascination! Ah, if you only knew how many times I started to come here and then turned back, wretched and discouraged, angry with the fate that had ordained it thus! If you only knew how many sleepless nights I've spent thinking over it, lamenting, wishing I had never left Australia, or that I had found you free! You appeared to me from the first instant I beheld you as the true realization of my dreams. You do not know the power of your beauty. You do not know how it has taken possession of me, how it has claimed me as its own and fettered me in chains that will never break. No, you do not know. But when I entered this room just now I felt that not another hour should pass before I had told you of my passion, before I had entreated you to show clemency, to have pity, and to be merciful."

He had pronounced the last words supplicatingly, with his arms stretched out towards her in a practised attitude, but before he had finished speaking, she had risen, and stood undecided, looking away from him, flushed, and with a frown upon her forehead.

"Mr. Johns, I cannot listen to you. It's not right of you to speak to me like this. It's the first time anyone has said such things to me. It's wrong. I'm sorry for you, truly sorry, if you are so—I mean if you care for me so much, but in future you must think of me as a friend—a friend who wishes well to you."

She spoke agitatedly, almost confusedly, and he thought, "If she's on the *friend* tack, it's so much gained."

He said, "I know I must be mad to hope, to dream, and yet I cannot help it. I am as unable now to cease loving you as the moth to refrain from flying round the flame. If you tell me that we can never be but friends, you crush me. My life henceforth will have no meaning, will be rendered hateful, odious. The woman I adore will be chained to a man she cannot love—for I *know* you do not love him—while *I* shall be condemned to be a witness of such sacrilege."

Quickly he drew near to her and whispered in her ear—

"Lucy, my darling Lucy, do not take all hope away from me. Leave me a little ray so that I may find strength to go on living. Think of the unjust sacrifice you're making, think of its cruelty, its uselessness. I cannot, no, I cannot, look upon that perfect form, those lovely eyes, those perfect lips, without feeling that my reason is deserting me, that I am growing giddy, that I must not, will not, listen to any but the voice of love."

He saw that she was breathing fast, as if deeply moved. Thinking the moment opportune, he clasped her round the waist, and tried to kiss her.

But he found, to his disappointment, that he had gone too fast, for, instead of submitting, as he had thought she would, she disengaged herself with sudden energy, and, placing her hand upon the bell knob, said excitedly—

"If you attempt that, I'll ring."

He saw that she was in earnest, and that, for the moment, there was nothing to be done. To retrieve himself, he cried in a repentant tone, upon his knees—

"Oh, forgive me. I was mad and not able to control my passion. It was a sudden fit. I was not responsible. Say that you forgive me."

"I forgive you," she said slowly, and he fancied that her eyes glistened.

He rose, and, after pressing her hand in silence, left.

CHAPTER SIXTH

WHEN Johns left Princes Gate, he felt that he had risked much. He had not expected so much firmness on the part of Mrs. Dawson. She had appeared to him in the light of a woman tied to a man much older than herself and of coarser origin. He had considered that she was secretly regretting her enslavement, and would not refuse to avail herself of an opportunity of making it less hard to bear. But instead of that, she had made a show of virtue, had silenced him by threatening to ring the bell! The mistake was certainly annoying, and he scarcely knew what its effects would be. There was the danger of her refusing to receive him now, and that would seriously upset his plans, impede his progress. Why, then, had he been so hasty? Why had he not shown more patience and more prudence? Why had he not been more skilful? Well, he hadn't, and that was all about it. He wasn't going to quarrel with himself.

And as he reflected over it in bed that night, he reviewed the behaviour of the wife of the proprietor towards him since he had known her. He thought of the mildness of her rebuke after his first attack, the readiness with which she had consented to receive him, and he remembered a certain softness in the expression of her eyes when she was speaking. It was not long before he came to the conclusion that after all he had not much to fear. He had studied women well enough to know that his protestations of undying love could not have been entirely in vain; that it was impossible that some of them had not flattered, if they had not moved her. For that reason alone, he was sure that she would refrain from telling her husband a word of what had passed. No, that she would not do. He could feel easy on that score. Perhaps, indeed, she had been more strongly hit than he suspected. Did one ever know with women? and was not the very moment when they were upon the point of giving way often the time when they seemed most firm? Who could tell? The morality of women depended so much on circumstances! Educate them more? No, by God, he wasn't in favour of *that* notion.

Still, there was no doubt that the method which had succeeded with Mrs. Weber was not the one he ought to have employed with Mrs. Dawson. The conditions were not the same. The wife had more to lose than the widow, and therefore he should have been more careful. Although in reality, as long as there was no harm done to his own prospects, her severity didn't matter so very much. It would certainly have been easier if he had had chambers somewhere. He could have asked her to come to see his curios, his photographs, his trophies, and if she had come—oh, then, the result would hardly have been doubtful.

Yes he must move to better quarters as soon as he could afford it. He was sick of the squalid meanness of his surroundings. He must change them as soon as possible. If he could only raise £50, that would put him on a better footing and enable him to decently equip himself. Of course, his salary would be a little higher now; but he would have so long to wait before he would be paid, and he was weary of the expedients he was forced to use. He wanted to be fed decently and to be lodged decently.

The next morning being Sunday, he asked himself what he should do; whether he should call on Mrs. Dawson in the afternoon as if nothing had occurred, or whether he should let a little time elapse before going to her house again. After mature reflection, he decided to take the latter course.

In the afternoon, however, he was seized with a sudden longing to see Mrs. Weber, and although he had made no appointment for that day, he decided he would call on the chance of finding her at home. He was prompted, also, by a kind of curiosity to know where she was, and if possible what she was doing on an afternoon when she did not expect him.

When he arrived at Carsdale Mansions he was told that Mrs. Weber was at home, and on entering the drawing-room he found Parker with her. They were seated before a little table on which was a liqueur stand, and were smoking cigarettes.

Johns fancied that she started slightly when he was announced, but she rose at once and welcomed him as she would have welcomed an acquaintance who had called by chance.

Parker, although he shook hands cordially with Johns, did not seem to the young man to be much pleased with his visit, and for some time, while they were speaking of the meeting and the prospects of the radicals, there was a reserve which was the more apparent because they did their best to hide it.

Occasionally the conversation drooped, and there was a silence which Mrs. Weber would break by starting a new topic. Now and then, also, Johns surprised Parker, whom he was watching narrowly, casting a furtive glance at the clock upon the mantelpiece. But Johns, who wanted to remain after Parker left, began an explanation of the lecture he was preparing, and which, he said, was to be called *The Spirit of the True Radical*. He meant to embody in it all the principles of the leaders of the party during the last ten years, and to add some observations of his own.

"Quite right," said Parker, though with less enthusiasm than he generally evinced. "You can't do better."

Johns thought, "He's sure of his election, and he doesn't trouble about me now."

He pretended to be perfectly oblivious that he was in the way, as he suspected that he might be, and when half an hour had been thus spent, Parker left, after ceremoniously taking leave of Mrs. Weber.

When the door had closed upon the member for North Aldgate, Johns took the seat which he had just vacated. Without alluding to Parker's presence there that afternoon, he said, gravely—

"I came, Ellen, to tell you something that will trouble you, I fear."

"Oh, what is it?" she exclaimed, anxiously.

"I'm thinking of returning to Australia."

"Of returning to Australia!" she repeated, as if she did not realize his meaning.

"Listen, Ellen. I've been reflecting since Thursday, when I left you after so much happiness! so much happiness! that journalism here is a poor trade, since I'm actually in want of a miserable £50 to pay my creditors. I feel a strong repugnance to speak of such things to you, but if I did not, you might think I was hiding something from you. When I came over, I had spent nearly all I had, and although I haven't been here many months, I've been obliged to run up bills and to contract debts which must be paid. At present I can't pay them, and for a paltry sum I'm to be condemned to lose, or to no longer see, the only woman I have ever loved. My fate is indeed hard."

She burst out laughing.

"And it's for the enormous sum of £50 that you, with your abilities, are thinking of giving up the game! John, you've been too many days away from me, and you've been worrying about trifles as men sometimes do. What is £50, I should like to know? You'll have to let me lend that large amount at 25 per shent."

He answered, still with gravity, "I thought you knew me better, Ellen, than to speak like that."

"But it's ridiculous. Everybody says that you'll get on. It's only a question of a little time. You really must let me be your usurer for once."

But he knit his brow.

"Ellen, I beg of you not to speak of that again."

She was silent for a moment; then she said, "At all events you're not off by the next boat. I'm not going to despair. I know it will be all right. For £50! It's too ridiculous! No, my Johnnie, you're my property, and all the creditors in the world ——"

He seized her in his arms and kissed her.

"Ellen, my little Ellen, whatever happens I shall always love you!"

She whispered presently, "Why didn't you tell me you were coming, John? I wouldn't have promised to dine this evening with the Dawsons!"

"Talking of them," she added; "do you know, I believe you've made an impression on Lucy, you dreadful monster. She looks quite peculiar when I speak of you, and she generally tries to change the subject. That's a pretty sure sign, you know. If she weren't married and so strictly principled, I should be inclined to be a little jealous."

"Jealous of Mrs. Dawson!" he said, deprecatingly. "That would be indeed folly!"

"Who knows! If I were a man, I think she would attract me."

He stayed with her until it was time for her to get ready for the Dawsons, but before he left they arranged to dine together on the Wednesday.

As he was leaving she enquired, "Do you still wish to have your letters addressed to the office of the paper?"

"It's just as well," he answered, "in fact, it's more convenient."

In the street, as he was walking home, thinking over what had passed, he muttered, "What a fool I was not to say a hundred," and he was ill-humoured all the evening at the thought. Returning home early, after dinner, he went to bed at once.

The next morning he began his new work at the office. It was his duty to make comments, chiefly on politicians and political events, in strict accordance with the paper's tone. It was necessary that all the acts, whether good or bad, of the opposition should be held up to ridicule or to contempt; and that the errors of the radicals should be converted into proofs of wisdom. The theory was that the "party" was never wrong, and its opponents never right, and Johns grasped that readily. Not only did he show ingenuity in working round his subject, but he also evidenced a capacity for "hitting hard," which Tarte prophesied would worry the rival organs. This new employment had the advantage of bringing him into touch with the members of the staff, and it gave him access to the editorial room. Coulston was by no means pleased with it, but Johns performed his work without troubling himself about him, and Boyd, since the Aldgate meeting, seeing the favour in which he was held by Dawson, was forced to be more conciliatory.

While Johns was engaged in scanning the papers on the Tuesday morning before writing his paragraphs, a messenger came in and handed him a letter, registered. He was not surprised when he recognised the handwriting of Mrs. Weber on the blue-marked envelope. As there was no one in the room he opened it at once, and a piece of paper fell from it, which he picked up and unfolded. It was a Bank of England note bearing the word "fifty" in German text in the right-hand corner.

He breathed a sigh of satisfaction, and then read the letter, which ran thus—

"My own Johnnie. It is really too ridiculous that you should be worried for the sake of fifty pounds, and I insist— mind, I insist—on your accepting this little note. If by any chance you were to return it to me, I would be so deeply hurt that I swear I would never speak to you again.

"Remember, seven o'clock on Wednesday. Ever yours, Ellen."

He placed the note in his leather letter case, but the letter he tore into small pieces, which he put into his pocket, preferring, as a measure of precaution, not to trust them to the paper basket.

Then he muttered, "That's all right," for the feel of the crisp bank note had dispelled the regret he had felt at first at not saying he was in need of a larger sum. He experienced a feeling of relief. His road now appeared to him much straighter, and that very evening, when his work was over, he started westward in search of better quarters.

He would have liked to obtain rooms in the authentic Grafton Street, off Bond Street, in which he was supposed to live, but after a search, as he was unable to find any there, he wandered about until, in Jermyn Street, he discovered two which, though small, seemed suitable. They were furnished with more taste than is usually to be found in what are termed apartments, as though some festive bachelor of taste had furnished them himself. Johns engaged them without hesitation, and told the proprietor that he would come in on the morrow. No doubt the rent would make a large inroad on his present income, but the £50, judiciously expended, would enable him to hold out until his position mended. He walked down Piccadilly conscious that he had an address of which he need not be ashamed, and feeling several degrees higher in the social scale—now that he was transformed into a fashionable bachelor. He had only to find a trustful tailor, and the transformation would be complete.

Then, as he was anxious not to remain an hour longer than was needful in Grafton Street, he hurried home to tell his landlady of his departure and to pack up his belongings. As his wardrobe had increased since his arrival, the black portmanteau would not suffice, and on the way he stopped at a shop and ordered a large "Gladstone" to be sent to him immediately.

His landlady received his announcement that he was going into rooms in Jermyn Street and that he wanted to pay his bill, with some astonishment, for it was not often that her "gentlemen" left her to go to a more expensive neighbourhood. It was generally the other way, she said, with a grin, as she fingered the sovereigns he gave her, but, of course, it was nice to rise in the world, and she hoped he would continue doing so.

When he had packed everything ready to leave the next morning, and was going out again to dine, he suddenly thought of Maggie, and at once he felt a revival of affection for the pale-faced girl who seemed so lonely. He had not been to see her lately, and he wondered how she was getting on. It was only right that he should say good-bye.

In answer to his knock, a feeble voice invited him to enter. He entered, and as there was no one in the parlour, he passed on to the next room.

In the middle of a large bed, at the side of which was a little table bearing a medicine bottle and a glass, Maggie's head appeared above the covers, half hidden in a network of dishevelled hair, which spread itself upon the pillow. Her face was thin and colourless, and her eyes sunken. She seemed to be in pain.

Johns approached the bedside.

"Oh," she said, "I was going to ask you to come and see me. Ever since Saturday I have been so ill!"

She was interrupted by a fit of coughing.

"I caught a chill, and the doctor says it's settled on my chest, and he won't say when I will be better. Oh, and things have been going bad for me. Nobody seems to like me now. And Mrs. Reid says she can't keep me if I don't pay her, and I've got no money, not a farthing."

She hid her face in her pillow and began to sob.

John's features gave a nervous twitch. Women's tears made him feel uncomfortable, and he tried to find a few words of encouragement.

"Why, Maggie, what is the meaning of all this worry for a cold? Of course you'll be better in a day or two, and as for the money, my luck's been better lately, and I'm going to make you a little present."

Saying this, he thrust his hand into his pocket, drew out his purse, and taking two sovereigns from it he placed them on the table by the bedside.

"Oh, thanks," she murmured, "I thought you would try to help me when you knew."

He stayed with her a few minutes in the disordered room, with its odour of medicine and its air of misery, and as he looked at her, and listened to her hollow cough, he concluded that her spell down here would not be long. Then, as hopeless cases of any kind disturbed him, he left her without saying that he had come to say good-bye.

When he was outside he said, "She's mistaken *her* vocation with a vengeance," and he hurried off to dinner without thinking any more about her.

Early the next morning he left Grafton Street, with his now respectable new luggage. As the cab moved off he gave a last look at the house and mentally took leave of its genteel shabbiness, he hoped for ever.

The drive to Jermyn Street represented in his mind a translation to a sphere of respectability, a kind of minor apotheosis presaging a greater one. When he reached the house, he entrusted the luggage to the valet at the door, who received him with much deference. Then he hurried to the Strand, performed his daily task, and in the evening went to Aldgate, where he was advertised to lecture. There he addressed an appreciative audience, in the hall in which the electors' meeting had been held, on *The Spirit of the True Radical*, and his address was duly reported in the next day's *Planet*.

As he had anticipated, Mrs. Dawson had not told her husband what had passed, for the proprietor was friendlier than ever, often calling him into his private room to enquire how he was getting on, and chatting with him about his project of enlarging the paper by two sheets. Johns listened attentively, and offered a suggestion now and then, which Dawson received with favour. Sometimes Johns hinted that a larger circulation might be reached under a different system.

When the Wednesday came, he thought frequently throughout the day about the attitude he was going to adopt towards Mrs. Weber, and when he reached her door that evening, after a meditative walk from Jermyn Street, he delayed ringing until he had composed the countenance he had decided upon wearing. Then he touched the knob, and was admitted.

He entered the drawing-room, where the widow was waiting for him, with an expression of great solemnity. Advancing slowly towards her, he took her hand and raised it to his lips.

"Ellen," he said, "since I received your note I have been engaged in a constant struggle with myself. You confronted me with two alternatives—I must either accept your misguided offer, or else leave England and no longer see you. Well, Ellen, the trial was too great. I could not bring myself to lose you, and you see me here to-night, convicted in my own eyes and perhaps in yours."

But she took his hands and said, "My own Johnnie, how can you say that! I love you more for the confidence you have in me, and for letting me do the little I can for you, but for Heaven's sake say no more about it, or I shall feel that we are greater strangers than I thought."

He asked no better than to say no more; but he preserved a certain thoughtfulness and reticence all through the evening. He told her that he had removed to a small room in Jermyn Street, where rents were cheaper, because he wanted to economise until he had obtained the post he aimed at. But he could not receive her there, he said. It was too small and too uncomfortable. Besides, had they not found a means of getting over the difficulty of the servants? and as for the porter down below, his discretion was secured. They had nothing to fear —nothing.

He did not leave, this time, until two hours after daybreak the next morning.

The next day Mrs. Baxter was holding a reception, and as

Mrs. Weber had told him that Mrs. Dawson would be there, Johns was not a little curious to know what attitude she would adopt towards him. His own behaviour, he decided, must be based on hers, and there was no knowing what it would prove to be : he had a feeling that she would not be too severe, though with women one never knew. Of one thing he fancied he was sure. He thought he knew, with certainty, that when a man persistently made love to any woman, it was almost impossible for that woman to preserve herself from thinking of that man. Involuntary obsessions, such as these, often had an influence upon women of which they were barely conscious. At all events, he was going to have an opportunity of ascertaining. He really did not care, very much, whether she fell in love with him or not. He only thought of her as a sufficiently attractive blonde, who might advance his interests.

Although the season was drawing to its close, he was beginning to receive invitations from the majority of Mrs. Dawson's friends. Many of these—the unimportant ones—he had declined; for he wanted to increase his social value, and that, he deemed, could be best effected by showing himself exclusive. Among the few invitations that he accepted was that of Mrs. Baxter—the lady whom he had met, that auspicious evening, at the Berkeley.

As soon, therefore, as he could leave, he made his way to the Baxters' house in Portland Place.

He found, when he entered the reception-room, after being warmly received by Mrs. Baxter on the threshold, that he had come to one of those crowded gatherings which seem designed to flatten, to compress the unfortunates for whose amusement they are organized, and he was imprisoned, to his disgust, for many minutes in a dense crowd of people vaguely listening to a pianist who was invisible to most of them. Johns, on account of his short stature, felt himself buried in the throng, and it was in vain that he stood upon tip-toes to try to catch a glimpse of either Mrs. Weber or Mrs. Dawson. He could see nothing but the backs of the people immediately before him. This sort of function, in which he had no chance of making himself seen or heard, irritated him extremely, and he swore that he would never come to one again unless it was greatly to his interest to do so.

When the pianist had finished there was a slight slackening, and it became possible to make an attempt to move. Johns took advantage of it to disengage himself, and he was progressing slowly round the room, when, suddenly, he found himself face to face with Mrs. Dawson.

Gravely, with that impressive gravity which he knew so well how to assume, he held out his hand to her, saying with a long sigh, "Mrs. Dawson!"

Embarrassed, she said, apparently at random, "Isn't it crowded here to-day?"

He looked about, and seeing a recess which had been constructed on the verandah, said, "Oppressively! Let us go over yonder." And perceiving that she seemed inclined to follow, he made a passage for her through the throng.

A poet of the long-haired tribe was preparing to recite, and the occupants of the recess were coming out to listen. Soon, therefore, they were alone, seated upon a red divan amid the foliage of some giant palms.

He did not ask her if she wished to listen to the reciter, but exclaimed, "Ah! if you knew!"

"What?" she asked, timorously.

"What I have suffered! What I suffer!"

She looked down quickly, and he continued, "But do not be afraid. I have struggled with myself, and I have succeeded, heaven knows with how much pain, in subduing, not my feelings, for that is utterly impossible, but myself! No, you have no need to fear. I have disciplined myself; I have brought myself into subjection. I am the most harmless, the most humble of your admirers. Will you not have confidence in me?"

"I want to have confidence in you," she said, in a low voice, which seemed to him to tremble.

The words of the reciter penetrated indistinctly to them in a confused medley of sounds and rhymes and sentiments.

"Will you give me a proof of that?" he asked.

"But how can I?"

"Listen for a moment. I want to speak to you more earnestly, more explicitly, than I can here—in this place, which will be filled again as soon as that poet stops. Not, believe me, to cause you the slightest apprehension—that is all over now—but I entreat you, I implore you, to give me an opportunity of telling you all that I have in my heart to say, all that I *must* say some day if I am to relieve my mind of the weight which burdens it. I feel that you will not refuse to tell me where to meet you, what day, what hour. Choose the place that suits you best, be it park or picture gallery, or where you will, but tell me quickly where and when. If you refuse, this will be the last time you will see me. Unless I have your friendship, I shall go back to Australia."

She looked troubled, anxious, and replied, "But it's impossible, how can I?"

"You can meet me to-morrow at the National Gallery at four."

"Oh, how could I?"

"That poet will have finished in a moment. I entreat you, I implore you, to say yes or no."

"Oh, you must not ask it."

"Yes or no?"

"Must I really?"

"Ah," he murmured, quickly, "you have taken a sad weight off my mind! You have given me new hope, you will not regret that you have agreed to come. You will never have reason to regret it—never!"

"But remember, if I consent to come, it is only because you have given me your word that you will not speak to me again as you did last time we met."

He thought, "She's getting tedious with her virtue," and he said, "Alas, yes! I have bound myself in fetters. Those fetters I shall never break."

But at that moment there was a slight rustle amid the palms at the entrance of the recess, and Mrs. Weber, escorted by Parker, entered.

As Johns rose, the widow gave him a sharp glance which, after scrutinizing him, passed on to Mrs. Dawson. Johns met it by a calm smile and a look which included the widow and the politician.

After greetings had been exchanged, Parker said to Johns, "Mr. Johns, it is often my duty to congratulate you now. I hear your lecture was very well received."

Johns answered, "Very well. The gentlemen of Aldgate are more appreciative than I thought."

Then, as by this time the recitation was over and the recess was beginning to be filled, Parker, who seemed to consider it incumbent on him to speak to Mrs. Dawson, took a seat beside her, and Johns another next to Mrs. Weber. And as the conversation in the already filled recess had become noisy, the widow was able to say to Johns without being overheard, "So you preferred solitude to poetry this afternoon."

He answered quietly, "Like you."

She glanced at him enquiringly, suspiciously, and asked, "What do you mean by that?"

He answered, smiling, "Not more than you, by your first question."

Then he whispered almost in her ear, "Don't be silly, Ellen!"

For some moments she was silent, while he was thinking, "I must steer carefully to-day."

Why Parker was so often with her he did not seek to know. There might be one reason, there might also be another. For the moment it didn't matter. It would be time enough to find out later on. He continued presently, "I was looking for you everywhere, but in that crush I could not find you, and now I'm obliged to get back to the office, as I'm over head and ears in work."

"Till Wednesday then," she said.

"Till Wednesday."

Johns excused himself to Mrs. Dawson and to Parker, and stopped on his way out to say a few words to his hostess and to her ugly daughter. Then he left, and walked home satisfied with his afternoon.

He scarcely imagined that Mrs. Dawson seriously believed he would have carried out his threat of leaving England if she had refused to meet him, and the fact of her accepting the excuse as easily as she had done proved, he thought, that there was just that balance of desire which he had often remarked on the part of women.

On the morrow, although he had not had time to be dressed by the tailor in his street from whom he had ordered a complete wardrobe, he composed a fairly presentable exterior with a new silk hat and patent boots. Having finished his work early, he left the office shortly after half-past three, and hurried along the Strand. When he reached the Gallery, he mounted the long flight of steps, two at a time, in his anxiety to avoid being recognised by anyone passing in the street. Beneath the peristyle he asked himself whether he should wait for her in the vestibule or at the entrance to the first room, up above. After a moment's reflection he decided on the latter course. He entered, therefore, and mounting to the first floor, took up his position behind a glass-panelled door, whence he could see the entrance wickets.

His feelings were by no means as intense as the day when he had waited for the widow at Victoria; but still he watched the entrance narrowly, and scrutinized the ladies who came in alone. Some entered hesitatingly, with the demure air of women going to a rendezvous, casting side-glances as they ascended the marble staircase. Others passed up quickly, looking straight before them and disappearing in the Galleries. Johns thought, "I'm not the only one who's expecting an *inamorata*." Bands of foreign tourists, Baedekers in hand, their travelling bags strapped across their shoulders, were ascending the wide staircase, looking around them with that lost air peculiar to tourists. Little shop assistants, out of work, carrying a book or journal with which to pass a quiet hour in the Galleries, were descending leisurely, and a few youths with dirty hands and faces moved along as if in awe at the impressive architecture. Some entered through the entrance above which Johns was standing. Others went in by one of the doors on either side. As Johns was pacing to and fro before the door, one of the custodians in uniform was eyeing him with apparent curiosity, guessing, no doubt, the reason of his presence there; while from the Galleries beyond came the clattering sound of footsteps on the hard oak floor.

At length, after he had been waiting for at least ten minutes, he saw a lady pass through the wicket hurriedly, and recognizing Mrs. Dawson, he hastened down the stairs to meet her. Without giving him her hand, she said, "Let us go quickly where we won't meet anyone."

He answered, "I know the exact spot," and he led her in silence through the fine Renaissance galleries to a little room which, being devoted to mediæval art, attracted but few visitors.

Around them on the walls were paintings in the strangest of perspective. Knights in armour, lance in hand, were riding towards weird castles which seemed to be suspended from the clouds of an ultra-marine firmament. Monks on their bended knees were beholding fat-faced angels in the sky. Virgins, with and without the Child, were depicted, some with joyous, some with sorrowful expressions. Martyred Christs and holy men were shown before the farthest of receding backgrounds. There were gilded triptychs and quaint ecclesiastical presentments.

Leaning against the hand-rail before the portrait of an ascetic saint in a gothic frame, Johns said, pointing to the picture, "Is not this art of the middle ages wonderful? Look at that saintly man, look at the serenity, the magnanimity, the grandeur which is depicted on his placid countenance! Does he not really seem to be a man far more than human?"

"Oh, yes, he does," she answered, "but what was it, Mr. Johns, that you were so anxious to see me for to-day? You said, you know, that you had something to say to me—something that would be different from anything you've said as yet."

"Eternal curiosity!" he thought, and answered, "Yes, Mrs. Dawson, yes, I did. I wanted to tell you that from the day I met you, my life, my being has completely changed. Till then I had hovered from one ideal, from one admiration to another, vaguely, wantonly, and lightly—satisfying mere whims and fancies, always realizing their hollowness, their transcience.

But from the day I met you I knew that I was definitely chained to one ideal; I knew that I should never in the world find one more perfect. What then did I do? I told you of the love which had come to me, I spoke of the divine feeling of which I had grown conscious, I endeavoured to excite your pity. But you were as inflexible as adamant. You bade me choose one of two sad alternatives. Either I must treat you as a friend, or I must never speak to you again! Rather than lose the ideal I had found, I accepted the hard conditions, and it is as friends to-day that we are here together. But friendship is of many kinds, and it was to tell you how I understand it that I entreated you to come. Only one great boundless friendship can satisfy, can comfort me. A friendship as perfect as you are perfect, indissoluble as long as we have life, a friendship in which a sweet community of thought, a perfect confidence will reign. Convinced as you are now that you can trust me, you will tell me all your cares and I will tell you mine. A rare and beautiful reciprocity of feeling will grow up between us, which will help us both to live, which will relieve the burdens we both have to bear. Whenever we are alone together, and I hope that now it will be often, we will call each other by our Christian names, we will have no secrets from each other, we will live in the firm hope that one day we will be united."

Unable to think of any more variations of the same air, he stopped, turning the gaze of his piercing eyes upon her.

"That," he said, "was what I had to tell you!"

She continued looking at the picture of the saint, and after a lengthy pause, which Johns refrained from interrupting, said, "Oh, but is not that a dangerous kind of friendship?"

"Not now! Not now!"

"I've told you that I want to trust you, haven't I?"

"You have, you have."

"Well, then, I will try to offer you that friendship, and it will be your fault if I don't succeed."

"Oh, Lucy, Lucy," he exclaimed, "how happy you have made me!"

"Have I really?——John."

"That's promising," he thought, and he began to tell her how they would arrange to meet as often as they could, so that the sacred flame of friendship, as he called it, should never for one moment flicker. They would accept the same invitations, go to the same theatres, to the same shows, and there would be a feeling of association, of companionship, which would be subtle and intense—a feeling such as only higher minds could know. And then, if they grew tired of meeting always before strangers, before whom they could not talk even in the language of pure friendship lest it might be misconstrued, they might try to meet somewhere where they would not be troubled by, perhaps, malicious listeners. And since he was speaking of such a possibility, why should he not tell her that he had a pleasant little sitting-room in Jermyn Street, where they might meet, and where he had some curiosities he longed to show her, some photographs which he wanted her to see. And after all, why should they hesitate, why should they defer the realization of a project which was harmless and so natural? Why should she not pay him a little visit the very next afternoon—between five and six, as a diversion from her shopping? How she would be welcomed and respected! And how he would be gladdened! Oh, why should it not be? Yes, let it be!

For some minutes he waited for her answer, looking intently at her, guessing the struggle which was taking place in her woman's conscience, feeling that success was already half assured.

Presently she said, "I wonder if I might! But think how dreadful it would be if I were seen! Who would believe that it was merely as a friend?"

He thought, "Who indeed!" and answered, "But no one will see you, Lucy, no one. A bootmaker has a shop on the ground floor, and one entrance serves for both. The street is as quiet as any in a country town. There's no risk, absolutely none."

"But someone might call to see you!"

"They wouldn't be admitted. Every precaution shall be taken."

"And do you really think I should?"

"Ah, it will be such a charity!"

"Well, then," she said, slowly, "I'll try; but mind, if anything should happen, I'll never come again."

He thought, "She's precious willing"; and once again he reassured her, telling her that her reputation would be as dear as her friendship to him; that he would guard it so jealously— so jealously that not the slightest breath of a suspicion would ever be allowed to tarnish it. Oh, she need not fear. He would promise that she would be without reproach.

And, either because she was convinced, or because she wished to seem so, she told him that she would place herself confidently in his hands, and that he might rely upon her coming.

He told her the number of the house, the hour at which he would be there to meet her, and then, as the mediæval saints possessed no further interest for them, and as Mrs. Dawson had to meet her husband at a jeweller's in Bond Street, after a few more assurances of confidence, he led her back to the great staircase, at the top of which they parted.

Left alone, Johns, as soon as she had disappeared, gave vent to a little laugh. "And I," he said, "who was almost taking her in earnest the other day. They're all alike—all semi-conscious beings, longing for what they fear, always to be overcome by patience and a few fine words!"

As he waited for Mrs. Dawson the next afternoon in his little parlour, he thought over his adventure. Whither would it lead him? Save that he was confident that the quickest road to fortune was through women, he had no very definite idea.

Women possessed a power of facilitating men's careers. Their love was often one of the best of levers to success. He was resolved to follow out this episode to its conclusion.

And then, was not Mrs. Dawson pretty? And ought he not to think himself extremely fortunate to have won her—or nearly won her—for he hoped she would not weary him with much more virtue now. Virtue was well during the preliminary stages, but it must not be carried to extremes—not certainly after a woman had consented to pay a visit to a man in his own rooms. Surely she would have sense enough to perceive that, and not waste time over that platonic nonsense for which he had no taste—which he held to be one of the inconsistencies of Saxons.

Surveying his room anew, he rearranged the collection of more or less authentic Indian weapons, which he had bought at an antiquary's in Bloomsbury, and which represented the native curios he was supposed to have brought with him from Australia. Then he sorted and put in order a set of coloured views of places in the island which he had discovered at a stationer's in Regent Street.

These things would serve as an introduction to more tender themes, and he was glad that he had been able to procure them.

When the little Buhl clock upon the mantel told him that the hour had arrived, he listened at the door, which he had purposely left ajar, for the sound of ascending footsteps on the staircase. He did not for a moment doubt that she wished to come; but he had a little apprehension as the minutes passed and the staircase remained silent, lest she had been prevented by one of those many reasons which hinder women who have social ties.

But presently his apprehension vanished, for he heard a light hurried step upon the stairs, accompanied by the rustle of a

H

dress. A moment afterwards the footsteps stopped upon his landing. He opened the door wider, and Mrs. Dawson, dressed in black and wearing a thick veil, entered.

"Oh," she said, as he led her to a seat, after divesting her of her parasol, "I was so terrified I might be seen."

He reassured her, and she looked around the room.

"What a charming little nook you have!"

"Lucy, it's a poor place in which to receive you!"

She rose and made a tour of scrutiny, and after she had curiously examined the ornaments upon the mantel shelf—some terra-cotta figures of Sicilian peasants—she stopped before the photograph of a lady in evening dress which Johns had placed there purposely.

"Who is that?" she asked, quickly, in a tone which did not sound quite free from jealousy.

"That," said Johns, "is a portrait of my mother when she was young."

He said this, not from a particular desire to raise himself in the social scale, but because he had remarked that some women have more confidence in men of whose families they know something.

"Your mother was a pretty woman, then," she said, and he answered with a sigh, "Ah, yes!"

"Is she living now?"

"Do not ask me that!"

"Pardon me," she said, "I did not know," and then, noticing the arms displayed upon the table, she exclaimed, "Oh, what savage looking things! Did you bring them from Australia?"

"Yes, I obtained them from the descendant of a chief."

She took a dagger and drew it from its sheath, then a spearhead black with age, and next a battle-axe, the edge of which was jagged as if it had been used in war. Passing to the photographs, she began to turn them over, but he begged her to allow him to explain them. Leading her to the long straight sofa, covered with a leopard's skin, he took a seat beside her. Then, holding the packet in his left hand, he placed the views, one by one, upon her lap, dealing them out with a short elucidation, and sometimes a little anecdote drawn from his experiences. She listened to him approvingly, asking questions now and then, or expressing her admiration. But gradually, as he held the photographs before her, he allowed his hand to linger on her lap, and as he had observed, while he was doing so, that she looked away and blushed, when he reached the last he tarried longer, leaning slightly over her.

He saw that she became somewhat flushed, and, thinking the moment opportune, without any preparation, he dropped upon his knees beside her, hiding his face in his hands and heaving a deep sigh.

"What is the matter?" she asked, nervously.

"Oh," he murmured, "it's too much!"

"What—John?" she enquired, timorously.

"The penance I have imposed upon myself. It's more than human nature can endure, more than a man can bear. It's terrible. It's killing me."

There was a silence. Then he continued—

"I thought that I was stronger. I thought that I had disciplined my feelings; but now I find I cannot conquer them, that they rebel. Ah, you will never know how sorely I am tried!"

She said, taking up her gloves, "Oh, this is dreadful! Think of your promise."

But he had detected a want of firmness in her tone, and raising his head from the sofa and looking up at her imploringly, he commenced breathlessly, "Lucy, listen to me! I had made the firmest resolution that ever a man made to keep my promise, but all my resolutions vanish in your presence. The magic of your beauty, the charm which emanates from you like perfume from a rose, intoxicates and overcomes me. When I look at you so lovely in your pure blonde splendour, I am seized with a subtle feeling as if I were confronted with something irresistible, with an influence which strikes into the depth of my existence, and chains me hopelessly in bonds of the profoundest love. Oh, I know it's wrong of me to speak of love again, but there are impulses against which one cannot struggle. You are the only woman I can ever love, for you are the ideal of all my dreams. You are love itself in its most perfect and superb expression."

He paused a moment to study the effect his words had had, and seeing that she looked away from him, he sprang quickly from his knees to his seat beside her on the sofa. Then, encircling her waist in a passionate embrace, he drew her to him, while the pile of photographs fell clattering upon the floor. "Oh, Lucy, it's useless to go on struggling. We are neither of us strong enough to do it; we cannot fight against inevitable things; it's too cruel, it's torture which we should not bear!"

She had not tried to free herself, but her head was still turned from him. All she seemed able to ejaculate was, "Oh, how dreadful!" and "you've not kept your promise."

Seeing that her presence of mind was fast deserting her, he then continued—

"Listen to me, my little Lucy; we could be so happy, so supremely happy! Our lives would be one long happiness, one constant joy. I believe you love me, yes, I believe that now. Why, then, should we suffer? In the name of what frigid virtue should we go on suffering? You are married to a man you cannot love, who is unworthy of you, and I am free! What is to prevent the realization of our dreams?

But now she made an effort to move from him.

"Oh, I cannot listen to such things. I must leave you now—I cannot stay, you promised that you wouldn't, and it's right not of you."

She spoke disjointedly, and in broken phrases, and, encouraged by her weak resistance, he gathered his forces for a supreme attack.

"Lucy, it must be, there is no help for it. The power which commands we must obey. We were destined for each other, moulded for each other. We belong by nature to each other. Fate wills it. It *must* be."

Without waiting, this time, to see what effect he had produced, he implanted his lips on hers in a long deep kiss. And now he felt that she no longer resisted seriously, and that his triumph was assured.

But knowing, by this time, the woman with whom he had to deal, he thought it wiser to avoid haste, and he changed his tone of firmness for one of tenderness and gratitude, thanking her for having made him happier than he had ever been in his existence, and asking her to trust to his discretion and his love. But he soon discovered, to his annoyance, for he was tired of inventing epithets of love, that she needed more persuasion still—since she now began to tremble for the consequences, as a woman brought up in principles of strict virtue is wont to do. She asked him if he had reflected how disastrous it would be if they were discovered, declaring that she would kill herself rather than face exposure, and imploring him to reason, to reflect. If he would only think more calmly, he would see that she was right. Oh, why was it she had met him, since he fascinated her so dangerously? And what would he himself think of her if she yielded to him? He would think, perhaps, that she had already been unfaithful to her husband, while she could swear that she never had. Oh, what was it that attracted her to him so strangely? Why must it be that they could not love—as friends?"

But at the word "friends" Johns interposed vehemently—

"No, Lucy, that word must not be used again between us. You are too generous to wish to prolong my penance. You *know* that there is no escape from the fatality of love," and he caught her in his arms again.

More than half subdued, she laid her head upon his shoulder, saying—

"Oh, John, I never thought it would come to this!"

"Lucy, it was inevitable."

"Oh, but I must go, I cannot stay."

"No, Lucy, you won't go *now*."

Then he persuaded her to rise, his arm still encircling her waist. He wanted to show her round his little room again, he said—his little den, where he spent hours thinking of her, in that chair over by the fireplace, dreaming of her beauty. One night, he said, he had come in tired, and had gone to sleep in that same arm-chair, dreaming that she was by his side, and then when he awoke and found that it was but a dream, oh, then the room had seemed so empty and his life so grim! And now she had come to grace it, and he wanted her gaze to rest on every object, so that when she was not with him, he could look at something on which her eyes had rested.

As they approached the door which led into the next room, and which was partly hidden by a thick oriental curtain, he felt her stiffen in his grasp and try to pass it quickly. He was beginning to lose patience. He asked himself how long she was going to play the maiden.

This resistance on her part necessitated another journey round the room, which, as there was nothing left to examine or to linger over, soon brought them back to the same spot.

But Johns now thought the prologue had lasted long enough, so, tightening his hold of his companion's waist, he drew her with him through the curtained doorway, while she murmured plaintively, "Oh John! oh John!"

CHAPTER SEVENTH

TWO hours afterwards Johns, who had just taken a tender leave of Mrs. Dawson, was sitting in his arm-chair, smoking a cigarette and thinking. He could not help admitting that, all things considered, the novel conquest he had made had not been very difficult. No doubt he had had to overcome some final scruples, and to listen, also, to a little exhibition of remorse; but, in the end, he had obtained the victory.

Had this new enterprise procured him any satisfaction? he enquired of himself. Well, it had pleased his *amour propre*, and it augured well for future enterprise. But when he came to compare the charms of Mrs. Dawson with those of Mrs. Weber, he was obliged to own that the widow was by far the more delightful. There was a touch of reticence, of Puritanic reticence, about the wife of the proprietor, and, with her, sentiment of the pale, tender kind took the place of passion. Yes, it was undeniable, as far as his feelings were concerned, Mrs. Weber had nothing to lose by the comparison he had had an opportunity of making. And yet, and yet, he could quite imagine that, in certain moods, on certain days, in certain states of the barometer, the blonde would be as acceptable as the brunette.

Of course there was an element of danger in all this, and it was possible that the day might come when the house he had been building would tumble about his ears. But those were the risks of war, and they couldn't be avoided. Besides, he was scarcely anxious on that score, knowing very well that it wasn't often that women were willing to accuse themselves, and as for the precautions to be taken, well, he meant to take as many as he could. Fancy old Dawson now! How amusing

THE ADVENTURES OF JOHN JOHNS

it would be to study him, to see what a man looked like who was in his shoes. He laughed. How superior he felt to the whole office-full of scribes, now that he shared the wife of the proprietor with the proprietor himself! It almost seemed to him that he formed part of the proprietary! And certainly he could not fail to benefit by this. Had she not said, that very afternoon, in a tender moment, succeeding a remorseful one, that she would always have his interest at heart? Yes, women were made to be helps to men, and he smiled as he thought of the multitudes who toil and drudge for wives who bring them nothing except children and bad temper.

But the season was drawing to its close, and, though he had arranged to see Mrs. Dawson once again before she left for Homburg with her husband, he knew that the time was coming when he would be left alone; for even Mrs. Weber talked of going on the river in the autumn. He reflected that he must shape his course accordingly. How pleasant, and amusing, too, it was to think that he was increasing in Dawson's favour.

For, to the surprise of Maskelyne and the reporting staff, from whom he was now completely severed, he had gained free access to the private room, and he knew that they were not accustomed, at the office, to see men rise so rapidly. They began, he was aware, to look upon him with that kind of half-envious respect with which men of moderate capacity and little luck regard those who soar above them. And, in his own way, he felt a sort of friendship for the proprietor, who had been well advised enough to choose a wife like Lucy. He would do his best to humour him, and to see that his wishes were carried out, now that he had become to a great extent his confidential man.

At the office, Dawson had never been so affable as the day when, shortly afterwards, he told Johns that he was leaving for Homburg in a week, and that, during his absence, he wanted him to keep a sharp look-out on the *Metropolitan Gazette*, a Tory paper, which had lately been established, and which had interfered with the circulation of the *Planet*. If Johns detected any errors or inconsistencies he was to expose them in his daily paragraphs.

Johns promised that he would watch the *Metropolitan Gazette*. It would be hard if he didn't catch it tripping.

" How long will you be away? " Johns asked.

" About two months, I fancy," was the reply, and Johns reflected that that would be a convenient time for the elaboration of a little plan he had been forming in his mind. It would also relieve him of the somewhat awkward task of conducting two love affairs at once. Everything therefore was for the best.

On the Wednesday evening when he reached Carsdale Mansions and found Mrs. Weber waiting for him as usual in the drawing-room, his first impression, as he kissed her, was a sense of her superiority over the rival he had given her since their last meeting.

It was a warm evening; one of those sultry evenings at the end of a London summer when the air is still and heavy, and a languor seems to rest on everything—when the whole city seems plunged in a hot moist vapour. She was wearing a gauze frock of a delicate cream shade, which matched with her profuse black hair and her olive-tinted skin.

Johns thought, "If such a woman fancies me, I must be worth it, or there's another reason."

"How pretty you look this evening, Ellen! prettier than ever!"

"That's just what I hoped you'd say! I thought you'd like my frock. I've had it for the river."

"You're going then to leave me in my solitude!"

"Yes, but only for a little time, and you'll come down once a week at least. I've taken a little house at Maidenhead, just near to the water's edge, and surrounded by trees and bushes. A little paradise!"

"And you've arranged all that since I saw you last?"

"Of course! Why not?"

Johns agreed with her that there was no reason why she should not have done so, although, in his own mind, he thought the circumstance somewhat strange. The arrangement suited him extremely well, because it would give him a change of air, of which he was much in want, and some happy hours in a river-side retreat with her. For he had become accustomed to this intimacy now, and there would have been something wanting in his existence if these meetings had been suspended, even for a time. Altogether the plan suited him.

Presently she said—

"I've a little quarrel to pick with you. Why did you not tell me you had been promoted?"

"Oh," he said, with a shrug of the shoulders; "can it be called promotion?"

"At anyrate it was a change, and you know how interested I am in all that happens to you."

"I was hoping to surprise you with a greater change later on."

"Editor?" she asked.

"Who knows!"

"Oh, my little Johnnie, how I love you for your pluck!"

He smiled, and after a moment's reflection, asked, "But how did you know of this?"

"Oh, that's my secret, and I'm not going to disclose it. Since *you* were mysterious, I shall be so too."

"Mrs. Dawson told you?"

"No, you're wrong. On the subject of Mr. Johns, Mrs. Dawson is particularly silent."

"Yes," he said, with a puzzled air, "I wonder why that is."

"I suppose she's smitten too. Even old Mrs. Baxter is raving about that Mr. Johns who tells such pretty stories."

"Ah! Ellen, as long as *you* admire me, what matters all the rest?"

She placed her hands upon his shoulder and looked into his eyes.

"Oh, those wonderful eyes of yours which no woman can resist. Swear that they are faithful eyes."

"By all the gods!"

"My little Johnnie, if they were not, I've told you what an enemy I could become."

"Fixing the rivets again," he thought. Then, contemplating her, he said, "How pretty you must look when you are angry! I imagine that your own dark eyes, my Ellen, must flash like a meteor, and the lines of your delicious mouth must curve with a magnificent defiance. You must be superb as Nemesis."

"John, that's dilletantism."

"It's admiration!"

"Nonsense."

They both laughed, and the evening passed as other Wednesday evenings had. Before he left, Mrs. Weber promised to write, should they not meet before she left, to tell him the exact day and hour when she would expect him on the river.

A few days afterwards Johns received a letter from Mrs. Dawson. It was merely a line in pencil, and ran thus—

"I cannot be at Jermyn Street till six to-morrow."

He looked at this message several times, for its brevity and the haste in which it had apparently been written attracted his attention. He had almost expected an effusion after what had passed, and this laconic note surprised him. However, the important thing was that she was coming. He would wait to see what she had to say.

On the Saturday at six, therefore, he waited for her in his

rooms. This time there was no need of curios, and he put away the arms and photographs into a corner as likely objects to excite remorse should she be inclined to be remorseful. It was never wise to give women too much opportunity to think; and little objects of the kind, when they had served their purpose, were best put out of sight. He had had placed, however, upon the table, a vase of large white roses which spread a delicious, almost enervating perfume in the room.

At a few minutes past the hour she arrived, breathless with the haste with which she had come up the stairs.

As soon as the door was closed, he tried to seize her in his arms, but she passed him hurriedly, and making for an armchair threw herself into it. Then, without taking off her gloves or veil, she cried excitedly—

"Oh! if you knew what I have suffered, how I have accused myself for giving way to you, how terrible it was to face my husband when I knew that I had deceived him, and how I trembled lest I should betray myself. I never thought I should feel so guilty! Every moment since I was weak enough to come here, I have realized how guilty I have been. It's terrible! It's terrible! You took advantage of me. It was wrong of you; and I've come to tell you that our intimacy must cease."

He thought, "And she's come *here* to tell me that!" and he answered with a superb gesture of calm purpose—

"So you've come then to tell me, Lucy, that I must end my life because I am unable to refrain from loving you?"

She looked at him through her veil as he stood before her, with his arms folded, and she seemed to ask herself if he was in earnest.

"Oh! why," she cried, "did I ever see you? Why did I ever allow you to speak to me of love? I must have been mad, mad. This morning my husband asked me why I seemed so troubled. I almost confessed my fault. It was to save you that I refrained—not for myself, for I would have felt far happier had I confessed, whatever might have happened."

Johns by this time was beginning to perceive that the remorse of Mrs. Dawson was not without some danger. If she could even contemplate the possibility of so disastrous a revelation, it was evident that he must arrange things better. How tiresome she was! Why couldn't she accept the situation quietly? He judged that a change of manner would be expedient, so he said, walking to and fro, looking on the ground, "Lucy, every word which you have uttered has been as a knife cutting me. If your contrition is so great for having loved me, you need fear no more. I will trouble you no longer."

"What will you do?" she asked.

He stopped before her and gazed into her face.

"What will I do?" he repeated. "You will learn that soon enough."

Again she looked at him as if uncertain.

"Oh, John, how you torture me!"

He took a seat beside her and said gravely—

"Lucy, there is no help for it. You must either be mine unhesitatingly or you must lose me." Then changing his tone quickly, he burst out rapturously. "Lucy, Lucy, let us talk no more of separation. You are mine by all the laws of nature and affinity. It's right and fitting that you should not belong to such a man. You owe it to your beauty to disregard the bond which has been imposed upon you. You *must* disregard it, for you love me. I know you love me. I can see it in the bottom of those deep blue eyes. I can hear it in the echo of that soft, pure voice, in the curve of those lovely lips. You have been fretting because you haven't realized that the tie which binds us is a thousand times more powerful, more beautiful, than that which binds you to your husband. Lucy, your conception of it all is strangely wrong. You must have confidence in me. You *shall* have confidence in me, and I forbid you henceforth to do outrage to your truest feelings."

She remained silent, her hands clasped and her gaze fixed upon the floor, while he, with a dexterity acquired by previous experience, began to unpin her veil.

"Let me divest you," he said, "of that forbidding thing."

She offered no resistance, but continued to look down.

"Do I even know," she said, "if you would be true to me?"

He answered, "I forbid you to doubt that."

And the tone in which he said this was so peremptory that she almost started.

Then, seizing his opportunity as soon as he had removed the veil, he confirmed his words by kissing her.

"Oh, Lucy, Lucy. No more recriminations, no more self-accusations; there is no law, human or divine, which can reach us now."

Stimulated by the contact of her lips and the warmth of her half-yielding form, he began to pour into her ears a whole vocabulary of love, of epithets used many times before, of accents meant to penetrate into the very depths of a woman's nature.

And she listened to him as she had done before, under the influence, again, of the attraction to which she had before succumbed.

"Oh!" she said, with a heavy sigh, "I'm too weak, too weak!"

And when the inevitable had happened, when he had proved to her that she was indeed too weak, and the time had come for her to leave, her farewell was as tender as her greeting had been cold. She would write to him from Homburg very often, though she feared that he would not be able to reply, because her husband would be with her. But that need not trouble him. He knew now that she was his, and that she trusted him. She wanted him to think of her often, very often, till they met again. And if she had regret in future, she would overcome it. She knew that he would guard her reputation jealously. He was so kind, so good!

Suddenly she remembered that she had something she wished to tell him.

"Do you know, John, my husband said this morning that he was beginning to have had enough of Mr. Boyd."

"Did he?" said Johns, quickly.

"Yes; and if he hadn't had an agreement with him for a year longer, he said he would have dismissed him, because the circulation was diminishing. I thought you'd like to know."

Johns thanked her for the piece of information, and gave her a parting kiss of unfeigned gratitude.

"Good bye, John—think of me!"

"Good bye, Lucy. You will be always in my thoughts!"

Johns returned to his room in a reflective frame of mind. The news which he had learned seemed to him so important that he thought no more of the victory he had just achieved. He knew that the circulation had been going down of late, and that Dawson was annoyed, and now he knew from the best of sources that the proprietor attributed the cause of the falling-off to Boyd. That was a piece of knowledge which might be precious. He resolved for the second time that he would make use of Dawson's absence to prepare his plans.

Being exceptionally busy at the office, he did not see Mrs. Weber again before her flight to Maidenhead, but in a few days he received a note from her telling him that she would expect him on the Saturday. He was to bring flannels, the note said, because they would have boating, and he was to come by the two o'clock train as she wanted to meet him at the station. Above all, he was to let her know if he would take that train.

He replied to her note by telegraph, because he preferred to answer women so. It showed solicitude, and was infinitely less compromising than a letter. Besides, it was so much less trouble! During his intimacy with Mrs. Weber he had seldom communicated with her otherwise, having told her from the commencement that the post was much too slow a medium when he wanted to write to *her*.

On the Saturday afternoon he took the train at Paddington, and after a short journey he arrived at Maidenhead, where Mrs. Weber, accompanied by a young girl he had never seen, was waiting for him in the station.

As soon as she had recognized him she advanced alone to meet him, and whispered, hurriedly, "I've taken a room for you in a house close to mine. A little niece of mine is with me for propriety."

"Prudent Ellen!" he answered, smiling.

She handed him a slip of paper on which was written the address of the house he was to go to, as well as that of her own villa.

"You had better go there alone, and come afterwards to take us on the river."

He did as she advised, and in a few minutes he was driven with his luggage, through the shady roads, to a house at the end of the townlet—one of those houses which are let in the summer months to couples seeking the river as the scene of their love episodes. Having been shown into a comfortable bedroom, he quickly changed and left for "The Retreat," which he found, on enquiring, stood only a little further down the road. "The Retreat" was a square white house, more than half hidden by the trees and shrubs with which it was surrounded, and approached by a gravel path between two stretches of green sward.

Johns opened the wooden gate and made his way along the path to the ivy-mantled door on which the sun was shining gaily. A bright little servant maid opened the door to him and led him to a long narrow drawing-room opening at one end upon the garden, and at the other upon a lawn which sloped to the water's edge.

Mrs Weber, in boating costume, was waiting for him.

"Oh," she said, throwing her arms around his neck and kissing him. "How delightful it is to have you here, my Johnnie."

And she looked at him with the long admiring look of a woman in love—a look of passion and of great longing.

He complimented her upon her costume, vowing that he had never seen her form more perfect than in the soft white flannels, or her face more pretty than surmounted by the wide straw hat she wore.

"The reason I could not have you here," she said, "is that one is apt to meet people whom one knows, but, of course, you won't lose anything, my Johnnie, for being *supposed* to sleep out yonder at the lodgings."

"Ah!"

"And to show you how careful one has to be," she continued, "who do you think I have found, to my surprise, has taken a house down here?"

"I haven't an idea."

"The Parkers."

"The husband and the wife?"

"Of course."

He scarcely thought that the "of course" was obvious, but he said nothing.

The niece now entered, and was introduced to Johns as Miss Brabant.

Whenever he made a new acquaintance, Johns surveyed the person narrowly, thinking that every man or woman whom he met might in some way have an influence on his career; that there was no circumstance in life, however small, that had not its effect on a man's fortunes.

Thus, while shaking hands with her, he observed her carefully, settling in his mind that she was plain, that she was thirty, and that she bore the stamp of poverty. Evidently a poor relation to be treated with politeness, and noted as unimportant.

The niece, in answer to Mrs. Weber's question, expressing herself ready, they left by the drawing-room exit, and, crossing the lawn, descended to the boat which was moored to the river bank.

"Are you good at sculling?" Mrs. Dawson asked, and Johns who, when a boy, had rowed his father's boat, with its heavy oars, many a time in a rough sea, replied—

"You shall judge."

"That sounds promising."

The two ladies sat in the stern. Johns, after taking off his coat and tucking up his shirt sleeves, displaying a pair of muscular and hirsute arms, took his seat and put the skulls into position. The sculls, which he had never used before, although of the usual weight, felt to him ridiculously light. He thought it would not be difficult to row for a whole day with such feather-weighted things.

And when he began to scull, he did so to such purpose that the boat soon travelled at a pace which Mrs. Weber and the niece declared was quite delicious, as they gave themselves up to the pleasure of being drawn through the thin light air of the summer's afternoon.

The river looked its best. The reaches were vieing with each other in placid dignity, and the colours of the foliage and meadows were matched in richness by the deep blue of the sky and water.

The boat, gliding along so quickly, made a crisp rustling sound, and left a long wake behind it. It seemed as if Johns, angry with the stream, were using his strength to punish it.

At length Mrs. Weber said, "I'm afraid, Mr. Johns, you'll tire yourself if you row like that."

But Johns, on looking round, had just perceived a boat a long way up the stream, going in the same direction as themselves, and at once the spirit of emulation which was in him, and a desire to give a still more abundant proof of his prowess, made him wish to overtake it.

"I want to catch those people up," he answered.

"But they are a mere speck."

"Oh, they'll soon get larger."

Whereupon he continued rowing with redoubled vigour, without pausing a minute to regain breath, although, unaccustomed as he was to sculling, he was expending much more energy than was really needful.

Gradually he gained upon the distant boat, until the ladies could discern its occupants, a man rowing and a lady steering.

"By God," he said, "I must get up to them before they reach the lock," and although he was becoming red in the face, and the muscles of his arms were swollen, he went on steadily.

But as they crept nearer, the people in the other boat seemed to have understood Johns' intention, for the man now began to ply his sculls more energetically, so that it was problematical who would reach the lock gates first.

Suddenly Mrs. Weber bent forward and said to Johns, in a half whisper, "Good heavens, it's the Parkers. I've made him promise to back you up with Dawson in case they should want another editor. Don't you think you'd best not beat him?"

There was not a moment for reflection, for Johns, in spite of Parker's renewed efforts, was gaining on him fast. At once he slacked speed, and allowed the boat to glide along towards the lock mainly by its own impetus.

"I grudge him that," he said, "but I suppose there was no help for it."

It was not long before they reached the lock, where the Parkers, who had by this time recognized them, were waiting.

There was an exchange of greetings, reserved on the part of the ladies, cordial enough on the part of Johns and Parker.

"So you were trying to beat us?" the politician said, with a smile of self-complacency.

"Yes," said Johns, resignedly, "I tried and failed. You row well, Mr. Parker."

Evidently pleased at the compliment paid to the prowess of his mature years, Parker enquired how long Johns had come for, where he was staying, and how the *Planet* was getting on, while the ladies indulged in feminine amenities.

But, as Mrs. Weber wanted to continue past the lock, and the Parkers were returning, they parted company after their chat was over.

"He's come on the river with his wife," said Johns, "how excellent a husband!"

"Perhaps he cannot help himself," suggested Mrs. Weber.

"Perhaps not."

They spent the remainder of the afternoon upon the river, and returned to "The Retreat" as the sun was setting with great splendour over the wooded hills.

Johns, although he did not own it, was exhausted. On the other reaches he had been unable to refrain from distancing the boats he met, and the exertion had so severely tried his strength that when they reached the bank he was unable, for a few moments, to rise up from his seat.

Noticing his paleness, Mrs. Weber enquired quickly, "What is the matter, Mr. Johns?"

The question made him rouse himself. Pulling himself together with a great effort, he rose and stepped on to the bank to help the ladies out.

But his hand trembled as he did so, and Mrs. Weber gave him an anxious look.

"You're ill," she whispered; but he shook his head and smiled.

A moment after, the niece having discreetly left them alone together in the drawing-room, Mrs. Weber, seizing Johns' hand, exclaimed—

"My Johnnie, why are you so pale? You've strained yourself. I know you have," and she flew to the door to order a servant to bring some wine.

"Oh, my little Johnnie, you must not be so imprudent. You

rowed splendidly this afternoon, but it was too much for any man. I'll never allow you to do that again, never."

He smiled again, feeling a calm pleasure in being pitied.

A large glass of sherry, swallowed almost in one gulp, revived him somewhat, and he was able, although giddy, and with a droning in his ears, to walk back to his lodgings.

While he was changing, after having rested a few minutes upon his bed to endeavour to regain his faculties, he cursed his folly. To run the risk of being ill, and obliged to give up the game for the sake of showing two women what he could do in sculling, was nothing less than rank stupidity. He would not try that again unless for some reason more important than the present one. No matter, he had shown them that he could beat that old ass Parker, and there was some satisfaction in the thought.

When he had finished dressing, he still felt so weak that he was obliged to take a draught of brandy from the flask which he had brought in his portmanteau—a draught that would have been sufficient to stagger a man with a less resistant head.

After this, he felt somewhat revived, and leaving presently, he walked along in the twilight to "The Retreat."

As he approached the place, and was thinking over his afternoon's experiences, the thought struck him that this house upon the river, considering the sum she had already given him, was a rather large expense for a widow who was supposed to be in straitened circumstances. For it was a pretty villa, and he knew that its rent in the summer months could not but be high. There was something in this which he did not understand, and when he came to think of it, it was a curious coincidence that Parker should be at Maidenhead at the same time as Mrs. Weber, even though his wife was with him. Was it possible that the widow was Parker's mistress? What reason had he to suppose so? None that was at all definite, no doubt, and yet all the little indications which he had noticed, put together, amounted to a suspicion, to a feeling that there was something to be observed, something perhaps to be discovered. He was guided by his instinct chiefly, but in these affairs it had seldom led him wrong. But then, if there was really anything between them, why should she have taken so violent a fancy to him? Why should she continue to talk of marriage? Marriage! He didn't think much of *that* idea! As if it was usual to marry in that way! But perhaps Parker wanted to shift his burden on to other shoulders, or perhaps, again, she thought him a good speculation—a man likely to get on. Perhaps there was an understanding between them! Oh, by God, they'd find, if that were so, that they'd counted without their host. But why should he trouble himself about that now, when for the moment everything he wanted fell into his mouth so easily? She was fond of him, of that he had no doubt. What his own feelings were towards her he didn't care to analyse. He only knew she was a damned fine woman.

Thinking thus, he unlatched the garden gate and ascended the gravel path again. Mrs. Weber met him in the hall, and led him to a little room but a few yards square on the right of the front door where, she said, they could be quiet for a few moments before dinner.

As soon as the door was closed, she threw her arms around him, crying—

"My poor Johnnie, who looked so pale just now! And is he better now? Oh, how he frightened me!"

"Don't be silly, Ellen," he said, laughing; "I'm all right now."

"But you don't look it, my poor John. You look terribly fatigued. You shall rest *here* to-night. I'll be your nurse, and you shall be kissed to sleep."

But the prospect did not please him. He felt that he was tired out, and he wanted to get back to his own rooms as soon as he was able.

"No, Ellen, I must go back to-night. I'm too tired, much too tired."

"Oh, but that doesn't matter. Say you'll stay, my Johnnie."

But he shook his head, thinking it well that she should long in vain for once, and by no means reconciled to the idea of leaving early the next morning, as he thought he would have to do.

As if she guessed his thought, she said—

"You won't have to leave early to-morrow morning. I'll say that you're too tired to go home, and you shall have the most charming little room and the softest little bed you ever slept in in your life."

"Ellen," he answered, "your prudence is deserting you. As if anyone would believe that I was so tired that I couldn't walk a few hundred yards. No, it can't be managed."

"As you wish then, John," she said, with a sigh of disappointment.

"But it won't matter," he added, presently; "I'm thinking of stopping here a week."

As he said this, he watched her narrowly, detecting, he was certain, a passing look of perplexed anxiety upon her face.

"Oh," she said, somewhat confusedly, "that would be delightful, but ——"

"But what, Nellie?"

"But I've promised to go to stay with—with some friends at Henley, on Monday, for a few days; until you come back again at the end of the week, you know."

"Can't you put them off?"

"I'm afraid I can't. They would be terribly offended."

"Who are they?"

"The ——, some relations of my husband's."

He thought, "I'd bet they don't exist," and said, "Well, never mind, we've yet to-morrow, Nellie. I shall be all right then."

Her face brightened, and she said, "Oh, yes, to-morrow you must, you will come to-morrow."

"Yes," he said, "I mean to."

The dinner bell then rang. He offered her his arm, and they passed into a modest little dining-room on the same floor, the walls of which were hung with portraits of the owner's family. Miss Brabant was waiting for them.

An English dinner was served them on a table decorated with a profusion of pink roses; but as the niece spoke little, and Johns, still tired, was somewhat taciturn, it fell to Mrs. Weber to sustain the conversation.

This, however, she appeared to find it difficult to do, and she seemed to Johns to be not quite at her ease.

While the dessert was being served a servant handed her a note. After looking at the address she put it in her pocket, which she seemed annoyed at not finding quickly, hidden as it was in the folds of her gauze dress.

But Johns had caught a rapid glimpse of the handwriting, although the widow had held the note before her only for a moment, and he felt as certain that it was that of Parker, as a little while before he had been convinced that she was inventing an excuse.

All this, he thought, would have to be dexterously sifted.

The niece, who it seemed was musical, played them some symphonies after dinner.

Before the clock struck ten Johns left.

When the Monday morning came, after a Sunday passed in quiet ease upon the lawn under the shade of the thick trees, Johns, who had reached his rooms at dawn, was lying on his bed reflecting.

As he had kissed her while taking leave, he had told her that he intended to take an early train to town, and as the morning light came streaming through his window, he was asking himself whether he would return that day or whether he would remain yet one day longer.

She had been to him all that a women could be to a man, and yet, all the time, he had suspected that she was hiding something from him. He had a very strong suspicion that there was something of interest to learn by staying. But if he were to stay and watch, there would be considerable danger of being seen, and that must be avoided. After much deliberation, therefore, he decided that the best plan was to go to town and to return by an evening train.

Accordingly, having settled upon this course, he rested for a few hours longer. Then he rose and left for Paddington at eight. At the office he wrote all day, and in the evening, when his work was finished and he had dined, he left again for Maidenhead.

It was dark as he alighted from the train at the little station, and he made his way towards "The Retreat" with a curious feeling of expectancy, with which was mingled a little jealousy—just so much as he permitted himself to indulge in sometimes.

There was no moon, but the sky was lit up brilliantly with stars; and Johns, invigorated by the cool night air, charged with the aroma of the laurels in the shrubberies, walked along reflectively.

Keeping close to the wooden palings, he slowly approached the house. If what Mrs. Weber had said were true, the place would be in darkness, but if, on the contrary, she had not left, there would be lights, as usual, in all the windows.

The trees and bushes prevented him from ascertaining until he had almost reached the gate; but as soon as the square white house came into view, his curiosity was quickly satisfied. There were lights in all the rooms!

He gave a little laugh, and then, as he fancied he perceived a blind being drawn aside in the drawing-room window, he withdrew again into the darkness of the palings.

But he had not remained there more than a few minutes reflecting on the discovery he had made, when he heard a footstep in the road. It was coming towards the house from the opposite direction.

Moving up as close as he dared to the garden gate, Johns waited until, presently, he saw a thick-set figure looming into view. Soon he recognised the conical felt hat which Parker wore, and an instant afterwards, the round fat face of Parker, as he turned it in his direction while stooping to unlatch the gate.

"By God," said Johns, as he watched the form retreating along the path, "I know *this* time."

He turned on his heels, and walked back to the station.

CHAPTER EIGHTH

DURING the absence of the Dawsons on the Continent, Johns was not idle. Not only did he watch the *Metropolitan Gazette* as he had been asked to do, but he also watched, and closely, the doings of the *Planet's* chief.

He had noticed, in the afternoons after the first editions had been sent out, that Boyd, who was supposed then to receive callers, shut himself up in his room, refusing to see anyone save Coulston, and he had perceived that even Coulston, who he had learnt was a relative of Boyd's, never entered the editorial room without previously knocking loudly at the door, and waiting till he was asked to enter. If there were any orders to be given during the latter part of the afternoon, they were sent through Coulston, who was Boyd's lieutenant in the same way as Johns was latterly, to a great extent, the right-hand man of Dawson. And sometimes Johns would go into the ante-room, filled with people waiting for an interview which they had little chance of having, and sympathise with them. He would tell them that he for one was truly sorry to see them wasting so much valuable time. But what was to be done? Some editors had curious notions of exclusiveness, notions which he, personally, did not like. It seemed to him, he told them, that the more fresh blood was let into a paper, the better it progressed. And then, were they not all brother journalists and entitled to consideration? They listened to him eagerly, for they knew that he was on the staff and regarded as a man with a good future—a man to be conciliated, especially as he often hinted that, if he were editor, the whole literary republic would have access to him. And they felt that, although he was powerless to help them then, he might, later, be a useful man to know.

"How hungry they must be!" Johns would say to himself as he saw some of them come, day by day, on the bare hope that Boyd would see them for a minute in the ante-room on his way out, and he would laugh at the tenacity with which they returned to such a hopeless market for the product of their brains. And how cheap brains were, how cheap! And how great the gain for those who knew how to exploit them well! All this was a lesson for the future.

One day he asked Tarte if he knew why Boyd closeted himself in the afternoons of late, but the old man smiled enigmatically, saying, "Must not an editor indulge once a day in the delights of correspondence? He's answering his letters."

"Oh, answering his letters, is he?" Johns repeated, trying to guess the meaning which seemed to lurk behind the old man's words.

"And is that so engrossing an occupation? Are you sure you don't mean drinking whisky?"

"He might be doing both. He may find one as pleasant as the other. Ah, what a mighty thing it is to be an editor!"

"Why are you so mysterious, Tarte? Don't you trust me?"

"You'd think me foolish if I did."

"Curious old chap," thought Johns, "but smarter than I fancied."

He reflected over this for a few days, not knowing what to think of it, but terribly desirous of making a discovery which might enable him to put a spoke in the editor's wheel; and one morning, as he lay in bed waiting for the valet, he had a sudden inspiration. Yes, of course, why not? Why had he not thought of that before? Did he not know from the best of sources that Boyd's position was a weak one? Yes, he could safely try. Perhaps he would discover something, perhaps there was nothing to discover. At anyrate his curiosity would be appeased. "Tarte," he said, in the afternoon, as he was sitting before him at the same table, "I've a question to ask Boyd about this par on the *Metropolitan Gazette*, and I'm damned if I'll ask Coulston. I'm going into the sacred presence myself at once."

Tarte gave a grin and an approving nod.

"I congratulate you on your intrepidity, my friend. You're what the French call a *struggle-for-lifeur*."

"Yes, by God, I am."

Saying this, he rose from his chair, buttoned his frock-coat, and, taking the slip of paper with him, made for the private door of the editorial room. When he reached the threshold, as there was no one in the passage, he stopped to listen.

But as he could hear no sound coming from within, he seized the handle of the door, turned it rapidly, and entered.

What he saw repaid him for his trouble.

Boyd, seated next the typist at the long table, was reading a letter which he was holding in his left hand, while his right hand was encircling the waist of the fair-haired amanuensis, whose head was resting on his shoulder. Johns had appeared so suddenly, that he had been able to take in the little scene before the surprised pair had time to move.

Abruptly, and with flushed faces as soon as they became aware that Johns was looking at them, they separated. The lady remained in her seat in a rigid posture, her face wearing an expression of outraged modesty. Boyd, however, started to his, feet, and turning his pair of vinous eyes angrily upon Johns, exclaimed—

"What do you mean, sir, by coming here against my orders?"

"I meant," said Johns, with perfect equanimity, "to consult you, Mr. Boyd, about something of importance to the paper; but as I see you're *particularly* busy, I'll take another opportunity."

And without waiting for an answer from Boyd, who, speechless with rage, stood glaring at him, he retired as quickly as he had entered.

When he returned to Tarte's room, he resumed his seat as if nothing had occurred, and when Tarte asked, "Well, was your interview a pleasant one?" he answered, "It's *my* turn, Tarte, to be mysterious."

But when the day's work was over, he strolled homewards in a happy frame of mind. "With the little typist!" he muttered, as he walked up the Strand. This was the little blonde, with a plump figure, whom, at one time, he had thought of conquering himself! How fortunate that a prudential instinct had restrained him, for now he possessed knowledge which he intended to make use of. It was plain that Boyd was hurrying to his own destruction. He had heard it whispered that he had been drinking hard of late, and now he had taken to make love to typists in the editorial room! Such shocking immorality must not be permitted to continue!

From this day onwards he worked with an increased zest, not because he liked work, for in reality he hated it, but because he was sustained by the hope of attaining an ambition soon. Boyd had not referred to his intrusion when he met him the next morning, and had affected not to see him. That alone, he thought, was a sign of fear.

In the meantime he went to Maidenhead as usual at the

week's end, and though he carefully refrained from saying a word to the widow of what he had seen that night in the shadow of the paling, his manner towards her changed. Knowing that his position was a good one, he became less tender, troubled himself less to make love speeches, was more exacting and more hard to please. Grumbling at the precautions which they had to take to keep their intimacy secret, he vowed that he was tired of the river, and that he wouldn't be sorry when she returned to town. For now he could not kiss her without thinking of the burly politician to whom she would offer those same lips as soon as he had left her, and who, perhaps, was paying the rent of this riverside retreat. How the arrangement was conducted; whether Parker was aware or not that he was anything more to her than a possible husband to take her off his hands, Johns had no means of knowing. In reality he scarcely cared. Things would work themselves out by themselves, he thought.

And she, perceiving the change in his behaviour, pretended to attribute it to overwork, and increased in kindness and attention, spoiling him in every way she could imagine, trying to bring a smile upon his face. Why was he so preoccupied, so serious? What was there she could do for him? Was he pressed again for money? What was it that was troubling him?

But even these questions, proofs as they were of her solicitude, annoyed him, and he would tell her curtly that he was well, that he wanted no more money, and that he would be much obliged to her if she wouldn't scrutinize his looks so narrowly. He didn't like it. No man liked it, and he least of all. And he would sit smoking the Havanas which she always kept for him, in moody silence, or sometimes, when they were alone, he would rise suddenly from his chair, and going up to her, would kiss her violently, almost brutally, and then resume his seat and continue smoking.

And she would contemplate him gravely, wonderingly, as if trying to divine the reason for this inequality of temper, and there was a feeling of constraint between them which only disappeared during the moments of strong passion.

One Sunday in the middle of September, as he was sitting smoking on a garden seat beneath the low verandah, looking at the passing boats with their freights of pretty women in dazzling light costumes, she came and sat beside him. They had spent the morning on the river, and had returned for luncheon. Throughout the trip he had been taciturn and moody, rowing leisurely and without spirit.

"John," she said, in a soft tone, "why won't you tell me what is on your mind? I cannot bear to see you so changed towards me."

But he wasn't in a humour to be conciliated. He had had enough of those eternal questions. He had nothing on his mind, he said bluntly—nothing but his work.

"It's not true," she said, with a sudden flash of anger, "you have. I know you have, or you wouldn't sit there thinking gloomily as you're doing now. You're treating me as I don't deserve."

He looked up at her sharply to guage the extent of her indignation, and to determine whether it was menacing.

"I've done all a woman can for you," she continued, "and this is how I am repaid."

There was no doubt about it—this time he had gone too far. She was getting vexed, and as he stood towards her at that moment, he didn't want her to be vexed.

"My dear Ellen," he replied, "you are quite wrong. If I have hurt your feelings in any way, believe me it was unconsciously. I've been overworked for the last six weeks. I fear that's made me bearish, and, perhaps, neglectful."

He felt that this was rather weak, but he could think of nothing better.

"Is that the *real* reason?" she asked, suspiciously, and he assured her that it was.

"Oh, forgive me, then, my Johnnie; I ought to have known that you were working hard." And she looked into his eyes with an expression of subdued passion.

"There's no one in the house this afternoon," she whispered. "Come, let us make it up."

"Now?" he asked.

"Oh yes, now."

And they disappeared into the house.

During the absence of the Dawsons, Johns had received several letters from the wife of the proprietor, letters which gave him considerable satisfaction to receive. They stirred up recollections which he prized, because they seemed to him to be a link with the people on whom his career depended. And what serious compositions these notes were! He never read them without smiling. They were variations on every chord of sentiment, by a woman whose illicit love struggled against the principles of virtue in which she had been trained, and who by nature had never been intended for the part she had been made to play. Now they were warm and hopeful, now sorrowful and timorous; but in none of them did she repeat the recriminations which she had made at her last visit. Her chief solicitude was to know if he were thinking of her, if he would be always good to her, and careful of her fame. And as she had asked him not to answer her—a request he was only too anxious to comply with—he was relieved of even the trouble of writing letters. "But what I ask myself a hundred times a day," she wrote, "is by what magic you make me love you. I had never thought it possible to love a man as I love you. What women say of you is true. You charm them by your voice, your look, your presence. And I ask myself how long you will continue loving me, you whom so many women like. John, shall I confess it? I am dreaming of the day when we shall be back in London, when I can come and see you in your little room in Jermyn Street!"

Then followed tender injunctions for his health, and hopes that he would not work too hard.

And though, as a last precaution of departed virtue, she omitted to sign her name, he did not fail to preserve these letters carefully. The mere possession of them seemed to him a guarantee for his own future.

At length, one morning at the end of the month, he received a note from her announcing her return in a few days. She was tired of Homburg and the people she had met. She was dying to be home again. Previously she had enjoyed her stay at Homburg, had interested herself in its life and gaiety, but now she could only think of *him*. All else seemed to have grown pale and colourless. Oh, how she longed for the day when they would be together once again! And at the bottom of the note he read, in a hastily-added postscript, "My husband says he is not pleased with the way the paper has been managed in his absence."

Johns thoughtfully replaced the letter in its envelope, and muttered to himself, "That's my chance; if I don't seize it I'm a fool." And he went down to the office the same morning with a determination to make a decisive effort as soon as the proprietor returned.

In the meantime he clearly realized the riskiness of his position. In a few days his two *inamoratas* would be back again, for Mrs. Weber was also returning at the week's end, and he would have to exercise all the caution he could command to avoid a blunder or an accident. He fancied he had studied women well enough to be aware that too much skill in dealing with them could not be employed, because one never knew what they might do when they thought themselves deceived or injured. He was playing for high stakes, and his play must accordingly be good. Now, however, that he was well clothed, well fed, well lodged, he felt himself equal to all emergencies. It was magnificent, he thought, to be so prized by women. How far could not a man go who was so favoured! And sometimes in the morning, as he was dressing, he would stand before his looking-glass studying his features, practising some subtleties of smile, now bright and gay, now full of changing shades of pathos. But the expression which he cultivated most was that intensely earnest, almost sorrowful arrangement of the muscles of his countenance which had so often proved successful in the course of his career. It was an expression which seemed to embody in itself a world of sadness for the ills of life, a longing for the ideal, a simple innocence with a calm dignity. It rendered all the emotions he was capable of feeling in his transient, objective way, and it was always at his command whenever he wished to make others think that he was feeling them. He thought, indeed, that the majority of men neglect to study their natural advantages; that many possess gifts which they fail to utilize from the want of the knack of introspection.

Yes, there was nothing like studying oneself! He knew *himself*, as Americans said, "derned" well. He knew, too, what he wanted, and he fancied he knew what he could do to reach it.

All through the autumn he had been reading steadily, filling up gaps in his knowledge and forming literary opinions, which he put into sonorous phrases and committed to memory, so that he might use them at a moment's notice before anyone he wanted to impress. Many of these he had tried on Maskelyne and the reporters. He had found they had produced a better effect than even he anticipated. Encouraged by his success, he learned by heart impressive passages from masterpieces, and he settled his likes and dislikes in literature so that he might appear to have decided tastes, resolved to extol enthusiastically the authors who took his fancy and to condemn uncompromisingly those who did not. It was no use having half opinions, and seeking the truth between two opposites. One must be either for or against a book or a work of art—unhesitatingly. That was the only way in which one could be striking.

Now and then, when he wanted to read books which he could not afford to buy, he would go to the Museum and consult them in the reading-room, but the sight of the circular maze-like room, with its population of emaciated literary hacks, working like slaves at their melancholy drudgery, gave him a cold shiver down his back. The place seemed to him dangerous to frequent. For he felt instinctively it was the refuge of the unsuccessful, and unsuccess in some way seemed to him contagious. He felt imprisoned under the great dome, and as if cut off from the life of the outer world. He spent as little time there as he could. It was a place of poverty, and he had seen enough of poverty. His appetite was whetted for better things. Literature, if taken too seriously to heart, seemed to him a pitfall; but as a means to attain an end, he had a high opinion of it. He devoted as much time as he was able to French literature, with which his semi-Gallic nature was in sympathy. A good acquaintance with it, he considered, lent distinction and a certain superiority.

At length the Monday morning came when Dawson was expected in the Strand. Everybody in the office felt that their fates were in his hands, and as he had hitherto been in the habit, after his summer holiday, of making changes in the staff, his return was awaited with a general trepidation.

Johns left home earlier than usual that morning, and reached the *Planet* before Dawson had arrived. He had deliberated whether he should attack the proprietor on his entrance to the office, or wait till the latter had had an interview with Boyd. He decided, eventually, that he would see Dawson as soon as possible.

He thought it probable that the proprietor would first enter his own room before calling for or going to see the editor, and therefore he seated himself upon the sofa of that room, reading a morning paper.

It was not long before Dawson, brisk and florid, walked in with the firm step of a master. He seemed surprised when Johns rose and advanced to meet him.

"Good morning, Mr. Johns," he said, in an official tone, "you see I'm back. I'll speak to you about your column later on. It was well done. I was pleased with it."

Saying this, he looked at the letters on his table as a signal to Johns that he wished to be alone.

"Pardon me," said Johns, gravely, taking a seat near Dawson's desk, "if you find me in this room, it's not by accident. I've come here with a purpose. I've come in the interest of the paper."

Dawson began, "I'm sorry, Mr. Johns, but this morning I'm too busy."

Johns, however, did not move. He knew there was going

to be a struggle of will between them, and the sooner it began the better. He continued, "I'm sorry also, Mr. Dawson, but what I have to say cannot be deferred."

Dawson moved impatiently in his chair, and Johns pursued—

"During your absence, I've been studying the way in which your paper is conducted, and I've come to the conclusion that unless it's bettered, you will see the *Planet* sink—sink, sir, to a few miserable thousands daily."

Roused at length, Dawson answered—

"Explain yourself, Mr. Johns."

"Ever since the *Metropolitan Gazette* was started, our circulation has been dwindling week by week, day by day. In the last three months it has been tumbling down at a break-neck pace. The paper's on the road to ruin, to extinction. It's falling from the place it held to the level of a murder sheet, and that not popular. And what are the reasons for this disaster? They are two, Mr. Dawson, two. The first is that the *Metropolitan Gazette* is a great deal better at the same price, and the second that your editor is unfitted for his post."

Dawson, during this speech, had been showing signs of alarm and irritation.

"This is a grave accusation," he said, "to make against Mr. Boyd."

"It would be, if I were not prepared to prove it."

"That's the only thing left for you to do."

Johns perceived the threat which Dawson's words conveyed, but he was fairly launched on his enterprise now, and he must go on to the end.

"An editor," he said, "who for the last two months has refused to see all callers, and who has shut himself in his own room, making love to his own typist, oblivious to the peril which besets the paper, is totally *unfit* to be at the head of a journal such as this."

"Do you mean to insinuate ——," Dawson began, but Johns stopped him.

"I insinuate nothing—I state what I have seen."

"What you have seen?" said Dawson, fairly starting from his seat.

"It's the least thing one can expect of an editor," Johns continued, "to have some sense of decency, and this man, whose drunken tendencies cannot be unknown to you, is destitute of any."

Then Johns related carefully the scene which he had witnessed — the editor surprised with his arm round the typist's waist during the business of the afternoon.

He spoke, he said, with great reluctance, and solely in the interest of the paper.

Dawson, when he had finished, was silent for a moment. Then he said, "And you affirm that you saw this?"

"I am ready to take my oath before Boyd himself."

Dawson was again silent.

Johns, thinking that he had gained a point, resumed, "And that is not all I have to tell you. I have to say that I, personally, cannot continue to serve under such a man. If Boyd is to remain, I must ask you to accept my resignation."

This was a bold stroke, as he knew well, and if he had not had information from the best of sources that Dawson was dissatisfied with Boyd, he probably would not have made it. Dawson said—

"I don't know that there's any hurry about your resignation. I should advise you to wait to see what changes may take place between this and a few months hence.

"A few months!" repeated Johns; "in a few months the harm done to the paper will be irretrievable."

"You don't suppose that, even if what you say were true, I should be likely to dismiss Boyd at once."

Johns rose from his chair. He could speak better standing. "Listen, Mr. Dawson," he began, "*I* offer myself as editor."

"*You?*" said Dawson, with astonishment.

"Yes, I! I am ready to guarantee that, if you appoint me editor, your circulation will not only regain its former figure in three months' time, but will go beyond it. The paper wants fresh blood, fresh life. It has been going too long upon its old lines, and the public has found something better for its money. Dismiss that drunken fool, entrust me with his post, and I'll turn you out the smartest thing in London, sound and bright, written by younger men, and a thousand times more interesting than the flimsy stuff he's been producing."

Dawson stared at Johns as he had stared at him when he had first asserted that he could do anything.

"Do you mean to say," he said, "that you think you could edit the paper with the experience you have?"

"I don't *think*; I'm sure."

Dawson smiled.

Johns said, sharply, "I've made an offer, Mr. Dawson, and a serious one. It's for you to consider whether you accept or not. All I can tell you is that if you don't, I'm going to start a paper of my own. I'm promised strong support from Australian capitalists."

And seeing that Dawson still looked sceptical, he continued—

"You think perhaps that is a mere boast, but you'll find it's not, and to be frank with you, if I have not already closed with them, it is because I don't consider there is room for another evening paper. I would prefer to edit yours, which is properly established. Remember what I have said. I undertake to resuscitate your paper."

Then, bringing his fist down upon the desk with a loud thump, he said—

"By God, sir, I'm the man you want. I've got the 'grit' you want, the brains you want. I'm not one of those kid-glove journalists with their academic snobbery, but a man who knows his public and how to please them. I've taken the measure of every available editor in London, and there isn't one, not one, that is of any value who would leave his post to come to you unless you offered him the salary of an ambassador. If you, to your misfortune, got in one of those sublime asses from the universities who emprison journalism within the bounds of their own narrowness, the fate of the *Planet* would be sealed."

"Perhaps you're not aware," said Dawson, "that I'm offered the services of Briton Howard, who conducted the *Evening Herald* for six years, and who is now editing a weekly paper."

But at this name Johns made a bound across the room that caused Dawson to start half out of his arm-chair.

"Of Briton Howard!" he cried, contemptuously. "A man whose habits are those of a street cur, a vapid mediocrity who killed the *Evening Herald* as everybody knows, and who is killing the *Weekly Journal!* Why, you might as well appoint old Tarte."

Dawson said, "I'm learning something new," and for a few moments there was a silence which Dawson was the first to break.

"Boyd has an agreement to the end of the year," he said.

"And what of that? Wouldn't it be a thousand times cheaper to pay him off than to let him ruin you?"

Dawson's air of scepticism had now changed to one of thoughtfulness. He said, "You arrange things very easily, Mr. Johns."

"I can carry them out as easily."

"But you have no plan to offer, no programme?"

"No programme!" Johns repeated. "Haven't I!" And then he proceeded to unfold a whole scheme of ameliorations, partly drawn from his imagination. More room would be given to foreign news and to literature. The personal gossip would be made more accurate, interviewing would be conducted on more skilful lines, the financial column was to be made a gold mine by a method he had seen practised in Australia, and, above all, new blood was to be introduced.

He continued to develop his ideas for at least ten minutes, and when he finished, Dawson, rising, said—

"Very well, Mr. Johns, I see you at least know what you want to do. I'm going to make inquiries, and I'll let you know about your offer in a day or two."

Johns said, "As you please," and left the proprietor to his correspondence.

He had launched his venture, and it remained to be seen now whether it would be successful. He believed that Dawson was alarmed, and he counted upon that as a factor in his favour. He also thought he had impressed him, but of course it was impossible to be sure. All through the day he was restless, unable to chain his thoughts to work, and he paced up and down Tarte's room until the old man asked him what the matter was.

"You'll know that soon enough, Tarte. I've run a chance for all it's worth—that's all."

In the evening when he reached his rooms, two letters were awaiting him. One was from Mrs. Weber, to whom he had been obliged to give his new address, and the other from Mrs. Dawson. He opened the latter first. It ran—

"Dearest,—I am coming to you at half-past five to-morrow.—Lucy."

"Good," he thought; "she'll bring some news."

Then he opened the other—

"My own Johnnie,—I expect you to dinner to-morrow night as usual. Yours ever, Ellen."

"Damn it," he said, "why couldn't she choose another day?"

He replaced both notes in their envelopes and put them in his pocket, feeling nervous and unsettled.

The next day he reached the Strand in a peculiar state of mind, not knowing whether this was going to be his last upon the paper, or whether he was suddenly to find himself its editor. He had slept little the previous night, for he had been revolving in his mind what he would do in this case, and what in that, and as he mounted the office stairs he tried to discipline himself by giving himself a hit in the chest with his clenched fist. In the morning he saw neither Dawson nor the editor, but he heard that they had been closeted together for a long time. No one in the office knew what was happening, but it was the general impression that there was "something up."

Towards two o'clock, however, as Johns was passing through the corridor, he saw Boyd leaving Dawson's room.

His face was flushed, and he seemed excited. He almost stumbled against Johns in passing.

"Oh, that's you, is it?" he said, as he perceived him—"you cursed sneak!"

Johns's face lit up with a sudden gleam of pleasure. If Boyd called him a cursed sneak, certainly he must have had a row with Dawson, and if so, who knew? perhaps the chief had taken his advice.

"Fool!" he said, with a shrug of his shoulders, and then, as Boyd was already half down the stairs, he turned upon his heel and re-entered his own room. Here he sat waiting in a kind of dogged calm succeeding to the agitation of the morning, forcing his mind to remain in a sort of vague suspense, so that he might keep his coolness for whatever might occur. And he sat there digging holes in his blotting pad with a pair of scissors, to the surprise of his companion, who looked up at him now and then above his glasses. At length, as the clock struck four, the acoustic tube gave a shrill whistle, and Tarte, after replying "Yes" through it, applied it to his ear. A moment afterwards the old man answered, "Yes, Mr. Dawson," and replaced the tube upon its rest. Then, turning to Johns, he said, "Dawson wants to speak to you."

Johns rose at once. Now he would know something.

With a firm step he crossed to Dawson's room and entered.

"Good afternoon," the proprietor said, with something like a smile. "You may be surprised to hear that Mr. Boyd and I have fallen out."

"No, not surprised," said Johns, imperturbably; "it was inevitable."

"Therefore, as I have decided to dispense at once with his services at a considerable expense to me, the editorship is vacant."

"I have already asked for it, and I ask for it again."

"And do you mean to tell me that you feel yourself equal to the task of conducting the paper?"

"Really, Mr. Dawson, this is not serious! Not only am I capable of conducting it, but I will pledge myself to save it."

"But are you certain that you can do all you say?"

Johns thought, "He's in a fearful funk," and said, "I can only repeat that, should you not appoint me, I should be compelled to leave you."

For some moments Dawson remained silent, moving a paper weight upon his desk from one side to the other, as if in thought.

Johns stood motionless before him, with his arms folded.

At length Dawson rose, and, facing Johns, said slowly, and as if with effort, "Very well, then, I'll try you for three months."

"No," said Johns," I can't undertake to do it in three months. I must have six."

"Must you, really?" asked Dawson, nervously, again reflecting.

"I must."

"Then I suppose I must say yes."

"That," said Johns, without moving a muscle of his face, "is satisfactory. When do I commence?"

"To-morrow."

"Very good."

Then they settled details, and decided upon the course to be pursued, and when Johns left Dawson's room it was past five.

Suddenly he remembered, as he looked at his watch, that Lucy was coming to his rooms that afternoon, and, without stopping to tell the news of his appointment, he rushed down to the street and, jumping into a passing hansom, was driven to Jermyn Street at once.

Editor! He, John Johns, was editor of a London "daily," with that delicious sense of power, and more than two sovereigns a day! How easy it was, after all, to make the world believe in you! How men, and women too, were influenced by talk! Oh, it was a fine thing to understand humanity—a fine thing indeed!

As he drove along, the shops, the people in the streets, even the autumn sky, seemed to smile on him. There was a glamour of success in everything. An editor! There was an editor driving in that hansom, and he almost felt that the people in the streets should know it. Now that he had got his foot in the stirrup in real earnest, a hundred new horizons revealed themselves to him in the rosy future. His life seemed suddenly to have a higher value in the world's plan. He was a master now in one of the fields of intellect. He was a personage; he was somebody.

The hansom stopped before his house, and, throwing the man twice his fare, he rushed up the stairs to his own rooms.

He had not long to wait. A minute afterwards Mrs. Dawson came.

"And has he told you, John?" she enquired, breathlessly, after the first embrace.

"That I'm to be the editor?"

"Yes."

"Yes, Lucy, it's all settled."

"Oh," she said, joyfully; "do you know it was all decided last night when Mr. Parker came to dinner. It was he advised my husband to appoint you. I said as much as I dared about you too, and then he hesitated and said he didn't know if you were fit. As if my John isn't fit for anything! At last, when Mr. Parker spoke so highly of you, he said he thought he would. How can I tell you how pleased I was when he said this morning, before he left, that he had decided in your favour! I knew you were anxious to be editor, and I wanted you to have this news to-day on my return."

"Oh, Lucy," he exclaimed in an enthusiasm of unfeigned gratitude; "how much I owe to you!"

An hour afterwards, when she had left, he went to the nearest telegraph office and telegraphed to Mrs. Weber—

"Sorry, too busy to come to-night," after which he dined quietly at Verry's.

CHAPTER NINTH

SINCE his promotion, a new life had commenced for Johns. It was no longer his duty to please others, but it behoved others to please him, and, from the day he took up the reins, he showed that he was not to be pleased easily. He had undertaken to revive the paper, and he thought that this could be done only by the strongest efforts of all connected with it. Therefore he made them work at fever heat, never satisfied with their performances until they had given all that their brains could furnish. He forced Coulston to resign, and appointed Maskelyne, whom he knew to be without too much ambition, in his stead. The typist he sent away, as he wanted no petticoats about him. To the frequenters of the ante-room he kept his promise, and gave each of them a few minutes' interview; but, as he rarely saw the same man twice after he had, as he expressed it, got his measure and found him wanting, the ranks were considerably thinned, and the unappreciated were more disaffected than before. "It's the old story," Tarte would say to them as a sort of consolation, "and they're all alike. You'd do the same, my friends, if you got upon that perch." With Dawson he had assumed, from the first day, an attitude of independence, totally refusing to be controlled or checked, as Boyd had been, and forcing the proprietor to pay prices for good articles which made him tremble. But as, during the first month, the god of circulation whom Dawson worshipped showed signs of clemency—that is, as the sale increased in an appreciable measure—he made no objection, and was, indeed, beginning to have a kind of timid respect for Johns.

But Johns thought that a paper wasn't to be recruited by merely sitting in an office chair, and he set out in pursuit of journalistic talent, frequenting the circles where he could meet it best, and seizing upon it when he found it.

Since he had been made editor, invitations rained upon him from people he had once met casually, and who now were anxious to see the young and brilliant editor who had sprung up quickly in their midst. Rumours had been spread of his extraordinary adventures in Australia, and every one wanted to see the man who was also said by some to possess a remarkable attraction in women's eyes. And, as he was receiving a fair salary, he was in a much better position than previously to meet the calls upon his purse which society now made, and to return the hospitality of useful people in a variety of ways.

For Mrs. Weber his promotion meant a disappointment, since he had told her that, far from getting married immediately, as she had anticipated, they would have to wait until his position was assured, *at least* until the six months of his probation had expired. And she was still more disappointed when he declared to her that his work would now prevent him from coming to her house as often as he wished. He continued to pay his weekly visit, most weeks, although he left long before the morning; but the extra visits in the afternoon, or on odd evenings—those that were arranged from day to day at the hazard of events, the meetings that she prized the most—he had said he would be forced to discontinue now. And she would ask why this should be. She knew that he went to see other people. Why should he not come to her? But he explained that, in his new capacity, he was forced to go as much as possible into society, especially into political and journalistic sets, where he had a chance of recruiting writers and of learning news. She was obliged to accept these reasons, the truth of which it was so difficult to test.

One day he said, "Do you know, Ellen, that there are a hundred hungry dogs watching me, to see how I get on, and ready to scramble for my place?"

"Oh, but you are so clever and so well supported," she replied.

But he said hastily, thinking of Parker, "I don't *want* to be supported, Ellen. I intend to *fare da se*."

She said, "Do you know, my Johnnie, that when I hear everybody talking of you I feel as if they were trying to steal you from me? If any woman dared!"

And she frowned, while her eyes flashed.

At other times she would question him narrowly upon his doings since their last meeting, the people he had met, and the invitations he received, with a minuteness savouring of suspicion, which annoyed him, and made him declare, each time he left her, that he wouldn't stand it long—pretty and enticing as she was. He would have wished to give her back the money she had lent him, although, to do that, he would have had to stint himself, his expenses having already risen beyond his income. But she had told him once that she would take it as a sign of rupture if he did so, and he didn't want to go so far as that. For he knew very well he would seek long before he found her equal. Only she took it much too seriously. Why could she not be like the wife of the proprietor, who trusted him and did not give him half that trouble, and who, since her return from Homburg, had improved both in beauty and in common sense?

The winter passed in this way, and at the commencement of the new year Johns had already lifted the *Planet* a long way out of the mire into which it had fallen. Dawson, now entirely subdued, allowed him a free hand, and when the spring came, thanks to the talent he had been able to recruit, and to a series of stirring events which he had known how to take advantage of, the paper had regained its old position.

In the meanwhile he had made the acquaintance, at a luncheon of journalists, of a young man called St. George, a young man of means, who, having some literary leanings, affected the society of journalists and authors. From the first Johns had been interested in him. His quiet, well-bred air, the faultless way in which he dressed, the old Norfolk family from which he came, and above all, the entrée which he had to some of the most exclusive sets in London, made him of especial interest to Johns, who had been thinking for some time that the society he moved in was not the only one to which he might attain. He commenced, therefore, to cultivate St. George's friendship, and as few resisted him when he laid siege to their affections, it was not long before St. George and he were friends. He would allow the young man to sit with him in the editorial room in the afternoon whenever he liked to come, and once he had flattered him considerably by publishing a short poem which St. George had written. Often they would dine together, and Johns soon became a candidate for election at one of St. George's clubs, where politics were not a bar to his admission. In a remarkably short space of time they had become firm friends.

One evening, while Johns was with St. George in his bachelor flat in Piccadilly, smoking in a little warmly-draped recess, carpeted and lined with Persian rugs, and lit by an

Oriental lamp hanging from the ceiling, the young man said, after a puff of smoke—

"Who do you think was asking me about you, Johns?"

"I can't guess."

"Lord Stanfield."

Johns knew vaguely that Lord Stanfield was a kind of patron of literary men, a sort of Mæcenas who was fond of inviting men of letters to his house, and who was reputed to have shares in periodicals.

He said, "I shall be glad to know him."

"My dear fellow, I should be delighted to introduce you. There is only one slight difficulty. Lord Stanfield is interested in you, and has a wish to see you. He was only afraid that your democratic notions, such as you made known in some speech or other once, might be a little obstacle."

"Oh," said Johns, laughing, "that's nothing. I don't preach democracy in private life, and I've given up platform politics."

"Well, if you think you can put politics aside, I'll take you to Berkeley Square to-morrow."

"My dear St. George," said Johns, with a discreet smile, "there's nothing so adaptable as politics."

St. George laughed; and it was agreed that they should call the next day, which happened to be that on which Lady Stanfield was at home.

Accordingly, on the morrow, at five o'clock, Johns and his friend drove to the Stanfields in Berkeley Square.

It was a large brick house, wearing that air of sober dignity, indifferent to outward show, which characterises the houses of a London square. They were at once admitted and shown up to the drawing-room. This was a large and lofty room, furnished in the style of twenty years ago, with gilded chairs and tables, gilded mirrors, and crimson hangings and chair coverings—a room which seemed to mark an antipathy to change, a contentment with the tastes of formerly.

Lady Stanfield was sitting near the fireplace in a high-backed arm-chair. She was a thin woman of about fifty, with a narrow face and a pair of lifeless eyes, though she wore an unmistakable air of dignity and breeding. She was surrounded by a ring of visitors, in which the male element predominated. Her husband, who rose on the entrance of St. George and Johns, was a tall man of about sixty, with iron-grey hair and a short beard. His face was intelligent and thoughtful, his carriage graceful. As St. George had seen him at his club the night before, he was quite prepared for the visit. He advanced and shook hands cordially with Johns as his friend introduced them.

"Mr. Johns," he said, leading him to Lady Stanfield, "Mr. Johns, the young and brilliant editor of whom we have sometimes heard."

Lady Stanfield made a slight bow to Johns, and shook hands with his companion, after which her husband led the former to a seat and began to talk to him.

"Mr. Johns," he said, "you're no stranger to me by reputation."

Johns answered, "Reputation, Lord Stanfield, is a misleading jade."

"Even when she's favourable?"

"Often even then."

Lord Stanfield laughed.

"We have heard of you, Mr. Johns, in a vague kind of way as a meteor in our midst. It has been said that you came, you saw, and you conquered. Is rumour right?"

"Oh," said Johns, with a broad smile, "I came, certainly—and saw, but I don't consider that I've conquered."

"That sounds almost ambitious. An editorship in the flower of youth is rather difficult to get, I fancy. At least, I'm told so."

Johns said, "Mine is a modest post. Our strength lies in numbers; but, alas! we are tied to the tastes of a certain public."

Then suddenly assuming his earnest air, he said, "Ah, Lord Stanfield, if you only knew what it is to have a longing for a standard which one cannot reach, to feel a craving for good literature, and to be condemned to produce nothing but mere journalism! I have naturally tried to group around me as much talent as I could, but I am obliged to adapt it to the needs of our readers. It is no light task, I can assure you, to conduct a paper under such conditions."

Lord Stanfield said, with a shade of malice in his voice, "I can understand that readily, but I suppose it is one of the conditions of the radical press. You've perhaps not chosen the field best suited to your tastes."

Johns said, "In following one's destiny, one does not always choose."

"I suppose not," Lord Stanfield answered, reflectively, adding a moment afterwards—

"Did you not help Mr. Parker some time ago with his Education Bill?"

Johns thought, "How well these lords are posted"; and he

answered carelessly, "I did. Mr. Parker explained his views to me and I applied them—that was all."
Lord Stanfield gave a reflective "Oh."
"But," said Johns, "what, after all, are these views of politicians which differ in each camp? They're held to-day, and to-morrow they're abandoned. We live in a constant world of change."
Before Lord Stanfield could reply, the door was opened, and a lady entered, who was announced as Mrs. Humphreys.
Johns looked at the new arrival, whom Lord Stanfield had advanced to meet. She was a woman whom he judged to be about forty, or perhaps a little older, and she was rather stout. Fair, with regular features which had been handsome once, but which suggested now the sad fugacity of things, her face, beneath the rouge it bore, seemed by its surfeited expression to denote a life of ease, of opulence, of satisfaction. She appeared to Johns, as he noticed the studied, almost juvenile, simplicity of her little brown cloth jacket, and the plainness of her dress, to belong to that class of women who are never reconciled to growing old, and as something about her, he could scarcely tell what—an aroma of wealth perhaps —excited his curiosity, he resolved to observe her closely, fancying that she would be worth the trouble. She was evidently a welcome guest, for Lady Stanfield asked her to take a chair at the side of hers, and they appeared to be on terms of intimacy. St. George seemed to know her also, for he had shaken hands with her.
As soon as the peer returned to his seat, Johns continued speaking to him. What subject could he start, he asked himself, so that he might attract attention to himself? For he thought it was not much use to come to such a house and remain unrecognized by the majority. So, trusting to his voice to create its usual effect, and to literature to do the rest, he forced Lord Stanfield into a discussion of the works of a young poet who had lately come somewhat into notice and whom Johns had met. Having first ascertained that Lord Stanfield did not think this young aspirant, with an exotic name, a genius, he broke out into a sudden diatribe against his verse.
"Never," he said, in a deep tone, "surely never has a more vapid mediocrity tried to foist his imbecilities upon the public. His doggerel is an insult to English letters, and it's marvellous to me that even a printer should have been found to print it."
Then, seeing that the visitors were beginning to look round,

and thinking that he had perhaps been too crushing, had seemed perhaps too trenchant, he softened his tone, continuing—

"And when one thinks that this is the country of the divine Shelley, who left behind him so beautiful a model for all who were to follow him, one can but pity this innocent young man. Ah, Shelley was a great magician! Surely he was the truest poet of this century!"

He had assumed so sorrowful a countenance, he seemed to realize so deeply the loss which the nation made when it lost Shelley, that several of the visitors were still looking at him, and Mrs. Humphreys turned to Lady Stanfield, seemingly to ask a question.

But Lord Stanfield said, "No doubt Shelley was a great poet, but he was singularly ignorant of the nature of the ills which he deplored."

And suddenly Johns thought of the "Masque of Anarchy" and the "Ode to Liberty," and said, "Of course, I know that Shelley was a visionary at times, that his imagination led him beyond the bounds of sober reason; but how superb he was in his illusions! In what inimitable notes he scourged the tyrants which his brain created!"

As Lord Stanfield assented by an "Oh, no doubt," there was a pause, during which the conversation was resumed among the visitors.

Presently Johns said, as he perceived Lord Stanfield rising, "Who, might I ask, is that lady speaking to Lady Stanfield? Her face reminds me of a lady I once knew."

"Her name is Mrs. Humphreys. Would you like to speak to her?"

"I would."

They crossed the room to the fireplace, and Lord Stanfield said, "Mrs. Humphreys, here is Mr. Johns, of whom you may have heard."

Johns bowed, while Lady Stanfield said, by way of explanation, and in a tone which was not quite free from condescension, "Mr. Johns is the editor—the young editor, I should say—of a paper called the *Planet*."

Mrs. Humphreys said, "Oh, yes, I've read of Mr. Johns. The *Sphere* had several paragraphs about him the other day."

"Yes," said Johns, with a quiet smile, "they are good enough to trouble themselves about me. It amuses them to make of me a kind of legendary person."

"Indeed," said Mrs. Humphreys, laughing, and showing a set of faultless teeth, which somehow scarcely seemed to Johns quite natural.

And as he thought that women are always a little grateful to those who take the trouble to interest and to amuse them, he exerted himself to obtain the suffrages of his two hearers. Speaking without ceasing, passing from one topic to another without pausing, so that they might continue to give him their attention, presenting many pictures to their imagination, he did his best to dazzle them, studying their faces all the time as if they were barometers to indicate the effect he was producing. Theatres, novels, art—the trinity on which social conversation lives—he attacked them all with lightness and originality, although somewhat dogmatically and with many gestures. From the first he saw that he could amuse Mrs. Humphreys easily, but to do the same with Lady Stanfield was more difficult. He guessed that those cold grey eyes of hers had seen a great deal of life, and he fancied she possessed that British aversion to over-demonstrativeness which made him always feel uncomfortable when he came across it. So he moderated his tones, towards the end, lest she should think him "loud"—a thing which would have touched his *amour propre* considerably. At length, when by a queer turn of phrase he was able to raise a smile upon her serious face, he esteemed it a little victory. She was evidently thawing.

Presently, however, he was forced to give up his place to a new arrival, and as Lady Stanfield was busy taking leave of an old man, with white hair and a bent back, and two ladies who seemed to be his daughters, he was unable to come to the front again, and for some time was forced to become a listener.

But a little later, as he was looking towards his friend—who was chatting with a pale-faced girl in black—to see if he were inclined to leave, Mrs. Humphreys, from whom he had been separated in the change of seats, passed him on her way out.

She said, in passing, "I'm always at home on Wednesdays, Mr. Johns, at 60 Grosvenor Place."

He replied, with a low bow, "Not another week shall pass then, before I give myself the pleasure of a visit."

He spent a few more minutes speaking to a young man, whom he did not know, about the change of government. Then he left with his friend St. George, promising Lord Stanfield that he would come again, since he was good enough to ask him.

When they reached the street, St. George enquired, "What do you think of them?"

Johns answered, "A remarkably nice family; I'm much obliged to you, St. George, for introducing me."

St. George said, "They're inclined to be rather sleepy, and I think you woke them up."

"I didn't say too much, did I?"

"No, not a bit, although at one time I was getting rather fidgety."

"Yes, of course, because of Shelley's anarchy; but I made up for that, I hope. By the way, who is Mrs. Humphreys?"

"Mrs. Humphreys is the widow of a Mr. Humphreys, which Mr. Humphreys was a wealthy man, who left his widow something like six or seven thousand a year in consols, besides a house in Grosvenor Place."

"Oh indeed," Johns said, much more impressed than he cared to let his companion see, "and is she a friend of yours?"

"Not exactly that, but I go to see her now and then."

"That means, I suppose, that you've no desire to take the place of the late Mr. Humphreys?"

"None whatever. Fifty if she's a day. No, my boy, I want something fresher, and thirty years less ancient.

"Yes," said Johns, "all that is very nice—when one can afford it."

Then, to change the subject, he continued, "And what is it that Lord Stanfield has a share in?"

"He's the principal owner of the *Centenary Review*."

"Oh," said Johns, reflectively, "influential in every way."

"Yes, very. You won't regret your visit."

Johns answered, "I should say not."

They had reached Hyde Park Corner. The sun was setting over the Roman arch, tinting the wall of the hospital with a soft shade and reflecting its fire in the windowpanes, while some pure white clouds were floating calmly over the great park.

St. George said, "I must leave you now, as I've got to call on a friend at the Bachelors', but remember, you're coming to my rooms to-night at ten. I've my little actress and her sister coming in to supper. We shall be only four."

"Is the sister nice?"

"You shall see. I promise you you'll not be disappointed."

"Then I'll come, St. George," and upon this they parted.

Johns walked down Piccadilly slowly. He was in a somewhat uncertain frame of mind, for he was asking himself whether he had made a good impression at the Stanfields. Those big people were so reserved, so enigmatic, that one could not read them as easily as others. And yet he thought he had made the most of the opportunity, and it was a fine thing to have gained admittance into that set—a fine thing indeed. For, after all, these were the people who ruled England, who held all that was worth having in their hands, whose influence was in reality as great now as ever it was, although their titles were but nominal. As if anything ever really changed in England! Never! And it was evident that a man had much to gain by frequenting such favoured people. Already he felt himself a degree higher in the social scale than he had the day before, now that he numbered a peer among his friends. And when one thought that democrats in England were only too delighted, as a rule, to be hoisted to a title! Down with the House of Lords, they cried, and they wanted to be Lords themselves. Of course, and quite right too. It was necessary to have a higher caste than the mere peddling middle classes. It was necessary there should be a set of men who were held to be the flower of the race, the "cream," as the French had it, the pick of its men and women. And whether it was necessary or not, these Lords existed, and that was enough for him.

And what about this widow, with her house and consols, her girlish manner, her little waist and ample bust? Surely she, too, was somebody worth knowing. A woman who moved in such society as that, was not the widow of a soap boiler. No, evidently she belonged to the authentic aristocracy, the real aristocracy, that into which he had so much wished of late to enter—a very different sort from that represented by the Dawsons and the Parkers. Faugh, the Parkers! What if they *did* live in a big house; they could only get a few rough politicians like Parker himself to come to it. And the Dawsons too! Was not Dawson an old grocer who had wanted to rise a peg by owning his own newspaper? What a set of nobodies! Perhaps some day he'd be able to do without them.

And as he walked along he continued to speculate upon the possible usefulness of the people he had met that afternoon, letting his imagination take him into ambitious places. How full of opportunities London seemed that evening in the fading light! How alert and pleasant was the aspect of the streets, how gay the traffic gliding through this thoroughfare of opulence, with its tasteful shops and its palatial clubs! How admirably it was all arranged for a man who could help himself! There were so many fools who couldn't, who thought and toiled and yet were never ready at the proper time, who were obliged to eat the bread of poverty. By God, he'd eaten that bread once, and its taste remained in his mouth still. There should be no more of *that* for him if he could help it.

Three days afterwards, upon the Wednesday, Johns, scrupulously shaved, and wearing an immaculate frock coat, with a flower in the button-hole, knocked at the door of Mrs. Humphreys' house in Grosvenor Place at five o'clock. He was not doubtful as to the reception which awaited him. The invitation the widow had given him was too cordial for there to be any chance of its being bad, and it was with an air of calm assurance that he gave his name to the man who opened the door to him.

"A fine house," he muttered to himself, as he mounted the wide stone staircase and noticed the Corinthian pillars of red marble on either side of the recess, and the high stately doors of walnut wood, surmounted by deep mouldings serving as pedestals for sculptured busts, "a monumental house."

St. George had given him some further information about Mrs. Humphreys since the visit to Berkeley Square. His friend had told him that she was a widow for the second time; that her last husband, the son of a large landowner, had died two years previously, and that Society had had something to say about the way in which Mrs. Humphreys had observed the marriage vow. There was a story of a certain captain, and another of a foreign count, for whom she was said to have been by no means adamantine, and there were other little anecdotes of less importance, which St. George had said he had forgotten. One thing was certain, she was left exceedingly well off. She was also without children.

Johns had expected to find a drawing-room filled with visitors, and he was somewhat surprised when he saw that Mrs. Humphreys was alone.

Almost hidden in the corner of a couch, near the high French window in a spacious room which was a model of harmonious elegance—a room suggestive of warmth, well-being, comfort—the fair-haired widow was seated reading. She wore a thin black muslin dress (although the weather scarcely seemed to warrant it) which was simply made and gathered round the waist by a silk band. The only jewelry she wore, besides a diamond ring, was a pearl-headed pin, which was passed through the knot of her hair.

"How good of you to come to-day," she said as Johns advanced towards her. "Very few of my friends know that I'm back in town, and I've only had two visitors this afternoon."

Taking the exceedingly white hand she held out to him in his, Johns said, "I'm delighted to have come so opportunely, Mrs. Humphreys, and all the more delighted to find you quite alone, because it affords me a better chance of making myself known to you. Had I come when you were surrounded by your friends, I would have been one among a number, and I should have had to be content with only speaking to you for a few moments. But that would not have pleased me. For do you know, dear Mrs. Humphreys, that when we met the other day, I had a quick presentiment that we should soon become acquainted, that we should soon perhaps be—may I say it?—friends. For I have always realized that there are natures with whom I have immediate sympathy, faces that interest me, that attract me at first sight, and need I say that when I saw you this phenomenon occurred?"

"Really?" she answered, with a smile of pleasure, "it's kind of you to say so, and I must confess, on my part, that when I heard you were Mr. Johns the editor, I also felt I should like to know you."

Johns looked grave.

"Only because I was Mr. Johns the editor?" he asked.

"Well, no," she explained, with a little laugh which exposed a row of wrinkles, "perhaps not on that account alone."

"Ah, I trust not!"

"But you really do ask curious questions."

"Prompted, I assure you, by a sincere motive."

"Mr. Johns, I've been told that you're a great flatterer. Is it true?"

"No, it is certainly not. I never flatter unless I can admire. Then it's no longer flattery."

Mrs. Humphreys smiled again without replying, and Johns thought, "She can't talk much at anyrate."

Presently he continued, "Ah, Mrs. Humphreys, if you only knew," and then he paused a moment, for he had brought out this phrase, which had stood him in good stead before, without having decided what was to follow after.

"If you only knew," he pursued, "how gladly I came here this afternoon, knowing that I would meet sympathy! As I told our friend St. George, if I had forty papers to attend to, that would not prevent me keeping my promise not to let a week pass by before I came to see you."

And then, feeling that he was perhaps carrying the sympathy motive too far, he said, "What a charming house you live in, and what perfect taste the arrangement of this drawing-room shows! There are some people who are born with the instinct for the beautiful! They embellish everything they touch!"

"I'm afraid," she said, "that a great deal of the credit is due to the decorator. I only gave a few directions—just a few, you know."

"Ah, but it is just those few that give the *cachet*, as the French say, to the whole room. That magnificent rich piano-covering, with its delicate gold-embroidery contrasting so finely with its crimson velvet! It was not the decorator who chose that chaste design. No, Mrs. Humphreys, it was the owner's taste!"

"Really, Mr. Johns, you will soon make me believe that I'm a born artist."

"You would be believing nothing but the truth."

She gave a little ringing laugh which sounded too young for her.

But Johns, noticing an indifferent piece of work which seemed hardly in keeping with the remainder of the furniture, exclaimed—

"And that beautiful tapestry over yonder against the wall, you will not tell me that *that* was chosen by a decorator!"

"Oh *that*," she said, "I worked myself when I was quite a little girl."

"You did? You really did? Marvellous! It's the finest piece I have seen for years. The colours are blended with the greatest skill, the execution's admirable. I have never seen Mary Stuart look more queenly. It's truly a work of art."

Mrs. Humphreys could only murmur, "Really, Mr. Johns!" though she was evidently pleased.

"Ah," he said, "you love art! You have that aspiration towards art which gives zest to life and lifts us out of the banality of things. You have travelled and compared. The art treasures of the world have no secrets for you, and if I am not mistaken, those lovely glasses on that little Louis XVI. table are from the land of Dante."

Mrs. Humphreys hesitated, looking somewhat puzzled.

"Yes," she said at length, "I think we *did* buy them at Madrid—or somewhere like that, you know."

Johns with difficulty suppressed a smile. He made a mental note—"Art and literature, blanks."

Then he attacked other subjects—their mutual friends the Stanfields, and St. George—finding, as he suspected, that on those subjects, as well as on the general doings of society, Mrs. Humphreys had a store of knowledge which she imparted in the easy, discreet tone of a woman of the world. Whether her education in her youth had been neglected, or she had little aptitude for learning, Johns did not know, but he was nevertheless quite sure, both from the way she spoke and from a certain something in her manners, that she had always moved in the best circles.

She said presently, "I met Lord Stanfield yesterday in Bond Street, and he spoke of you. I fancy he thinks highly of you. He said you were likely to make a mark."

"It's very kind of him," said Johns, "and I've quite made up my mind to try."

She continued, "Only if I might ask a question, why are you editor of one of those papers that—well, that no one sees?"

This time Johns smiled openly.

"It isn't given to every one, Mrs. Humphreys, to choose his lot in life. When I came over from Australia, that was what fell to me, and I couldn't consult my tastes."

The widow almost seemed surprised, but after a moment's reflection she said, "No, I suppose one can't very well in those cases, but of course you won't remain for ever at the—the ——"

"The *Planet*," Johns interposed.

"Pardon me, I could not recollect the name."

"One cannot see into one's own fate," he said.

With something like a sigh she answered, "Ah, no, one cannot! No one knows that so well as I," and there was a pause which Johns thought it better not to interrupt. Possibly she was trying to think of the late Mr. Humphreys.

The pause was interrupted by the entrance of a servant with a tea tray. Mrs. Humphreys poured Johns out a cup of fragrant tea in a chaste Sèvres cup. After he had taken a few sips, feeling stimulated, he recommenced—

"I once knew a man who said he could control his fate, and how do you think he tried to do it?"

"Really, I have no idea."

"By simply doing the opposite of what he wished to do. If he felt inclined to take a walk, he stopped at home; if he wanted to stay in, he took a walk; if he wanted to smoke, he didn't; if he didn't want to smoke, he did, and so on—contradicting all his tastes. Only the worst of it was, when he didn't want to die—he did."

Mrs. Humphreys laughed.

"Well, now, I," continued Johns, "don't believe that fate can be controlled, and I am perfectly convinced that I was predestined to meet you, Mrs. Humphreys; I am perfectly convinced that I made the acquaintance of St. George and that he took me to Berkeley Square the other afternoon, all because it was arranged by fate. Nothing will take that little superstition from me."

"Well, really, Mr. Johns, perhaps it was. We have already made so much progress in our acquaintance that it *does* seem as if we were meant to meet. I have always liked to know people like you who direct papers. The Press is such a power!"

L

Johns thought, "Where did she pick *that* phrase up, I wonder?" and he said with gravity, "Yes, Mrs. Humphreys, journalism can be made to lead a long way, a very long way, indeed, but it's a life of many worries."

Then, putting down the tea cup, and suddenly bending forward in his chair as if he were moved by an earnest thought, he said, "Mrs. Humphreys, I've known you only a little while, and yet I feel extraordinarily tempted to ask a favour of you."

"Please do, I'm sure I shall be delighted."

"Will you let me come and see you sometimes when you're not surrounded by your friends, just like to-day, so that I may have something to look forward to in the struggle of the week, so that I may be able to tell myself that at least one hour of it will be free from worry, will be full of charm?"

"Oh," she said, smiling, "if that's all you ask, it's easily granted. The only little difficulty is that my friends, as soon as they know I'm in town, so seldom let me have an hour to myself."

"Ah! you are such a favourite!"

"But still if you will come and lunch with me sometimes, there will be no one then but my companion, Miss Sinclair, who is spending two days in the country. For you know I must have her by me: you're such a dangerous man, I'm told."

"No, no, not dangerous, and thank you infinitely. Yes, I will come to lunch with all the pleasure in the world. How I shall look forward to those days!"

"Don't thank me, but come on Saturday."

"On Saturday!"

So it was arranged, and Johns shortly afterwards withdrew.

As he walked home he said to himself, "They're all alike, those women. That one has quite enough experience of life to know that I was talking *rot*, and yet she liked it hugely. Yes, they're all the same. The most sagacious of them is delighted by a compliment, and the silliest goes simply into ecstacy. By God! though, seven thousand pounds a year, and only such a head to manage it! It isn't right. Some body's wanted to put order there. I wonder if ——. Why not?" and he sauntered through the Green Park homewards, indulging in a golden dream.

CHAPTER TENTH

AS the summer progressed, Johns's popularity among his new friends rapidly increased. His little stories, which he had endeavoured to make humorous, knowing that humour is always popular, had been pronounced inimitable. He had varied them with trite sayings and peculiar epigrams, which were soon repeated from house to house as examples of a novel kind of wit.

At the Stanfields he had become a frequent visitor, and by dint of perseverance he had succeeded in overcoming the frigidity of even Lady Stanfield. But what gave him the greatest satisfaction, the most pleasant feeling of security, was the advances he had made in the good graces of Mrs. Humphreys, who received him now as an old acquaintance. It was true that she continued to disapprove of the *Evening Planet*, as she called it, and had asked him questions about his family which he had found it difficult to answer, but he believed so strongly in the power of human nature to conquer prejudice that he still nourished certain hopes which he confessed to no one, but which grew stronger as the days went by.

Unfortunately for their realization, two women somewhat blocked the way. Mrs. Weber was growing difficult to quiet. It was useless now for him to tell her that they must wait until the paper had outstripped its rivals; she knew from Parker that it was flourishing, and that Dawson had increased Johns's salary, declaring that he was simply indispensable. And sometimes, when she was particularly bitter and reproached him with not keeping his promise to her, he would be on the point of telling her that he didn't intend to listen any longer to her lamentations. But always that seductive beauty, which he had not yet seen equalled, even in the circles he now moved in, restrained him. Twice when she had wished to make a scene while he was with her, he had left the house suddenly without a word, and each time he had received a letter the next morning imploring pardon and promising reform. He had irritated her by refusing to introduce her to the Stanfields, on the plea that as a bachelor he could not do so, and by always objecting to her coming to see him in his rooms. She was nervous and excitable, tender and irritable in turns, and her thoughts, he knew, were always centred in the marriage question.

Mrs. Dawson, although more reasonable and resigned to seeing him only once a fortnight, since he had said his work prevented him from devoting more time to her, was so hopelessly engrossed in her passion for him that he was almost inclined to feel some little pity for her when she gazed into his eyes or nestled like a child in his arms, with the infatuation of a woman in love for the first time. And even on the days when he found her tiresome and burdensome, he could not help admitting that she possessed a certain naïveness in her love which was not without its charm. Besides, she never worried him like Mrs. Weber.

There were days, however, when both his mistresses annoyed and wearied him; days when he wanted to think of his own plans which he could not mention to them, and when he merely saw in them the means of a passing gratification; days when he wished, as soon as he was no longer with them, that they might each fall in love with other men, who would take them off his hands. Why couldn't they see that all irregular love affairs are doomed to fizzle out? How dense these women were!

One afternoon in June, however, an event occurred which brought matters to a crisis.

Mrs. Dawson had been spending an hour with him in his rooms in Jermyn Street. While she was putting on her gloves to leave, she paused to look at him admiringly, as he sat languidly in his arm-chair, sending puffs of smoke from his cigar upwards to the ceiling.

"Ah, Johnnie," she said, "you will never know how much I love you."

"Well," he answered, ill-humouredly, without looking at her, "I ought to know it, you tell me often enough."

She stopped in the act of buttoning her glove, and her expression changed.

"Oh, how unkind that sounds!"

"You think everything one says unkind."

She said, drawing nearer, "You are worried to-day about something—is that why you seem so cold?"
"Perhaps it is. I've more worries than you think."
"Why not tell me? You know my husband would do anything for you now."
"I should rather think he would, after I've stuck his paper on its legs again; but I don't trouble much about *him* now, I can tell you. He has to trouble about *me*. I should be curious to know," he added, glancing at Mrs. Dawson sideways, "what he would say if he happened to appear at the present moment."

But she shook her head and answered, "Don't let us talk of that. It's too dreadful."

"It isn't so impossible either. He came here one evening last week to see me—the old fool."

"Oh, John, please don't speak of him like that. I never loved him, never; but I can't forget that he married me without a penny."

Johns thought, "And this is the way you show your gratitude!"

"I'm afraid, John," she continued, "that those new people you have met have made you think less of us than you did before."

In spite of the mildness of the reproach, and the timid way in which it was made, Johns was vexed. In his irritable state of mind he construed this into a reflection upon his origin.

"Why not say at once," he said, sharply, "that you think I'm snobbish."

"No, John, I didn't mean that. You know I didn't."

"It sounded like it."

She could only sigh, "How unkind you are to-day!"

But he was anxious to get rid of her, and, instead of replying, looked at the clock upon the mantel-piece. After all, she was another man's wife, and therefore a dangerous person to be discovered on the premises in a country where the divorce laws were so stupid. He didn't want to spoil his chances by a public scandal, the damaging effect of which he knew. It was foolish of him to receive her there at all, and he made up his mind at once that before their next meeting he would write and tell her so. He had been acting with too much indecision, with a great deal too much imprudence. All that must be remedied—now that circumstances were changed.

After a few moments, as she did not move, he said, "I should think you'd better be going home; it's getting late."

But she still stood motionless, looking on the ground, and slowly a tear trickled down her cheek.

He rose now, and, approaching her, took one of her gloved hands in his.

"Come, Lucy," he said, in a voice that was rather softer, "what is all this about? You *know* we must be prudent."

"Yes, I suppose we must," she said, sadly; "I suppose I must go. Good-bye."

"Good-bye, Lucy, don't be upset. I'll write to you again soon."

With a faint smile she left.

"Ouf," he said, as soon as the door was closed; "she *has* taken it in earnest!"

He took a cigar from an open box upon the table, and was in the act of lighting it before sitting down to think over the situation, when the door was suddenly burst open, and Mrs. Weber, flushed and excited, rushed into the room.

Placing herself before him defiantly, her eyes flashing as he had never seen them flash before, she began—

"*Now* I understand your hesitation, you treacherous little cad! You wanted to wait until the paper had done this, until the paper had done that. You thought it better to be prudent; it wasn't the right month, and a hundred other lies. And all the time you had been stealing the wife of your own master. Oh, you little wretch, you *dirty* little wretch!"

Johns, who had turned pale, summoned all the dignity he could command.

"I don't understand you. What do you mean?"

Stamping her foot, she said, "You're not going to deny, I should imagine. It would be too feeble of you, since I've seen with my own eyes."

"Seen what?"

"Seen Lucy Dawson go away from here only a minute ago. I didn't think it possible you could have been such a sneak."

Johns was silent for a moment, counting up the issues. Then, when he had made up his mind as to the attitude he should adopt, he quietly struck another match and went on lighting his cigar.

Exasperated by his silence and this indifference, she almost shrieked—

"Well, have you become dumb as well?"

He answered, "Of your abuse I take no notice; you may think just what you please."

"Ha, you can't deny it! you can't deny it! To think that

I took pity on you when you were only a bit of a reporter, and did for you what no other woman would, and ———."
She paused a moment to reflect, and then, as if struck by a sudden thought, began again—"Oh, I see it all now. Long ago, when you were half-starving, when I spoke to her of you, she got confused, and would say nothing. No, because she was coming to these rooms to visit you, and all the time you were paying for them with my money! Oh you—you hypocrite!"

Johns had winced several times under the violence of the abuse, but maintaining, with an effort, his calm demeanour, he replied, "If it's the poor little fifty pounds that you're alluding to, my fine Ellen, I'll give you a cheque at once."

"I don't want your money, I won't touch it. You needn't think you're going to get off like that. I warned you once that if you deceived me, you'd repent it, and I intend to keep my word. Dawson shall know the kind of editor he has to-morrow."

But this time he was roused. "You'd better not," he said, "and if you'll wait a moment, I'll tell you why."

Saying this, he crossed the room to a secrétaire which stood in the window, and unlocked one of its drawers by means of a key which he drew from his pocket. Then he took from it a piece of paper, which he unfolded.

"On the 15th, 19th, 21st, 25th, and 31st of August," he said, glancing at the paper, "Parker was with you at Maidenhead under circumstances which it's needless for me to mention. From September of last year to the present time he has been a frequent visitor at Carsdale Mansions—never on Wednesdays —and at certain times he has stayed till the next morning. The dates are all carefully noted on this piece of paper, and I think it's useless to make any remark about it; only remember—that when I'm threatened, I know how to defend myself."

She remained speechless with astonishment, glancing alternately at Johns and at the paper he was holding in his hand.

"Oh," she said at length, "you've even been mean enough to have me watched."

"So you see," he continued, quietly folding up the slip and putting it in his pocket, "we can both denounce."

"You've no proof," she said.

"I've more than you," he answered, and for a few minutes they stood facing each other without speaking.

"After all," she continued presently, "what do I care? I've less to lose than you, and whatever you choose to do won't prevent me from acting as I please."

"Very well, we shall see who gets the best of it."

But as she stood before him in her defiant attitude, her eyes flashing, it seemed to him that she had never looked so handsome, and he advanced towards her and seized her arm. Then, drawing her towards him before she could resist, he said roughly—

"That's enough of that cursed nonsense. You know perfectly well we want each other!"

"Don't be brutal," she said, holding herself away from him.

"Will you keep your promise? Yes or no?"

Before answering, he looked into her face, and his peering eyes met hers in a gaze of mingled passion and defiance. Then, in a firm tone, he answered "No! —— I won't."

"Ah," she said, after a deep breath, "now you come out in your true colours. You refuse now, not because of Parker— what would he matter if you thought it to your interest to marry me?—but because you think that, now you've got in with those big people, you can do better. Oh, you little *cad!*"

"You'd better not irritate me," he said, beginning to lose patience, and stung by the reiteration of the word cad.

"Let go my arm, you brute!"

He released his hold, but with a push which sent her violently backwards.

"That's right," she said, defying him; "it's just what one might expect from a man of your origin. As if I didn't know that you were the son of an old fisherman. I've *my* sources of information, too."

"By God," said Johns, thoroughly roused this time, "if you don't stop I'll, I'll —— "

He faltered in the middle of his sentence, for his indignation was so great that it confused his thoughts.

"What will you do?" she asked, sneeringly; "I'm not afraid of you, you Guernseyman."

Johns, for reasons which he could scarcely have defined, had a particular dislike to be called a Guernseyman, and this last insult added gall to wormwood.

"What will I do?" he repeated; "I'll ——, by God, I'll put you out of here."

"You'd better wait till I go of my own free will, which won't be long, unless you want to make a scandal on the landing."

"What are you waiting for?" he muttered.

"To take a last look at an adventurer such as one doesn't often meet."

He sprang upon her, and, seizing her by the waist, dragged her to the sofa, and there they struggled with each other for a few moments, he, in a fit of exasperation, trying to force her into subjection, she battling against him with strength he had never known her to possess. At length, seeing a heavy paper-knife which was lying on the sofa, she seized it before he could prevent her and struck him heavily across the face. Then, as he released his hold, she sprang to her feet, and in another instant she was gone.

Johns, half-stunned at first by the blow he had received, and suffering pain from a contusion of his left eye, rose muttering an oath and went up to the glass. A round, red mark showed the place upon the high cheek-bone where the handle of the paper-knife had struck, and his eye, which he could only open with some difficulty, was inflamed and infused with blood.

" Curse her," he said, " she's bruised me for a week ! "

As he was smarting with pain, he rang the bell, and presently the valet came.

" Edward," he said, " I've fallen on that damned fender. Go and get me something for a bruised eye."

" Yes, sir," the man said, and vanished.

While he was gone, Johns, holding his handkerchief to his face, indulged in his reflections. What a devil she had shown herself as she stood there taunting him ! How her eyes had flashed with fire as she had called him every name she could invent ! Yes, she was a woman of the kind he liked, and yet henceforth she was going to be an enemy—curse her ! For there was no doubt about it, she was quite capable of carrying out her threat. In fact, there were nine chances to one she would. She had been smart enough to see that the consequences would fall heavier on him than they would on her in case of an exposure. He was quite alive to the danger of the situation, and he knew that his position was not yet so solidly established that a scandal, particularly one of this character, might not make the whole fabric tumble about his ears. Yes, he had got into an awkward corner when he least expected to, and there was no knowing how he was to get out. Although he had not told her lately much of his affairs, still she knew enough of them to do considerable harm. And the more he thought of it, the more numerous the weak points in his position seemed, and he began to call himself a fool for having delayed so long in breaking with her. It would have been so easy to have got up a quarrel about some trifle, and then refused to be propitiated, while now he had stupidly exposed himself to danger. Excited as he was by what had happened that afternoon, his imagination got the better of his reason and magnified the peril. Clearly he fancied he could see what was going to take place in the exact order of its happening. First, Dawson would learn from Mrs. Weber his intimacy with his wife; then he would lose his post of editor, finally a divorce suit would achieve his ruin, materially and socially. And the fond dreams he had been dreaming would vanish into thin air. Ah, that was a fine ending to a career which had begun so brilliantly, to success that had made all London talk! A pretty chance he'd have of beginning life again under such auspices! There would be little left for him to do but to go back to Australia and live again upon his wits. How was it possible he had been such a fool? As for Mrs. Dawson, whether she had seen her rival coming up the stairs or not he did not know; but he imagined that one woman under such circumstances would scarcely fail to see another. He felt quite sure that she would not be vindictive; but who knew whether she might not, conscience-struck, confess—as she had been on the point of doing once—when questioned by her husband? Oh, it was a fine imbroglio! He was sick of his own stupidity. He sat in his arm-chair thinking gloomily until the man returned with a lotion from the chemist, with which he at once began to bath his eye and his bruised cheek.

When he had finished doing this, he returned to the parlour. Pouring himself out a glass of Kümmel from the liqueur stand on the sideboard, he drank it, and then sat down to think.

Gradually now, as he felt a little calmer, his ideas began to form themselves into plans of self-defence. Perhaps after all things might not go so badly for him as he had thought at first, and in any case, if she accused him, it would be very difficult for her to furnish proof. He had never received Mrs. Dawson anywhere but in his own rooms, and as he had given her a key of the glass door on the ground floor (the front door was always kept open), no one, he thought, not even the valet of the place, had seen her—no one but Mrs. Weber, who, now he came to think of it, must have had the door opened for her by her rival as she was going out. It was thus they must have met.

Well, the first thing to be done was to send her back her money, and the next was to deny consistently, since so little proof could be brought against him, unless it were in the form of a few letters in ambiguous terms which he had been obliged to write to Mrs. Dawson at different times.

Yes, that was the only course open to him to pursue if Mrs. Weber carried out her threat, which, on the other hand, it was just possible she might refrain from doing when she reflected that she herself could not come out unscathed from any exposure she might provoke. Having resolved upon this course, he went to his desk, took a cheque-book from a drawer, wrote out a cheque for £50 to "self or bearer," and wrapped it in a blank piece of paper. This he placed in an envelope which he addressed to Mrs. Weber. Then he rang the bell again, and when the valet came he gave the letter to him to post, telling him that he would have dinner that evening in his rooms, and that he was not at home for anyone.

The evening was the gloomiest he had passed since he had been in Jermyn Street. In spite of himself he was tortured by a sense of insecurity, by an acute feeling of uncertainty. He could not read, for his eye still troubled him, and he sat in his chair after dinner unable to take his thoughts from the one question on which they were now centred—what was going to happen on the morrow? Tired of turning it over and over in his mind, he went to bed shortly after ten. But to his surprise he found that he could not sleep. It was the first time in his life that any mishap of his had been able to keep him awake, and he asked himself why it was so this time. He supposed it was because he'd never before been playing for such high stakes. Yes, that must be the reason. He hated suspense of any kind, and it had a great effect upon his nerves. When the morning came he jumped out of bed and looked at himself in the glass. The contusion round the cheek-bone was less inflamed, and his eye was rather better. He was not quite presentable, he knew, but still he thought that, even as he was, he had better go to the office to defend himself if needful, on the principle that the absent are always wrong.

He dressed slowly and carefully, and after he had taken a cup of coffee and a roll, he left for the Strand on foot. It was still early; the fresh morning air invigorated him and made him feel that his old spirit of combativeness was coming back to him. Nothing perhaps would happen that day; but if it did, he was now prepared to face it. He didn't want to think of the possibility of things going wrong. He would *not* think of it. And with this resolve he took his seat in the editorial chair and began his work, calling Maskelyne to help him and issuing his orders to the whole staff unmercifully, giving each at least three days' work to perform in as many hours. The Conservative *Report* had dared to sneer at them the day before, had it? Then Maskelyne was to write a paragraph which would make the whole staff of the rival paper smart and gnash their teeth. And Maskelyne, who knew very well from past experience that Johns would strike out the wrathful par from prudence before the paper went to press, smiled and began to scribble something. Towards eleven Tarte came into Johns's room with the face of an ambassador. His right hand resting on the top button of his long frock coat in a Beaconsfieldian attitude, his left placed upon the desk, he said, with his usual calm precision, "Mr. Dawson asks if you will be kind enough to step into his room."

Johns turned round quickly in his chair as though he had been struck, and faced the old man so savagely that the latter drew back a step, amazed. But Johns, after the first impression which the words had caused, had suddenly turned pale. He rose at once and said, "All right, I'm going."

Of late it had been Dawson's habit to come in to Johns's room when he had anything to say. The change that day evidently meant that Mrs. Weber had kept her word.

But from the moment he stepped into the room, he saw that his apprehensions were unfounded. Dawson received him as affably as usual, and requesting him to take a seat, began—

"I've asked you to come in here because I had to speak to you of something which is best mentioned where we are in private."

Saying this, he drew from his pocket one of those envelopes of a peculiar terra-cotta colour which are used to enclose telegrams, and drew a message from it.

Unfolding the pink sheet, he handed it to Johns who read, "Your wife is the mistress of your editor. This very day she left his rooms in Jermyn Street at six. Well informed."

"I need scarcely tell you," continued Dawson, "that this scandalous accusation took us by surprise. My wife, who is so sensitive on these matters, has been greatly affected. The mere thought that any aspersion should be put upon her reputation has upset her terribly. The reason I have mentioned this disgusting slander to you is in order that you may know that you have an enemy, as well as to give you an opportunity of perhaps discovering the author."

Johns, who had begun to breathe again, exclaimed—

"It seems incredible that there should be such blackguards! I am very grateful to you, Mr. Dawson, for showing me this so frankly. I have only a vague suspicion as to the author or the authoress; but until I have found out, I prefer not to mention names. It's the most odious piece of slander that ever was invented, and I'm deeply sorry that Mrs. Dawson should be so much disturbed. I hope that you will tell her that it should be treated as beneath contempt, and that if I am successful in discovering the perpetrator, he or she shall be punished."

"I thank you," said Dawson; "I have already told her that she must not trouble herself; but, of course, sensitive as she is, it affects her greatly."

Johns thought, "It must," and said, "Yes, no doubt, and I hope you will tell her how much I sympathize with her, and how much I regret the incident."

"I won't fail to do so," Dawson answered, "and now, let's talk no more about the wretched thing."

Then, noticing suddenly the mark on Johns's cheek, he asked, "But what's the matter with your face?"

Johns answered, "A stupid fall I had yesterday afternoon in Berkeley Square. Just as I was going to make a call I slipped on the pavement and fell upon the door-step. But it's nothing —a mere bruise."

Dawson's curiosity being satisfied, he said no more, and Johns, declaring that he was very busy, went back to his own room.

He was delighted at the turn things had taken, and amused at the credulity of the proprietor.

"Ha, my fine Ellen," he chuckled, "your telegram wasn't of much good. If you don't do better than that, you're not dangerous."

As long, he thought, as Mrs. Dawson was only "upset," as her husband called it, and didn't let her feelings get the better of her discretion, there was nothing lost. In fact, since the husband refused to listen, like the silly man he was, everything was for the best, and Johns indulged in reflections which were scarcely flattering to the intelligence of Dawson.

When he returned that evening, a letter was awaiting him. It was from Mrs. Dawson, and it began—

"Dear John."

"Oh," he thought, "if she begins like that it's all right."

"I cannot express the fearful trouble which has come upon me since I left you yesterday. I am so heart-broken that I can scarcely write. There is no need for me to tell you what has happened. You will have known it from her and from my husband. It was cruel to deceive me so! I, who trusted you implicitly, and who loved you as no woman ever loved before, I who would have shielded you from harm! How could I have ever thought that you would have been so faithless! Even now I can scarcely realize that you have been (perhaps for many months) deceiving me with my best friend! If you had seen the look she gave me as she opened the door, and heard the tone in which she asked me what I was doing there! I knew at once that she was going to see you, and when that telegram was brought, I knew her jealousy had made her send it. And I was forced to lie and act a part when my husband handed it to me across the table. I was certain then that you had been false to me, and the tears came into my eyes as he said it was a shameful slander, while I knew that it was true! Oh, how I wish that it were not!

"And now the past cannot be undone, and what has happened has quelled the love I had for you, and made me one of the most unfortunate of women. For I am unable to forget you, although everything is at an end between us. To deceive my husband pained me as you always knew, but to be deceived by the man I loved was terrible. Ah, if I could have foreseen all this that day when I was weak enough to come to see you in your rooms, and when you swore you would be true! but it is the fate of us women to trust, to love, and then to suffer. Good-bye, John, may you never make another woman so wretched as you have made your once loving Lucy."

"Your once loving Lucy," he repeated, slowly and approvingly, made rather serious by the tenour of the letter. "She's taken it exactly as I thought. Good little Lucy after all."

Had it been possible to dive into his thoughts at that moment, a curious medley would have been seen of satisfaction and assuaged fear, alternating with a few twinges of remorse, which assumed the shape of a vague feeling of discomfort. But the main thought which filled his mind was that the sky was clear again apparently, and that he could continue his career. That thought filled him with a calm sense of alleviation, and the same evening he dined pleasantly with St. George at a new restaurant in Regent Street.

The morning after this, as his eye was better and the round mark on his face had almost disappeared, he resolved to take a step which he had been contemplating for the last three months.

Towards five o'clock, accordingly, he left the Strand in a hansom for Grosvenor Place, where Mrs. Humphreys was expecting him. It was a fine summer's afternoon, and, as the air was clear, the London streets were looking as well as the disfigurement of their huge advertisements permitted. In passing the National Gallery, sombre in its besmeared grandeur, he saw a girl with a fresh and pretty face coming down the steps. And suddenly the sight caused him a sharp pang of envious regret. For Johns, like most men, had dreamed of an alliance some day with youth and candour, while now—well, he must take things as he found them, and make the best of his opportunities.

As he approached the house he thought of the baronet who was so assiduous in his attentions to the widow, and who had been a formidable thorn in his side throughout his acquaintance with Mrs. Humphreys. The baronet, he knew, had been ruined on the turf, and was past middle age, but belonged to a family which had been founded during the crusades, and Johns thought that, notwithstanding the widow's evident inclination for him, this baronet was still a rival against whom he must be on his guard. Whenever they had met at the house together, there had been passages of arms between them, in which Johns, more ready with his tongue, had generally been the victor. Undoubtedly the favour of the lady was on his side, on the side of his youth and dash, but then there was his origin, which he always felt had been an obstacle. No matter, men were strong and women weak. There were few exceptions to that rule, and certainly Mrs. Humphreys had never seemed to be one of them. It was, perhaps, after all, like so many other things, a question of pure will, and he intended to use his power of willing to the utmost.

Thinking thus, he reached the house.

Mrs. Humphreys received him in a little boudoir on the ground floor, the walls and ceiling of which were lined with a dark crimson cloth, festooned—the red shade predominating throughout the room, as if the widow had thought a red background the most suited to her complexion.

"You see," she said, with a coquettish air, "how good I am; I've given up a concert simply because you said in your letter you wanted so much to see me."

He answered, in a voice full of restrained emotion, "An angel is not better!"

"And now," she continued, "I hope you have something very interesting to tell me."

He said, "I have something on which the whole of my future life depends."

"Indeed," she said, moving a little, "what is it?"

He rose from the chair which he had taken on his entrance, and quickly, with a nimbleness which experience had taught him, took another and placed it at the side of hers.

"Can you not guess?" he asked. "Have you not been conscious that ever since the day when we made a pact of friendship there has grown between us a feeling which is something more, something greater than mere friendship. You remember how it happened that we met, and that immediately we both experienced one of those magnetic sympathies which are sometimes felt by two persons thrown together in the race of life. Ah, that day when we first met! I have thought of it so often since, so often! And what has happened? Oh, let me tell you. I have become conscious of a deep conviction that I have never met a woman who embodied so supremely the qualities of charm and grace which we men prize. You, Mrs. Humphreys—ah, why may I not call you Rose?—have fascinated, have impressed me so completely, that I am unable now to find pleasure in the society of other women. You have shown me that there is one woman in the world who can make me feel that it is good to live, that there is joy and satisfaction in existence."

He moved a little closer to her, and murmured almost in her ear, "I fancy I detect in the expression of that pure Greek face a lovely sign of reciprocity. Ah, Rose—I must, I will call you Rose—as the divine Shakespeare says, *what love can do, that dares love attempt*, and what I dare attempt is to ask you if you will be my wife."

She looked away from him with the air of a maiden whose hand is sought for the first time, and, as she did not answer, he continued—

"You are silent; you are perhaps weighing me in the balance with another; but let me tell you, Rose, that there is no other man among your friends who is so worthy of you, who would be so devoted to you as I. I am something better than a ruined baronet, for I am an actor on the world's stage, and my present avocation is only a stepping-stone to something higher. A baronet, indeed! *I* am on the path which leads much farther. *I*, only, can make you as happy as you deserve to be. Rose, do not keep me in suspense! Tell me if I am to be your husband!"

She answered, "But are you not afraid that I am perhaps not quite—that you are perhaps a little young to be my husband?"

"A little young!" he repeated, as if surprised. "Oh, there may be a few years' difference between us, but what of that, when nothing shows it, when you look as fresh and comely as your own sweet name? Rose, we should be an admirable match! You, with your dignity and beauty; I, with what they call my individuality. We should impress society. We should be the most prominent couple in all London!"

Then, putting his arm around the slender waist, he whispered gently, "Rose, my little Rose, I feel that you are going to consent. I see it in the tremor of those dainty lips, in the lustre of those matchless eyes. Say yes, and put an end to my suspense."

She said, "You were quite right when you thought that there was more than sympathy between us, for, shall I confess it? I, too, have always liked you. You are so clever, everybody says so, and so manly, and your face is more than handsome. If you really are quite sure that you would make a good husband ——"

But before she had completed the sentence he had imprinted a chaste kiss upon her forehead.

"Rose, my dearest Rose, how happy you have made me; why, there shall not be a more devoted husband in the world! You shall be my care, my whole solicitude!"

"Only," she added, presently, "there are some little things we must arrange. First of all there's the *Evening*—whatever it is—the paper. I shouldn't like you to continue doing that. It wouldn't do, you know, considering the set we should want to move in."

"Oh," said Johns, "of course I'll change it for something more congenial to our party as soon as I get an opportunity."

He said "our party" as if he had been born in it, and she pursued—

"Lord Stanfield could arrange that for you, I'm quite sure. He owns Reviews and things, and he's always so very kind when one asks him to do anything."

"Of course," Johns said, "of course, that can be settled easily."

What did editorships matter to him now?

"And then there's a question which is a little delicate. It's about your family, you know. I think you gave me to understand that they weren't—well, not the people one is quite accustomed to."

Johns waved his hand to reassure her.

"Don't be anxious on that score; my progenitors, excellent souls, shall never trouble us."

"Quite so," she said, approvingly, "and, of course, if you are asked, you might say they lived on their estates somewhere. People are so inquisitive, you know."

"Oh yes," said Johns, smiling, "my father does live on his estate of about a quarter of an acre, so it would be strictly accurate to say so."

Mrs. Humphreys laughed, and then they commenced a long chat about the future. Nothing should be changed in their existence. They would be married in a month, and they would travel. Then they would come back to Grosvenor Place, and everything would be well-ordered and satisfactory. Their engagement could be given out at once. Johns said that it would be quite unnecessary that his parents should be present at the wedding. No mention need be made of them unless it were to say that they were ill, and could not come, or any other little fiction of the kind, and no time would be lost in seeing Lord Stanfield about the change in his position. Mrs. Humphreys also thought that they might buy a Magazine, "or something," and that in that way her Johnnie would be his own master, and of course he acquiesced readily in such a proposition. And every day now, she told him tenderly, he must come to see her, without missing a single day, and he must go to her photographer and have a portrait taken of himself, so that she might keep it by her when he was absent, and she was going to give a big dinner to celebrate their engagement. She formed a host of projects of the kind, with all of which Johns expressed himself delighted.

Then, as he was leaving, with a touching coyness, she whispered softly, "Johns, you naughty man, you can give me a nice kiss."

He did not need to be asked twice, and with all the enthusiasm he could command, he pressed his lips on hers, thus sealing the bargain he had just concluded.

CHAPTER ELEVENTH

JOHNS left his rooms the next morning with a superb feeling of power and intensity. He was a new man. He was lifted an immeasurable distance above the heads of those he had come in contact with at the start of his career. In a little while he was going to control the revenue of an ambassador, to enjoy the independence of a capitalist. In another month he would be an important figure in society. All the luxuries and satisfactions a man can wish for would be his, together with a wife who, though certainly not quite the incarnation of his youthful dreams, looked well at times, and had that air of unmistakable good breeding which he admired. That morning at the office, as soon as he had heard that Dawson had arrived, he rang for Tarte.

"Tarte, ask Dawson to come in to me."

The old man asked, "Must the mountain now come to Mohammed?"

"Perhaps so, Tarte."

"Has Mohammed then married the rich widow?"

"No, but he's going to, my worthy Tarte."

"Ah," the old man said, as he moved away, "you're one of the great men of the earth."

Presently, after he had been gone a few minutes, Dawson entered.

"Good morning, Mr. Dawson," Johns said, without rising or excusing himself for asking the proprietor to come, "I've a little piece of news this morning."

"Indeed?" said Dawson, rubbing his hands, "something good for the paper, I hope?"

"I don't know about that," Johns answered, "I'm going to be married."

"I congratulate you. To whom?"
"To Mrs. Humphreys, of Grosvenor Place."
"What! not the widow of Stephen Humphreys?"
"The same." And he looked at the proprietor to study the effect the news had.

"Dawson in his surprise could only ejaculate—
"Well you are—you *are* a lucky man. They say she's worth three hundred thousand pounds!"

"About that," Johns answered, calmly.

Dawson reflected for a moment.

"Well, that *is* a piece of news, but I hope you don't intend to leave the paper."

"Not immediately, perhaps, but I shall want a big holiday to get married."

"Oh, of course, of course. A month, or even two."

"Most likely three."

"Three then it shall be," Dawson answered in his eagerness to keep so powerful a man.

"And now," said Johns, "I'm busy," upon which the proprietor was obliged to leave, which he did after repeating his congratulations.

In the office the news caused a great stir, and Johns was henceforth looked upon as a sort of superhuman person who could achieve anything he liked. Even the jealousies which his rapid rise had at first called forth disappeared before the magnitude of his success. Henceforth he was a man who could do something for his friends, and all wished to obtain his favour.

Everything went well until the night of the dinner party. When Johns arrived at Grosvenor Place that evening, half an hour before the time, as had been arranged, he found Mrs. Humphreys in a handsome and extremely low-necked dress waiting for him in the little boudoir which had witnessed their betrothal. From the moment he stepped in, he saw from the expression of her face that something was amiss.

"Why Rose," he said, "what is the meaning of this solemn face to-night?"

She handed him a telegram and said, "Read that."

He read, "You're going to marry a man who does not even respect the wife of his own master, who only sees in you a silly old woman with a money bag. Be warned before it is too late—One of his many victims."

"Who is this woman?" she asked rather sharply, as soon as he had finished reading.

Perfectly unmoved, he answered, "An adventuress with whom I was somewhat intimate before I became engaged to you, but whose acquaintance I have dropped. The telegram is a mere piece of jealousy, only worthy of contempt."

"But is what she says true about the wife of —— of the person, I suppose, who owns the paper?"

"It's a contemptible lie, as Dawson himself would tell you. I repeat, she's a mere adventuress, and this is not the first telegram she's sent to friends of mine."

"At all events," she said, "it's very disagreeable."

He had never seen her so annoyed, and he thought that he must make amends.

"Rose," he said, "do not be troubled for such trifles. Since I have been engaged to you, I have thought of no one but your own sweet self. I have banished from my mind all the women who used to pester me. You only, Rose, have shown me how great it is to love!"

"Still," she said a little softened, "you've been a reprobate."

"Oh," he answered, laughing, "my wild oats are all, all sown!"

Then, as usual, he began to chant the song of love, eternally the same, he thought, "Rose, my little Rose, can't you see that no other woman can exist for me? Can't you see that my whole thoughts, my whole life are centred in you? Do you not know that every moment of the day wherever I may be, your face, so perfect in its blonde repose, is with me? What can separate us now? Are we not destined for each other by all the laws of destiny and of affinity? What does it matter now what envy says of us? Are not happy people always envied? My little Rose, there will be no happier pair on all the earth. Ah, if I could express all I feel! But no, there are no words for it. Give me a kiss, my Rose."

And then, her serenity returning, she allowed him to kiss her, saying—

"Really, John, you're a great flatterer! A great flatterer!"

Presently, as the guests were beginning to arrive, they went up to the drawing-room, where Johns helped his affianced bride to welcome the party she had gathered round her to celebrate the third incursion into the married state she was on the eve of making. Amongst them were the Stanfields and St. George; a portly dean—a brother-in-law of Mrs. Humphreys, with his thin and ugly wife—a middle-aged relative; a judge and a general, both accompanied by their wives; and others whom Johns had never met before. As he exchanged a few words with each, acknowledging their congratulations, he was conscious of a delicious feeling of achievement. It gratified him greatly to feel that he had definitely forced these people to accept him as their equal, and the feeling was intensified, when, a little later, he descended the sumptuous staircase with Lady Stanfield on his arm. At dinner in the lofty dining-room, with its marble pillars and Pompeian air, its paintings by old masters, its luxuriously-appointed table, Johns was in a state of calm exuberance, and when a German lady with blue eyes and flaxen hair, who had a taste for social questions, started the subject of "the unfit," he said, "You say truly there is an infinite pathos in those wasted lives one meets with sometimes, in those half intelligences too good for common drudgery and yet not good enough for higher things. Think of the anguish with which they climb and climb, sometimes getting near the summit, only to drop back again into the pit of their own incompetence; think of the hope which dances before them like a delusive marsh light, of the chimera which yet allures them, because they prefer to be eternally deceived rather than give up the chase! And remember that it is all through no fault of theirs, but through an accident of birth!"

"Yes," said Princess Roltzau; "and it is for them that I would like to found an institution—an institution which would be a sort of Providence for the unfit."

Johns said, "The idea is noble, but impossible. There is no Providence for the unfit. They are as inseparable from their illusions as a drunkard from his bottle! No, Princess, *the revolver is their only providence!*"

He had pronounced these words with calm serenity, and when he ceased speaking, his hearers for a moment remained silent. He was conscious of a grateful sense of triumph. Was he not soon to be master of this palatial house? Had he not shown conclusively his own fitness?

He looked at his affianced bride at the head of the long table as if to offer her the homage of the impression he had made.

"Yes," said Lord Stanfield, who was seated opposite, "unfortunately that is true. Charity is powerless against ambitious incapacity."

Seated nearly opposite to him, next to his friend St. George, was a girl of twenty, with a beautiful fresh face and large thoughtful eyes fringed with long silk-like lashes, whom he had noticed when she came in with her father, a man of military bearing, whom Johns knew was a retired colonel.

During the time that Johns had been speaking, he had

noticed that her gaze had been fixed upon him. In her virginal white dress she looked, he thought, particularly lovely, and for a moment, in spite of his satisfaction, he felt a sudden pang of regret such as he had experienced that afternoon when passing the steps of the National Gallery. Oh, if that sweet young face had been his lot; if that dainty little hand, playing so delicately with a lily which had fallen from the vase upon the table had owned the thousands, and had been his *fiancée*, then would complete happiness have been attained! And when he glanced again at the end of the table, at the mature charms of Mrs. Humphreys, he was conscious of a sudden feeling of oppression, of a foretaste of something disagreeable with which he was henceforth to become familiar.

"By God, he mustn't think of it," and he took two mouthfuls of champagne to chase away the skeleton which had arisen.

Still he could not help remarking that St. George was assiduous in his attentions to his neighbour, and he wondered if this time his friend had found the ideal of his dreams. Ah, well, St. George could afford ideals, he supposed. *He* couldn't, and that was all about it, and as he looked down the table at the brilliant gathering of peers and heroes and law-givers, assembled chiefly in his honour, he could not help admitting that there were compensations for the part he was about to play.

When the ladies had retired Johns had plenty of work to do to enter into the good graces of his future relative the Dean, an ecclesiastic of great proportions, and with the other relative, a landowner in the North. They couldn't like his marriage, he knew that well, for it disappointed expectations which they certainly must have entertained. No doubt they had anticipated that, after having lost two husbands, the widow would not try again.

To the Dean he talked of chapters and convocations, giving him to understand that he had a high opinion of church charities, and that he looked upon the Church as the true distributor of alms, while to the other relative he spoke, to the best of his ability, of agriculture. He succeeded so well, indeed, that by the time they left to join the ladies, he had won approving smiles from both of them.

On the way up the stairs St. George whispered—

"I'll bet you were envying me at dinner."

"No," was the reply, "I've nothing now to envy anyone."

St. George gave a little laugh, and they reached the drawing room.

Johns went about from group to group, basking in the women's smiles which greeted him. Already he felt that he was looked upon, no longer as a scribbler, but as a man of means and station whose acquaintance was to be cultivated for something more than it was worth in little tales and epigrams. Many of the ladies wanted to know what Mr. Johns thought of this and what he thought of that, what were his favourite books, and if he considered the latest play of Ibsen was equal to his former ones, and they even went so far as to enquire his opinion as to the best places on the Continent in which to spend the summer months, although Johns had never been to one of them. But he was ready with an answer to all they asked, and he spoke with calm assurance, well knowing that his words and acts had now a golden prestige. Presently he found himself next to the young girl who had been his *vis-à-vis* at table. She gave him an engaging smile.

"I don't think you remember," she said, "that we've met once before at Lady Stanfield's."

Johns did not remember, but he replied, "You are wrong, very wrong, to think that, my dear Miss —— Miss —— "

"Douglas."

"My dear Miss Douglas. When I saw you opposite to me at dinner playing so daintily with that lily, I recalled your face at once. I take no credit for it. Who that has once seen you could forget?"

"You're quite equal to your reputation, Mr. Johns."

"I hope I am much better."

And he was about to begin, "Ah, if you only knew," mechanically, when he perceived Mrs. Humphreys glancing at him from the other side of the room with an uneasy look, a look of incipient jealousy perhaps.

Prudence bade him check himself, and instead of bringing out his phrase, he merely said, "and I'll come round presently to prove it."

Then, making his way to where his *fiancée* was sitting, he took a place beside her, murmuring with deep solicitude, "I hope you're not feeling tired, Rose."

With a look of tender gratitude, she answered, "No, John, thank you."

For the rest of the evening he remained near her, attentive to her every want, assisting her to entertain, and he was much amused when he heard a lady near him whisper to a friend during a lull in the conversation, "How devoted to her he seems." Yes, he was devoted, and not all the fair Miss Douglas's upon the earth would make him swerve in his allegiance to the woman who was going to endow him. His motto for the present was "Rose Humphreys," shortly to be called "Rose Johns." Rose Johns! It didn't sound very well; but that was of no consequence.

Before the party separated, Mrs. Humphreys whispered to him—

"Go and speak to Lord Stanfield about the Magazine. I've mentioned it to him already."

Lord Stanfield had just finished talking to the Dean, and he hailed Johns when he came up to him as the "hero of the hour."

"Well, what news has the hero of the hour?" he enquired.

"None, Lord Stanfield. The hero of the hour is rather sick of news."

"Of news, or of the democratic news sheet?"

"Of both, perhaps."

"Well, then, my dear Johns, you must join our camp."

"That is far from being an impossibility. I am convinced now that the largest quantity of intellect is on your side."

Smiling, Lord Stanfield said, "I thought you would come round to our views."

"But that is not all," continued Johns; "my future wife does not care for the *Planet*, and she would like me to have more leisure than it allows me."

"And you would like to edit a Review?"

"I think it would be more congenial."

"Come and lunch with me to-morrow, and perhaps something may be managed."

"With pleasure!"

And then as Lord Stanfield, who was leaving, held out his hand to say good-night, Johns said in a low tone, "If a trustee were required for our marriage settlement, would you be kind enough to act?"

"Oh yes, willingly."

When the party broke up Johns was the last to leave. Gradually the great drawing-room had emptied until the last black coat and the last bare shoulders had disappeared. Then the discreet little Miss Sinclair, whose engagement as companion was nearly over, having followed the retiring guests, Johns and his *fiancée* were left alone in the great drawing-room.

Mrs. Humphreys was standing in the middle of the room, and as soon as the door was closed, she said, "Oh, I'm so glad they're gone; come and let me look at you, my Johnnie." And then, seizing his hands, she scrutinized him narrowly as a mother would her child, while he looked into her face adoringly.

They remained in this posture for some minutes until he, wishing to play his part as well as it could be played, drew her towards him, whispering " My little Rose, I have never seen you look so queenly as you did to-night. In that lovely dress, showing that faultless neck and those matchless arms, you looked a perfect Hebe."

"Oh, did you think so, John?" she asked, crimson with delight. "It was only a little dinner frock of mine." Then continuing, "And you, my Johnnie, how well you spoke! How proud I was of you when they listened to you. You *are* so clever!"

"Ah, Rose, their admiration is my homage to your own sweet self!"

Presently, after he had kissed her with all the warmth he could conjure up, she queried, " And did you ask Lord Stanfield, my own Johnnie?"

"Yes, I'm going to see him about the Review to-morrow at his club."

"That's excellent."

They chatted for a little while until Mrs. Humphreys declared, with a laugh, that for the sake of her reputation he must leave. Then, as he was going, she said tenderly, " It won't be long now, Johnnie!"

He repeated, with an earnest glance, " It won't be long!"

Another kiss and he departed.

As he descended the broad staircase he felt himself a king; he felt that nothing now was wanting to his complete felicity. The little cloud which the telegram had raised was more than dissipated, and the horizon was serenely clear. The servants in the hall, knowing that he was soon to be their master, showed him to the door with infinite respect, and as his hansom was moving off, he gave a look at the lofty mansion with its imposing front, murmuring with pride, " My house."

And, as the day fixed for the marriage was approaching, Johns increased in his solicitude, sending his *fiancée* the choicest flowers he could find at Covent Garden, and calling twice a day to see her.

One thing, however, was still wanting to make his situation stable, and on the Monday preceding the wedding (which was to take place on the Saturday) he came to Grosvenor Place in the afternoon. He had a little business which he wanted to arrange, and he came as early as his work, which he still continued during the negotiations for the purchase of the Review, permitted.

"Rose," he said, "there's still a little matter which we have to settle."

"What is it, John?" she asked, indulgently, leaning back in the thickly-padded sofa. "What can I do to please you?"

"You can do this, my Rose. You can come with me into a dingy little office in Lincoln's Inn, and go through a matter of form with a grumpy old solicitor."

"With a solicitor?" she asked, with a slight movement of alarm. "What for?"

Johns felt a presentiment that he was going to have some trouble. He answered, gravely, "You see, Rose, a man is nothing without dignity, and you would not wish your husband to be in a monetary position inferior to yourself. My theory of married life is that all property should be held in common, so that the married couple may live together without having to discuss vulgar questions of self-interest. It gives the household, Rose, a better tone; it is more fitting, more becoming. My ideas of what I can achieve in the future are very great, and our fortune may be doubled. Whatever happens, I desire that there should be only one rule by which all money questions may be settled. As we have implicit trust in each other, there can be no objection to our signing a short deed which will settle things for the remainder of our lives."

Mrs. Humphreys was silent for a few moments, looking serious and thoughtful. Presently she said, "You want me to divide with you. But I have relatives."

He answered, "I see, Rose, that you misunderstand my meaning. It is not a question of division, but of apportionment. You, of course, will be at liberty, to make whatever will you like, and I, on my side, will be free to do the same. There will be nothing changed, only our relative positions will be clear, and mine will be more dignified than if there were no such settlement. You, on the other hand, will enjoy the extra revenue which I will bring. Lord Stanfield has consented to be trustee."

He continued a little longer in this strain until she, wearied by reasons which made her exert herself to think, and favourably impressed by the mention of Lord Stanfield's name, ended by saying—

"Oh, John, of course, what you say will be all right."

Delighted by this easy victory, he kissed her tenderly.

"Thanks, Rose. If you'll drive to Lincoln's Inn to-morrow, I'll meet you there at four, and it will be all arranged."

"Johnny," she said, plaintively, "Say you'll be always faithful to me!"

"Faithful," he repeated, "faithful until death!"

"Stay a moment," she said, rising and going to the other end of the room.

From a Louis XVI. writing table, the drawer of which she unlocked with a little key she produced from her pocket, she took a slip of paper.

"This," she said, handing it to Johns, "is what I have. I thought it might perhaps be wanted."

Johns glanced at the slip of paper rapidly, and saw that it was a banker's memorandum stating that Mrs. Stephen Humphreys possessed £156,750 in Consols and £59,000 6s. 8d. in India Stock.

Although dazzled at the simple eloquence of such figures, Johns nevertheless said, carelessly—

"Thanks. I'll give it to the solicitor. All in these two funds I suppose?"

"Yes, all. My late husband left it so."

Upon this Johns quitted her in an exulting frame of mind.

The next morning he telegraphed to the paper that he could not be there that day, and at ten o'clock he drove to Lincoln's Inn.

The solicitor he had selected for the work was a man who had a special reputation. His office on the first floor of a sombre building had been the birthplace of untold actions for divorce and slander and disputed wills. Everybody knew that he stretched the law to its utmost limits, and he was one of the busiest of London lawyers. He was considered to be certainly upon the road to knighthood.

Johns ascended the flight of stairs worn by the feet of litigants, and entered the outer office. He wanted to see Mr. Drew at once, he told the clerk—"at once."

"But he's very busy, sir," the clerk replied, "and there are some people already waiting."

"Tell him that I'm here, and that I *must* see him. Say it's a matter of life and death."

The clerk retired, and presently returned, requesting Johns to follow him. Drew was in an inner room, divided from the outer by a green baize-covered door.

He was a short thin man of about fifty, with a face expressive of great keenness and penetration.

"Did you imagine I was a doctor?" he asked, "to send such a message."

"No," said Johns, "I wanted to convey a notion of the urgency of the case and knew no other way."

"Well, the deed is ready with the exception of the amounts. Here it is."

Drew produced a document which Johns scanned rapidly and eagerly.

"Yes," he said, "that's pretty well. That gives me half the property; but don't you think, with a little more of your legal phraseology, we might go one better?"

"I'm open to a suggestion."

"Well, why could you not make it out in such a way that in case of the death of one of us, the whole fortune would go to the survivor?"

"Yes, it might be done. But would the lady sign it?"

"Oh, yes, she'll sign anything. You've only got to read it out in one of those legal monotones, and cram it with law phrases, and she'll sign it fast enough. The fee I intend to give, Mr. Drew, is a hundred guineas."

"Very well. But a new trust deed will have to be prepared. When do you want to sign?"

"This very afternoon at four. Here is a list of the amounts. Only two, you see. It's beautifully simple."

Drew took the slip, while saying, "But, my dear sir, there isn't time for it to be engrossed."

"It must be done," said Johns. "The clerk who does it shall be rewarded."

"Well, of course we'll try."

"And you'll succeed, I know, for you're a man of genius. I shall be back at four."

Saying this, he left precipitately.

At four o'clock, after having spent the intervening hours in the Strand, he returned to Lincoln's Inn.

After waiting a few moments outside the office, he perceived Mrs. Humphreys' carriage with its pair of bays and its men in dark green livery.

In spite of his assurance to the solicitor that all would go well, he was not without misgivings. He was conscious of a vague fear that all might still be spoiled by a mishap.

He was delighted, therefore, when Mrs. Humphreys in a dainty mantle and a bonnet surcharged with flowers, alighted gaily, giving him a sweet smile as she stepped upon the pavement.

"That's the prettiest bonnet that was surely ever seen," he said.

She whispered, "I chose it, John, because I knew you were fond of violets."

As they ascended the creaking stairs, he took her arm and pressed it tenderly, murmuring, "How much I love you! How infinitely happy you have made me! Only a few days more, my Rose! Only a few more days!"

They reached the office.

The clerk who had seen Johns in the morning advanced towards them, saying, "The deed is being finished now, sir. If you will kindly wait a moment, Mr. Drew will soon attend to you."

They followed the clerk to a little waiting-room, in which they were left alone.

Johns sat beside his future wife and took her hand.

"Rose," he said, "last night I had a frightful dream. I dreamt that I had fallen in the street, and that one of those gigantic waggons had passed over me. The horse's hoofs had struck me; I was dying. As my breath was leaving me, I murmured—what else could I murmur?—I murmured, Rose! Then when I awoke and found that it was nothing but a dream, that I was going to behold you, once again, this very day, I veritably cried with joy!"

"Poor Johnnie," she said tenderly, gazing into his face with the eager look of mature passion, "poor Johnnie!"

And he continued to chant the hymn of praise of which he knew she never tired. He was not fearful, now that he had guaged her character, lest he might go too far. He was quite certain that a woman so much in love, a woman, above all, who was so thoroughly an Eve, could not weary of the balm of flattery even if her inner conscience told her that it wasn't genuine.

When they had been there half an hour, no one had come to summon them. Johns continued talking, to prevent Mrs. Humphreys from thinking of the object of their visit; but he was secretly anathematising Drew for keeping him so long there in suspense—in suspense which was telling on his nerves. Unable any longer to remain still, he now walked round the room and examined the old French clock upon the mantelpiece, asking her if she admired it. Then he called her to see the sparrows which were flying to and fro from the window ledge to the roofs of the adjoining houses. "Poor little London sparrows!" he exclaimed. "See, Rose, how black they are!" She went up to the window and looked at the sparrows and remarked, "poor things," and then they turned over the pages of an illustrated paper which was on the table. At length, after another quarter of an hour had been spent thus, the door was opened and the clerk entered to ask them to step in to Mr. Drew.

Crossing through the outer office, they were soon in the solicitor's private room. Johns introduced his *fiancée*.

"I'm truly sorry," Drew began, "to have kept you waiting

so very long, but the fact is, I was not quite ready for you when you arrived."

"Oh," said Johns, "we have been amusing ourselves by looking at the sparrows."

They took seats in two high-backed chairs which were placed in front of the solicitor's table, and Drew continued—

"It's a pleasure for me to arrange these little matters, especially under such pleasant circumstances as the present. I feel sometimes as if I were a kind of parson, since it is my duty to marry the worldly interests of happy couples. Sometimes where there are differences of opinion between what we call 'the parties,' my task is by no means light; but in the present case it's very evident that we have perfect unity of views. By this deed, Mrs. Humphreys, you are placed on a footing of equality with your husband before the law, and you are relieved, for good, from troubling about your affairs. It is a deed of which I personally thoroughly approve, because it creates an honourable understanding between you, and puts an end to all uncertainty as to respective rights, if ever (though I do not think it possible) you were to have the smallest need to think of them."

Johns thought, "He's on the right tack," and remained silent.

Mrs. Humphreys was smiling pleasantly.

"I'm afraid what's written on this piece of parchment isn't exactly interesting literature, and if I could dispense with reading it to you, I would. But the law compels and I must obey. I will try, however, not to spend more time over it than is absolutely necessary since, as I said just now, there is in this case perfect harmony."

This remark was again received in silence, and presently Drew began to read, in a dry, professional tone of voice, a deed of settlement which, with a wealth of legal terms, gave Johns half the fortune under the trusteeship of Lord Stanfield, and the whole of it if his wife should die before him.

When, towards the end, Drew reached the portion in which the "demise" of one of the two parties was alluded to, Mrs. Humphreys looked up enquiringly, and Johns felt his pulse beat faster. But neither made a remark until Drew had finished reading.

Then Mrs. Humphreys said, somewhat timidly, "I'm afraid I don't very well understand these things. I always show them to my old family solicitor. Would there be any objection to my doing so with this?"

Drew tossed the deed upon the table, and said, with an

unmistakable air of offended dignity, "My dear madam, you have a perfect right to show it to whom you please; but I was under the impression that you came here to sign."

Mrs. Humphreys had become very red, and in her embarrassment looked at Johns as if she hoped that he might come to her assistance, but he, although in an agony of suspense, seeing that she had understood the sense of the last clauses, remained impassive.

For some moments there was a silence, and at length Mrs. Humphreys said, "Don't you think, John, that there's something at the end which is not quite right?"

She spoke slowly, and was evidently exceedingly embarrassed.

He replied, "My dear Rose, I really know nothing about it. I believe Mr. Drew has drawn up this deed in strict conformity with equity and custom. Of course, if you do not approve of it, that's another matter."

Torturing her gloves which she had taken off, Mrs. Humphreys said, "It's very awkward"; and Johns thought, "She's terribly perplexed."

He added presently, "I don't want to influence you, Rose, in any way; but it seems to me that now the deed has been prepared, and everything is arranged with Lord Stanfield, it would look somewhat odd if we were to change it—at least at present. Of course, you know we can make other deeds subsequently, and, as for your relatives, I'll take care that they're provided for—especially the poor ones. You won't find me wanting in good-heartedness."

She hesitated, looking alternately at Johns and at the solicitor, who, seizing the moment, bent forward, and said, insinuatingly—

"Then, do I understand you wish to sign?"

The unfortunate woman, whose feelings were being acted on by so many conflicting causes, stammered—

"Well—yes—I suppose it will be all right."

Drew pressed a nob upon his table, and, almost immediately, two clerks appeared.

"Just witness the signatures," he said to them, "of Mrs. Humphreys and Mr. Johns."

Then, handing a pen to the widow, he said, confidentially, "I really think you're wise."

She took the pen and wrote in the place marked in pencil, "Rosalind Humphreys," and the two clerks witnessed.

Johns, in the space assigned to him, wrote "John Johns," and again the clerks attested.

"There," said Drew, with a smile of satisfaction, as the scribes retired; "there's a tiresome formality over, and it only remains for me to wish you an extremely long and happy married life. I must ask you to excuse me now, for I've still many clients waiting."

So saying, he showed them politely to the door.

As they were going down the stairs, it was she now who clasped his arm.

"Promise me, John, that you'll be a good husband."

"Rose, can you for a moment doubt it?"

"No, John, I can't."

He saw her into her carriage, and, after promising to come to Grosvenor Place for dinner, he stood on the pavement for a moment, watching the retreating trap and murmuring, "Is it possible, at that age, to be so amorous?"

The woman who had driven off with her bonnet full of violets had made his fortune. Henceforth he was sure of living all his life in ease! Not only, by the arrangement, had he in reality conceded nothing of his own, but after her death, which, in the ordinary course of things, must take place before his, he was to inherit the remaining half of her hundred thousand. Oh, what a lucky day! oh, what a glorious day!

Whistling a tune, he jumped into a hansom and drove to Berkeley Square to tell Lord Stanfield what had been arranged.

CHAPTER TWELFTH

ON the morning of the wedding, Johns awoke with a feeling of intense felicity. As he jumped out of bed, a ray of sunshine was streaming through the window, and he hailed it as a happy omen. Men and nature smiled upon him now. His path was henceforth to be strewn with roses. He spent a long time dressing, longer than he had ever spent before, for his person, he considered, had acquired worth, and called for much solicitude. He had become a personage whose life was of some value in the world. If he were ill, he could rest and be tended like a prince; even if he died, he would be buried with great pomp. In short, he counted for something; he was somebody. When he had finished dressing, he surveyed himself in the long glass of the wardrobe in his bedroom, and felt satisfied. The lilac trousers of faultless cut were without a crease, and fell gracefully upon a pair of patent boots, the heels of which he had had made higher to increase his stature. The frock coat was not less perfect than the trousers, and the white silk tie, attached with a pearl pin, gave a delicate finish to the general appearance. Yes, he was satisfied; quite satisfied. From his bedroom he passed into the parlour, and sat down at his desk to write.

"My dear parents," he began, "When I wrote you last I told you that I was boss of a newspaper, and that things were going well. To-day I've gone one better. In an hour I'm to be married to a widow with lots of money and a big house to live in. She's a little older than I am, but that doesn't matter much. What I wanted was to be set up in life. My wife, whose name is Rose, is a fine woman with light hair and a pretty figure. She's a swell, too, by birth. So you see I've done well for myself, and I don't think you'll regret the money

THE ADVENTURES OF JOHN JOHNS

now for my education. In another week I'll send you a cheque to pay it back. In the meantime here is a note for £50. Rose sends you her love, and we both hope that you'll leave the old house and take a better one upon the hill, over by Grosmont, where we used to mend the nets in the old times before I went to school. Just say how much you want, and it shall be sent. Good-bye, my dear parents, I'll try to come and see you some day. Tell cousin Kate to let me know when she gets married, as I want to make her a little present. My address after this will be 60 Grosvenor Place. Your affectionate son, John Johns."

He had scarcely sealed this letter when there was a knock at the door, and St. George, irreproachably dressed in a frock coat, with a large gardenia in his button-hole, came in.

"Well, happy bridegroom," he said, taking a seat at the table on which the cloth was laid, "is breakfast ready? I'm very hungry."

Johns rang the bell.

"It shall be brought at once. It's very good of you to come so early."

St. George replied, "It's part of a best man's duty to be early." Then, scrutinizing Johns, he added—

"Why, Johns, you look superb—as well as an heir apparent!"

"That's what I *am*," Johns answered, with a grin, and St. George gave a discreet smile to show that he understood.

"Who ever would have thought that you would have married Mrs. Humphreys? I couldn't have done it myself, old chap."

"Why?" Johns asked, indulgently. "Is she not a remarkably fine woman?"

"She was one once."

"Oh, she's all right still, and surely it's no duty of a best man to criticise the bride."

"Pardon me," St. George said, laughing, "I'll say no more about it. In one way, too, I envy you; we all envy you. You're going to be such a big capitalist."

Johns answered, carelessly, "Yes, St. George, there's nothing disagreeable about *that*."

The breakfast arrived, and they chatted gaily over it.

St. George said presently, "I should think Miss Douglas will look pretty as a bridesmaid."

Johns gave his friend a sidelong glance.

"Exquisite. Do you mean to marry her, St. George?"

The directness of the question took the young man by surprise.

"I would to-morrow, if she would consent."

No more was said upon the subject, and they finished breakfast.

Then, as Edwards had announced that the carriage was at the door, they left together, after Johns had placed a white camelia in his button-hole. A short drive brought them to St. Margaret's at Westminster, in which the wedding was to take place.

On the journey Johns was taciturn, replying to his friend by nods and monosyllables, for suddenly he had been troubled by the feeling of regret which had once or twice before come over him. As he looked out of the carriage window at the busy streets, full of life and vigour on the summer's morning, he could not refrain from thinking how delightful it would have been if youth and beauty, as they were embodied in Miss Douglas, had been about to meet him at the church. But, alas! youth and beauty were seldom to be found in company with consols, and he might have spent his own youth seeking them! After all, he believed in fate, in the absolute necessity for accepting the good things which were offered in the shuffle of existence, without pausing to reflect whether they were precisely those one would have chosen. And yet ——!

Outside the grey gothic building nestling so curiously in the shadow of the high black Abbey, a crowd of the strange nondescripts who linger in church porches to witness the entry or the egress of a bride had gathered on either side of the red carpet which stretched from the outer railings to the door. Carriages were driving up in quick succession. As Johns stepped out of the brougham a dirty youth exclaimed, "'Ooray for the *Planet!*" and Johns acknowledged the greeting with a smile.

The church, as St. George and he walked up the aisle, was nearly full. A brilliant throng, drawn from the upper strata of society, had assembled to witness the marriage of the famous Mrs. Humphreys with the none less famous Mr. Johns. On all sides there were whispers as the two friends advanced, and Johns, conscious that all eyes were upon him, assumed his most dignified demeanour.

It was almost the first time he had entered a church of the Church of England. In his boyhood he had attended chapel with his parents, and sometimes in Australia while he had been a schoolmaster, but this was the first time he had taken part in any service of the Anglican community. The place, with its fluted columns, its gothic arches, and its stained-glass windows, had a certain stately harmony he liked.

When they reached the railings which divided the clergy

from the laity, and on the steps of which were placed four red cushions, St. George stopped and whispered—

"We must wait here for the lady."

Johns made use of the opportunity to look around. The church was already full. He saw before him a sea of women's faces, amid a wealth of colour, softened by the light which streamed through the high church windows revealing the black patches made by the sombre costume of the men.

Turning round again, he examined the choir full of boys in white, and he was looking at the organ when he suddenly perceived the portly Dean—Mrs. Humphreys' relative, who was to perform the service—standing at the extreme end, with his hands crossed, and motionless, in a devout attitude.

"That's the old chap who's going to join us," thought Johns. "Mustn't he detest me!"

He wondered if the Dean was going to give them much divinity to listen to. What a funny joke it was that that rotund old person should imagine that the road to righteousness lay through him, and that he was charged to unite him to Mrs. Humphreys. Charged by whom? Did anybody know? Could anybody say? except by pronouncing a name in three letters which had never conveyed anything definite to *his* mind. What a farce it all was after all, and what a set of simpletons the people were who could be impressed by that old fellow, in his white gown, with his well-fed frame and his seasoned nose! No matter, that dean was going to be useful.

Tired of looking at the Dean, he turned round again towards the people. In one of the front pews he recognised Dawson, who was looking at him with an expression of conscious approbation, as if to let the congregation know that he, and he alone, was the discoverer, the inventor of the bridegroom. Johns thought, "He's come alone; Lucy couldn't face it. Poor little Lucy! She wasn't so bad after all." A few rows lower down was seated Maskelyne, with his hair cut short as he had worn it since he had been promoted, and smiling sympathetically. Next to him old Tarte was looking on with a saint-like look of aloofness from the considerations of this world. "Poor devils," thought Johns, "ready to serve their master with the fidelity of slaves for the wages of mechanics."

Suddenly, however, his nerves underwent a little shock.

Seated in the front row within a few yards of him and watching him with a fixed stare, was Mrs. Weber. Instinctively he turned away, for there was something in the look she gave him which made him feel uncomfortable. He remained for a moment glancing down the aisle; then summoning his courage, he faced her and boldly returned her stare. But now, after a defiant gesture and a faint smile, she turned her head away.

Johns was thinking, "What pluck the woman has to put herself in the front row," when he caught sight of Lord Stanfield and his wife seated in the next pew with a whole bevy of acquaintances behind them. He bowed to the Stanfields deferentially, and he was about to turn a second time when St. George whispered in his ear, "She's coming."

Suddenly, in the lofty building there was a complete silence, and presently a noise of footsteps proceeding from the entrance. Then for a moment there was a lull, followed by a continuous rustle, as the bride, in a simple costume of light grey silk, came into view.

Leaning on the Judge's arm and looking down, the widow advanced slowly up the aisle followed by her bridesmaids—two winsome girls in pink, one of whom was Edith Douglas, the other a niece of Lady Stanfield.

"How innocent she looks!" Johns thought, although he was beginning to feel, in spite of himself, the impressiveness of the marriage scene.

Soon the bridal party reached the place where the two friends stood. Johns, who had been instructed as to what he had to do, after bowing to the smiling Mrs. Humphreys, turned and knelt beside her on the velvet cushion placed upon the step. St. George knelt on the right of Johns, and the Judge on the left of the bride.

The Dean, in the meantime, had reached the place where they were kneeling, and stood before them like a monument of sanction. Almost immediately, in a tedious drawl, he began to read aloud from a prayer-book which he held before him with both hands.

They were made acquainted in old English with the origin of marriage, its gravity, its mystical signification, the concession which was made by it to human frailty, the various reasons why it was ordained, and the respective parts devolving on the husband and the wife in the married state.

While the Dean was rolling out his periods, Johns amused himself by counting the buttons on his boots and the folds of his ample surplice, wondering how much of the conjugal doctrines he was giving forth the old man himself believed, but experiencing, at the same time, a vaguely soothing feeling, a sensation of a spiritual *douche*. The reading over, the Dean turned his back to the bride and bridegroom and walked up to the table in the apse with dignity.

St. George whispered, "You must follow," and Johns, with his bride and her relatives, advanced.

They were joined together by the Dean. Then, after the marriage questions had been asked and answered, after the Judge had made a gift to Johns of the person of the widow, after Johns had placed the ring on the finger of his bride, a short allocution followed.

Johns was to remember that marriage was a very sacred thing; that the duties of the husband were to protect the wife from the sorrows of existence, and to use the authority which was given him, with wise and tender moderation. Above all things he was to be unselfish and considerate, he was to avoid false pride in the commerce of domestic life, to pardon readily, to chide with kindness, and to be always faithful and sincere. Nothing militated more against the life of the family, as it was divinely constituted, than distrust. Perfect confidence must reign between man and wife so that conjugal ethics should be as pure and calm as a cloudless sky. These were the bases of the Christian family, wisely designed for the welfare of the human race. "You, Rosalind," he said to the bride, "I would exhort to prudence and to patience in the new life you are now entering. It will be your duty henceforth to be the solace and support of a husband whom you have promised to obey. In the hour of affliction, should it ever come to him, you will be his truest friend, and you will seek counsel of him in uncertainty and doubt. Blessed as you are with this world's wealth, it behoves you, more than many others, to be wise in the conduct of your daily life, and to remember that charity was ever the first of virtues. Banish from your heart all pride. Be just and faithful always. Let your union be a model of right living. Remember, my daughter, that life has but a transitory span, and that the time afforded us in which to do good works is brief."

He continued a little longer in this strain, and after he had ended his address the bridal party remained for some moments on their knees.

Then, as the first notes of the organ resounded in the vaulted church, ascending in a wave of triumphal sound, Johns and his wife rose, and moved slowly arm-in-arm towards the vestry, followed by the Judge, St. George, and the two bridesmaids.

But at that moment, as the nuptial march re-echoed in his ears, as he saw the sea of heads outstretched to catch a glimpse of them, his feelings underwent a change. Suddenly he felt that all this was admirable, that the Dean himself was the best of deans, the Church the best of churches, since in the brief space of half an hour they had made his fortune. It was well after all that there should be fat old deans to admonish people on their marriage day; it gave a peculiar kind of stamp to matrimony. It was all very right and proper, and the rich full strains which were coming from the organ seemed to him the most delightful he had ever heard. In the enthusiasm of the moment he was barely conscious that his wife was leaning on his arm. He was moving along in a state of high sublimity, with a delicious consciousness of power, a delightful sense of superiority. What a pleasant thing life was! How well he meant to explore and to enjoy it!

They reached the vestry and took up a position opposite the door to receive their friends, who immediately began to crowd around them.

Johns, in the enthusiasm of the moment, had a word for each, pressing their hands and looking into their faces with that expression of faithful-dog sincerity which had done so much for him in life. He would say to the men as they shook hands with him, "Oh, Sir James," or "Oh, Lord—promise me that we shall see you often in Grosvenor Place," or "I shall remember your presence here to-day a happy omen," or to others of small importance, "How kind of you to come! how glad I am to see you!" To the ladies he said, "And so you *really* have been good enough to grace our wedding?" or "How charming of you to be here!" and there was something in his manner which seemed to indicate protection, patronage, approval, as though he had been a royal personage wishing to be gracious to his subjects. He, and not his wife, was the centre of attraction.

One by one his friends shook hands with him, and for each he found a different kind of greeting. When Dawson approached with an air of familiarity and said loudly enough for those around to hear, while he pressed his hand, "I congratulate you in the name of the whole staff," he merely answered, "Thanks, Dawson," and turned to someone else. To Maskelyne, who approached him almost timidly, he said approvingly, "Well Maskelyne, so you've come to see me married!" while to old Tarte, who approached him saying, with a faint smile, "I always knew that you would be numbered among the great," he answered, "My worthy Tarte, you are a true philosopher."

When the Dean himself came in he said to him, "Sir, I thank you for your admirable discourse. I shall long remember it." To the Stanfields he showed much deference, appearing not to notice the curious smile with which the peer regarded him, the smile of a man of assured position studying a *nouveau riche.* Lord Stanfield, as trustee, knew the whole position of affairs, and was, Johns thought, in many ways a person to be cultivated always.

St. George had been so much occupied in talking to Miss Douglas that Johns had not exchanged a word with him, and he was about to cross to them so that he might thank them for their kind offices, when suddenly, to his astonishment, he saw before him Mrs. Weber!

Her presence in the church had seemed to him audacious, but that she should come into the vestry whither only those who had been invited to the wedding had repaired, seemed to him extraordinarily bold. Surely she didn't mean to make a scandal! And for a moment he felt alarmed.

But Mrs. Weber put an end to his apprehension by offering her hand and saying with a calm smile, and as if confident in the power of her beauty, "We shall meet again."

Johns glanced in the direction of his wife, and seeing that she was surrounded by a group of ladies, he pressed the daintily-gloved hand, and, brought suddenly again under the influence of the companion of his early days, he murmured in a low tone, "We shall."

No one was near them at the time, and Mrs..Weber moved away after giving Johns a penetrating glance.

With a sigh of satisfaction he pursued his original intention of crossing to Miss Douglas and St. George.

"Miss Douglas," he said, "and you St. George, how can I thank you?"

St. George answered, "For me it has been an intense pleasure," and he looked at the young girl in a pretty pink silk dress. As she played with her bouquet of white roses, her pure young face seemed to Johns more lovable than ever.

Glancing up, she said in a tone which scarcely seemed free from malice, "I hope, Mr. Johns, you're very happy."

Somewhat surprised at the singularity of the remark, Johns answered, "Ah!" in a way which left it doubtful whether he was rejoicing or deploring. "I hope," he added, "that we shall see you often, very often, in Grosvenor Place."

She nodded without answering, and St. George said, "I think, Johns, your bride is calling you," and Johns, looking round, realized for the first time, thoroughly, that he was not free.

Yes, his wife wanted him. It was time to go. It was all over. They were man and wife. Arm-in-arm they left the church.

What a triumphant drive back it was for Johns, in his own carriage, to his own house, at the side of his bride, who sat smiling placidly, apparently contented, happy! What a glorious feeling of possession and of power! How great it was to be definitely classed high up above the heads of untold thousands in this monster city! And, after all, how good of this woman to have placed him on this pinnacle!

When they reached the bottom of Victoria Street, his wife said, "Oh, Johnnie, at last we're married!" and he replied, "At last!" wondering if she had used that phrase before to either of her former husbands.

And then again, a few minutes later, as he ascended the fine broad staircase, followed by the congratulations of the friends who had already reached the house, he fairly swelled with pride. All this was his!

As they were going to leave by an early train for Dover, *en route* for Biarritz, it had been decided that there should be no reception. Mrs. Johns had wished the wedding to be a quiet one, and Johns had acquiesced. It was therefore only the bride's relatives and the intimate friends who were invited to the luncheon. These included Lord and Lady Stanfield, the Dean, the Judge, St. George, and the two bridesmaids, besides a few other friends and distant relatives.

With great dignity Johns took his place opposite his wife. Listening to Lord Stanfield's conversation, and refraining from looking towards Miss Douglas and St. George, he remained somewhat silent, with the air of a man who has no longer any need to talk to be appreciated. But when Lord Stanfield drank the health of the happy pair and congratulated Johns on his conversion to the cause of order (the name he gave his own party), Johns, who had now resigned his post on the radical print and who was to assume the conduct of the tory review on his return, in replying said, "It is indeed to you, Lord Stanfield, that I owe my conversion to the party of intelligence and of integrity. Henceforth I intend to battle in real earnest for it."

As everybody at the table were of conservative opinions, and would have thought it little short of madness to hold any other views, this announcement was received wlth a murmur of approval.

Lord Stanfield said, "We want your talent, Mr. Johns"; and Johns answered reassuringly, without any attempt at modesty, "Then you shall have it."

The Dean said, "It seems incomprehensible to me that there should be any other party," and the Judge agreed that he saw no necessity for any other.

Johns echoed, "No necessity whatever."

The luncheon lasted but an hour, and shortly after it the bride and bridegroom, in travelling costume, were seen into their carriage by the guests.

A week afterwards Johns and his wife were sitting after dinner on the terrace of the Casino at Biarritz. Johns, smoking a cigar, was looking up at the pure cloudless sky tinted with the last of the sun's rays. The air had a delicious coolness after a hot day, and from the building came the strains of a waltz performed upon an orchestra. Mrs. Johns, in a light muslin dress, with a light cloak thrown over her shoulders, was watching her husband as he sent the puffs of smoke curling skyward.

Johns himself would have found it no easy matter to describe his state of mind. He was conscious of two feelings which conflicted with each other—a delicious sense of immunity from future risks, and, at the same time, the sensation of a man in chains.

His experiences of the last three days had given him food for much reflection. He had had numerous occasions of knowing the nature of the bargain he had made. His wife adored him, idolized him, gratified his every whim, anticipated his smallest wish, but, alas! expected in return practical proofs of his affection which he was loath to give—which he gave with a reluctance he found it difficult to hide. Oh, the sense of a possibility of something better than this autumnal honeymoon, than this union of pure reason on the one side, and pure folly on the other! How could he help seeing constantly that his wife, with her cajolery unfitted for her age, must always be ridiculous? How was he to live day by day, week by week, and month by month in the presence of this woman who would not yield to the inevitable and accept the course of nature?

Was there, after all, anything more stupid than this eternal female instinct to combat decay, than this girlishness in evident maturity, this fierce tenacious egoism in decline? Ah! humanity was a very little thing indeed, and his view of it had been the right one! But now that he had made his compact, now that he had sold his youth for so magnificent a price, it was of no use to recriminate; he must steel himself in some way for the sacrifice he was called upon to make. After all, it wasn't so very terrible to feign a little love for a few years longer. There must be a natural conclusion even to the fiercest flame at an advanced period. And then, when this tedious honeymoon was over, would there not be compensations? Were there not always compensations for the man whose wallet was teeming with bank notes? Above all things, he must always be courteous to the woman who had given him so much. How grateful he would have been to her if she would only have considered him merely as an ornament, as a husband to be proud of, instead of wanting him to love her! But these were the circumstances, and he could not change them.

"What are you thinking of, my Johnnie?" she asked tenderly.

"Of nothing, Rose. I was enjoying the coolness of this terrace after the heat we had to-day at St. Jean de Luz. Look at those golden tints in that cloudless sky! They remind me of Australian sunsets which give one such a sense of infinite expansion!"

But the ideal side of his wife's nature had been left undeveloped, and she answered, in an ordinary tone of confirmation—

"Yes, it's very pretty, John, but aren't you afraid of taking cold in that thin jacket?"

"No," he said, with an almost imperceptible sigh of resignation, "I don't take cold so easily."

The light was waning and the calm was broken only by the distant sound of the waves of the Gulf of Gascony breaking upon the beach, and by the footsteps of the visitors going to the gaming tables.

Johns said almost to himself, and in one of the poetic moods which now and then came over him after too much materiality, "How beautiful the twilight is! Does it not always seem as though the day were dying for the last time, as though the darkness which is coming were to be eternal?"

His wife did not answer, and they remained seated there in silence until at length, when Johns threw his cigar stump from him, she whispered, "It's getting late, John; shall we look in at the tables before going back?"

He had an inward feeling of rebellion, for "going back" meant something very different for him from what it meant for her, but he replied, "Just as you like, Rose."

They crossed the terrace and entered the corridor of the Casino, from whence they reached the gaming room.

In a long lofty room some twenty persons—Spanish, French, and English—were assembled round a table at which the game of little horses was being played. There was not much animation, and the croupier, a stout man with his hair brushed up *en brosse*, was encouraging the lookers-on to stake. Two showily-dressed women of doubtful nationality, much past middle age, and belonging to the strange vague class that frequent casinos, were watching the game narrowly, side by side, each with a pile of silver and a few gold pieces before her. A young Spaniard, with a dark, short-cut beard and an olive-tinted skin, was staking with an air of unconcern. An old man, with white hair and clean-shaved face and a bent back, was placing his franc pieces philosophically, while a few amateurs contented themselves by staking now and then as their fancy guided them. Immediately Johns and his wife were offered seats, and they sat down at one end of the green cloth-covered table. To Johns a game which was limited to a few francs seemed petty now, and he watched the players with an amused smile, allowing his wife to stake instead of him. She, he soon saw, was in her element. She liked the sensation of gambling, he observed, for when, after a few losses, she won a little heap of silver, decided pleasure was depicted on her face. Johns, as he watched her, thought, "She's as I always knew her—matter, gilded no doubt, but matter."

Lazily he looked on as she played, troubled somewhat by the presence near him of a Spanish lady with a fine oval face and passionate dark eyes, who had just come in accompanied by a tall man who seemed to be her husband. Why were young and pretty women always to be seen so temptingly in the possession of other men? But the excitement of the game did not last, and after a tiresome series of alternate gains and losses, Mrs. Johns declared that the room was stifling, and that she would like to leave. Johns, resigned to his fate, rose slowly and they left. When they found themselves again upon the terrace, the moon was shining brightly, lighting up the façade of the building and throwing shadows upon the pavement.

"Let us go home by the sea," she said, "it's so nice to be alone, Johnnie, on a night like this," and Johns said, lighting his cigar, "As you please, Rose."

They took the path along the beach to the hotel, and when they reached a part which was deserted at that hour, she exclaimed lovingly, "Oh, my Johnnie, put your arm around my waist."

He did as he was bid, thinking that that, alas, was included in the bargain. Leaning with the stiff weight of her mature frame towards him, she murmured, "I never knew, Johnnie, what it was to love before, to love as you have made me love. How I shall care for you, how I shall cherish you, my prince, my pride, my darling clever boy, so strong, so handsome! Johnnie, you must tell me all you do and think, and I will tell you all *I* do and think. Oh, Johnnie, I'm afraid you've been a dreadfully bad boy, but now you'll be faithful to your little wife and never give her pain?"

"Yes, Rose," he said; "you won't have to complain of me, I fancy."

"You have such wicked, and yet such faithful eyes, my John!"

The waves were breaking proudly on the white sandy beach, the sea glittered like silver in the moonlight, and the high rocks at either end of the little bay were bathed in brightness.

As they were drawing near the road which led up to the hotel she stopped and said, "Kiss me, Johnnie! I like being kissed out here!"

Again he was forced to do as he was bid, saying to himself as he kissed her cheek, "It can't go on like this for ever though."

They walked up the lane in silence, and Johns asked himself a question. How old might his wife be? It was stupid of him not to have found out, but he had been so busy, and she so reticent, that the fact was he did not know. No doubt he could make a guess which had a good chance of being accurate, but then it would only be a guess, and he must, for many reasons, ascertain exactly. On his return he would make inquiries.

How long, he asked himself, could a woman keep up the illusion of love? How long could she expect to be attractive to a man? And the answer seemed to be—for ever! Yes, just as there were no bounds to female vanity, so there were no limits to a woman's faculty of self-delusion. Wonderful humanity!

They reached the end of the long lane and entered the hotel, a fine, square building standing in its own grounds on a slight eminence.

Crossing the spacious hall in which a few visitors in rocking-chairs were enjoying the cool air near the open door, they passed along a passage to their rooms.

On the table in the sitting-room, a small room furnished warmly with red velvet covering and hangings, they found a packet of letters from their friends. Mrs. Johns, to whom the majority had been addressed, took up the packet and glanced at the writing on the envelopes. Then she put it down again.

"What do they matter to me now? I'll read them some time to-morrow. To-night I don't want to think of anyone but you, my John, of no one but you, my darling boy!"

And she made him sit beside her on the sofa, placing his arm around her.

But he, glad of a pretext to postpone the inevitable sequel to her tenderness, replied, "There's plenty of time before us,

Rose. Just open some of your letters and see what they're about."

Reluctantly she rose and took the packet from the table.

"It seems so strange," she said, as she broke an envelope with a monogram, "to see Mrs. Johns."

He thought, "Very strange, when she's had three names already!"

"Yes, it's one syllable less," he said.

"Oh, but I'm so proud of it. Everybody knows of you, my Johnnie, and your name is better than many titles."

He thought, "What close appraisers women are!"

"Here's one from Edith Douglas. She says they're starting this week for Switzerland, and she asks to be remembered to you."

"Ah," he thought, "if she were only sitting next me at the present moment!"

"And here's one," she continued, handing him a letter, "addressed to you. I think it's from St. George."

Johns opened the note and read it.

St. George, after a few good wishes expressed in carefully chosen words, not altogether free from a delicately-veiled sarcasm, apprised his friend that he, too, was going to spend a month in Switzerland.

"That's curious," said Johns, "Miss Douglas and St. George are both going to the Alps."

She answered, "Perhaps they'll make a match there. What a nice couple they would make!"

"Oh," said Johns, shrugging his shoulders, "St. George is decorative enough, but he's a great noodle. I should think Miss Douglas had perceived it by this time."

"Ah! there are so few like you, my Johnnie!"

She went on opening the letters and glancing over their contents.

Presently she said, "Here's one from the Dean."

"What has the worthy man to say?" Johns asked.

Gradually, as she read, her face grew serious. When she had finished, she let the letter drop upon her lap and looked reflective.

Then, without replying to his question, she handed the letter to Johns.

In acid terms the Dean expressed surprise, astonishment, at having learnt from Lord Stanfield that Mrs. Johns had disinherited his children by a marriage settlement of so *unusual* a nature. Of course, she had a perfect right to dispose of her fortune as she chose, but it had always been understood that his sons were to be remembered in her will. There was no legal obligation, he pointed out, but there was a moral one, and moral obligations were binding on persons of their rank. He trusted that both her husband and herself would take such measures as would insure some fulfilment of the promises which had been made. Any other course of conduct he could not conceive. He expected an answer to reassure him without loss of time.

When Johns had finished reading the rounded sentences of the irate Dean, he said, "Oh, that's nothing. All you have to do is to write and tell him that his progeny won't be forgotten."

"Yes, but don't you think he'll want something more than an assurance?"

"Perhaps he may, but he can't have it. What business, I should like to know, has he to have nine children? It's rank improvidence!"

She was silent for a moment. Then she said, "Oh, my Johnnie, say you'll be faithful to me always!"

"Always, Rose, of course."

"I've read enough letters for to-night," she said softly, looking at the clock. "It's getting late."

He thought, "She means to have her money's worth."

Rising, he said, "I just want to smoke a last cigar outside."

She gave him a tender look and said, "Don't be long, my Johnnie."

He left, and in the hall he met the proprietor of the hotel who had shown him, ever since his arrival, a great deal of attention.

The little man, with a round jovial face, remarked, "Monsieur is going to smoke upon the terrace. It's a good idea. The night is perfect."

Then he added, with an air of great concern, "I trust Madame is quite well. I was afraid Madame was tired this evening after the drive to St. Jean de Luz."

"I wish she was," thought Johns.

He answered, "No, thank you, Monsieur Bouchard; Madame is always well."

"Ah, I am so glad. It causes me the greatest trouble when any of my visitors are ill. I have always been like that. I only have the pleasure of seeing them for a few weeks; but I am only happy when I think they are enjoying themselves as much as possible at Biarritz."

Johns, after lighting his cigar, left the hotel to stroll upon the gravelled paths in front of it.

There, in the stillness of the grounds—a stillness broken

only by the closing of a window or by the footsteps of an occasional visitor returning from the Casino—he indulged in his reflections.

He was rich beyond all the dreams he had ever formed, but, alas! he had parted with his liberty; he owed allegiance to the woman who had become his wife, and who no more satisfied his longings than a stale crust does the hunger of a hungry man. Ah! life that evening seemed to him less roseate than it had seemed upon his wedding-day. It appeared to him more dreary than he had ever thought it could be for a man as rich as he, and for a moment he stopped to ask himself whether he might not, by waiting, have done better. But no, hesitation in these things was fatal. He *must* reconcile himself to the existence which was offered him.

Thinking what a lottery life was, he walked many times up and down the path in the day-like brightness of the moonlight. Just as he had finished his cigar, a window on the ground floor opened.

Presently a voice called softly, "Johnnie."

He threw away the end of his cigar, and with a sigh went in.

CHAPTER THIRTEENTH

IN September, after a journey through the Basque country, the Johns's returned to town. The remainder of their wedding trip had been much the same as its commencement, and Johns had contrived to discipline himself into some sort of resignation to his lot.

It was a fine sensation, after all, to find himself installed in the great house in Grosvenor Place as master, to awake each morning in the luxurious bedroom with its damask hangings, its carved oak wardrobes and its satin-covered chairs, to exist in beautiful surroundings, with a dozen servants at command. It was no less pleasant, also, to assume the direction of the Review of which he had become editor and part proprietor, and for many weeks he was busily engaged making arrangements and studying editorships, such as those of Mr. Morley and Mr. Harris on the *Fortnightly*. He wanted to dazzle the literary world by the originality and force of his direction, and in order to achieve his purpose, he applied himself, as he had done before, with zeal, to the task of recruiting the best brains. *The Centenary*, he said, must have the highest talent in the land; it must stand at the head of all the periodicals. It must surpass them all. And either owing to the personal attraction which he exercised or to the curiosity which he excited, it was not long before his office in Bedford Street became the rendezvous of many of the best intellects in London. Johns, without a tithe of the knowledge his contributors possessed, would sit in his office chair and pontificate to them with a peculiar emphasis, with a quaint philosophy drawn from his experience of life, with a vigour which left his hearers wondering whether he was a charlatan or a great man, and generally inclined, they scarcely could tell why, to the latter view. Without ever saying anything that was absolutely new, he continued to give an impressiveness and interest to what he said, and, above all, he was careful never to make an error of fact, possessing a talent for working round a subject and not committing himself to statements whenever he was ignorant. They listened to him because he found the means to interest them, and they gave their articles to him in preference to giving them to editors who were less brilliant and less entertaining. In this way, by exercising a severe eclecticism, and by ruthlessly dispensing with the services of former writers, he soon raised the Magazine, if not exactly to the heights he wished, at all events to a fair position amongst its competitors

Mrs. Johns's drawing-room now became thronged by many of the aristocrats of intellect, who at times embarrassed her, and to whom she found it difficult to speak—an aristocracy among which her old friends were as strangers. She did her best, however, and had sense enough not to pretend to knowledge which she did not possess. There were amenities and satisfactions also for feminine vanity in the position she now occupied. It was amusing, too, to invite the aspirants she met to come and see her husband, and it pleased her vanity to notice how nervous they often were before him. Often she would promise her intercession to obtain an interview, like Josephine interceding with Napoleon for a *protégé*, or she would show commiseration for a candidate whose work had been rejected, although she would cease inviting him to call. While Johns was at her side, it was easy to manage the conversation; but when he was not there, she was forced to have recourse to—"My husband could tell you that," or "John would be sure to know," even when it was a question of what they had seen abroad, or the names of the places they had visited. For her mental indolence was such that she never troubled to burden her memory with foreign names. She had always found that wealth atoned so well for ignorance!

Henceforth she basked in the sunshine of her husband's fame, and seemed perfectly contented with the part she played, enjoying the sense of being the wife of a man whom everyone around him seemed to consider as a force of nature. It was true that some of her intimate friends were given to chaffing her at times for idolizing Johns, but she would answer, "Oh, but he is such a clever boy! Everybody says so." And what everybody said was always a law for her.

During the winter the Johns's, reserving themselves for the season when people more worth inviting than men of letters were in town, received little. Johns wanted to establish his

Review upon a proper footing, and the winter months were convenient for so doing.

One day, however, towards the end of December, when he was in his office talking to his secretary, a clerk came in and announced that a lady wished to speak to him.

"A lady?" said Johns. "It's one of those damned writing women! I won't have them at any price. Tell her I'm engaged!"

The clerk retired, but presently returned to say that the lady had not come on business.

"What is her name?" asked Johns.

"She won't give her name, sir. She says she must see you personally."

"Is she dark?"

"Yes, sir."

"And pretty, Simpson?"

"I should say so, sir."

"Show her in."

Johns had a strong presentiment as to who the dark and pretty lady was, and he said to his secretary as the latter was retiring, "I'm not in, Vaughan, for anyone."

Johns had had his room furnished with more elegance than is usually to be met with in editorial rooms. He meant not only to receive men who live by writing, but celebrities of all kinds anxious to see their names in print. He meant the Review to serve his purposes in many more ways than one. Thus, instead of the long table or the hard chairs usually to be seen in editorial rooms, he had a carved oak writing desk and a suite of red leather arm-chairs and divans.

Almost immediately a lady wrapped in furs was shown in by the clerk.

"I guessed it was you, Ellen," he said, as he recognized Mrs. Weber, "no one else would have such cheek."

She tossed her muff upon the sofa with a contemptuous laugh, and stood before him in a defiant attitude.

"I'm not so easy to get rid of as you think," she said. "I told you we should meet again."

"I don't *want* to get rid of you, Ellen, if you're reasonable."

"What do you mean by being reasonable?"

"Well, I can't marry you *now*, can I?"

"That's evident."

"But," he added, in a low voice, "if you are willing to be a good little woman again, why shouldn't things be as they were before?"

"Ha, ha," she laughed; "have you had enough of your antiquity?"

"My wife," he said, smiling, "is a charming woman."

"What a fearful humbug you are, John."

"What about Parker, Ellen?"

"I never see him now. He found out about us somehow and we quarrelled."

Johns thought, "And he's withdrawn supplies." He said, "And so you're a little lonely widow?"

"Yes, for the present. When will you come to see me?"

"By God," he said, with a sudden burst of enthusiasm aroused by her triumphant beauty, "I'll come to-morrow!"

"I thought you would," she said, with a quiet laugh. "I knew that that old woman wouldn't keep you from me long. It's no use to try to struggle against nature. It can't be done."

"No, Ellen, it can't."

Consoling themselves with this reflection, they were silent for a few minutes. Then he rose, and, darting quickly to the sofa, took a seat close beside her, and placed his arm around her waist. She was the sweetest, prettiest, most lovable of women, the only woman he had ever loved, he whispered, the only woman he could ever love. Of course he had had to marry. In certain cases a man couldn't go against his luck, but what of that? Everything could be so easily arranged when people made up their minds to be reasonable. They had many happy days before them now! Then, as there was a knock at the door, he left her quickly and resumed his seat before his table.

The clerk who entered said, "Mrs. Johns has called for you in the carriage, sir."

Johns answered, "Tell her I'll be with her in a minute," and then, turning to his companion as soon as the clerk had left, he said, "You see, Ellen, it's dangerous to come here. Don't come again."

"I won't now," she answered; "I'll expect you at four to-morrow."

After pressing her hand warmly, he took his hat and left before her, to drive home with his wife.

And in this way an existence soon commenced for Johns which was full of satisfactions, the drawbacks of which were so well compensated for that they ceased to be so hard to bear.

To avoid giving rise to comment on the part of servants, Johns engaged rooms in Pimlico, not far from Carsdale Mansions, where Mrs. Weber met him by appointment, and where, at each meeting, they would spend a few hours in the afternoon or sometimes in the evening, though not often, as Mrs. Johns always liked to spend the evening in her husband's company, whether they stayed at home or whether they went out.

And thus the months passed for Johns, who divided his time between his house, his office, and the daintily-furnished pair of rooms, which he kept filled with flowers so that it might seem, as he told Ellen, a true love's arbour. In her he found a companion to whom he could speak of his aims and projects with a chance of being understood, and gradually he fell into the way of discussing delicate questions with her, and of merely telling his wife the plain results of things. For he had soon perceived that the powers of comprehension of Mrs. Johns were equal to no greater task.

And for a time he took delight in making costly presents to Ellenita, as he now sometimes called her — presents of jewellery, which, considering the amount he had had to pay out of his current income for the purchase of the shares in the Magazine, were almost a strain upon his purse.

But he wanted Ellenita to be happy, and he thought that women are ever made so by the possession of these things. To relieve her of money troubles also, he had undertaken to pay the rent of her flat in Carsdale Mansions in remembrance, as he told her, of the joyful hours they had passed together there.

Never, in his life, had he been so happy.

When the season commenced, the Johns's inaugurated it with a series of receptions. The doors of the great drawing-room were thrown open once a fortnight to all who had a name in art and letters, as well as to the patrons by whom art and letters live. Johns's ambition was to become known to everyone worth knowing, so that when his name was mentioned, no matter in what circle, everybody should know the personality expressed by it. He had divided their acquaintances into three classes. The first was composed of those who were only to be invited to select dinners, such as titled persons, heroes, statesmen, or distinguished artists; the second consisted of relatives and friends, and of people whom it might be of temporary interest to know; and the third of minor personages, vaguely met and imperfectly remembered, but whom it was politic to invite to general receptions.

One day, as they were sending out the invitations for a reception of the latter kind, Johns remarked, "I should think, Rose, we might send one to the Dawsons. It's true that he owns a halfpenny print, but I assure you he's quite presentable, and his wife is a remarkably nice and rather pretty woman."

Mrs. Johns, who could not endure hearing other women praised, and who was inclined to be alarmed at her husband's extraordinary popularity with all the ladies of their acquaintance, answered, "They're rather vulgar people, I've been told."

"Ah! my dear Rose, no one who is rich is really vulgar now. Of course they don't belong to *our* class, but I assure you they'll do for a reception. Besides, who knows? we might convert old Dawson."

His wife replied, without the least enthusiasm, "Very well then. Send them an invitation."

Johns had absolutely refused to invite Mrs. Weber to his house on the pretext that his wife was terribly suspicious; but a feeling of curiosity, a desire to be seen in his present splendour, prompted him to invite the Dawsons.

Mrs. Dawson was a woman who could be relied upon, and who would never become troublesome, while with Mrs. Weber one never could be sure. It was not that he wished to recommence an intimacy with Lucy, but he had not met her since their rupture, and he thought he would like to see how she was getting on. He felt so secure in his position that he had no fear now of committing an imprudence.

In the drawing-room, on the first of these receptions, the Johns's were awaiting, at ten o'clock, the arrival of the guests.

Johns, who had been a little remiss in his attentions to his wife of late—staying with Mrs. Weber under pretence of dining at the club—wanted to make amends.

Approaching her, therefore, as she was reclining in a low armchair, he took her hand.

"You look a little tired, Rose. Are you not quite well?"

"Yes, thanks, John," she said, with a look of gratitude, "I only hope there won't be too great a crush this evening, And, oh, my Johnnie! all those women who flatter you so much, don't let them turn your head. Do you know that when I see them almost making love to you, I can't help feeling jealous? You mustn't listen to them, Johnnie."

"Don't be anxious, Rose," he said, with a quiet smile; "I'm steeled against their darts."

"Yes," she said reassured; "I've noticed that you don't encourage them. I know that I can trust you."

Then, reassured and brightened, she exclaimed, "Look, Johnnie, at my lamps! You haven't seen them properly."

And she showed him the new arrangement of the lights along the walls—a whim of her's to have little gilded cupids, perfect little gems of art, all round the room, each holding by the stem an orange which gave forth a soft pale yellow light, harmonizing with the furniture and decoration. "Aren't they pretty?"

But Johns, whom nothing, however small, escaped, had noticed them when coming into the room, and they had met with his entire disapproval. They were, he knew, terribly expensive, and they might, moreover, give rise to comments. Cupids, indeed, under *such* circumstances! But it was no use, women were eternally and irremediably foolish. To please her he rose and examined the metal figures with attention.

Then he said, "Charming, Rose. They are a proof of your good taste."

"You're quite delightful to-night, Johnnie."

Perceiving that the bunch of white carnations he was wearing was not well fixed, she rose and fastened it with a little diamond-headed pin which she drew from her own bodice. Then, retreating a little from him to judge the general effect, she exclaimed rapturously, "I never saw you look so nice, my Johnnie—my own prince!" and mentally he shrugged his shoulders, thinking "What an ass the woman is."

But the guests were beginning to arrive, and Mrs. Johns, adjusting her low-necked dress of yellow silk, took up her position on the threshold to receive them. Johns hovered about from door to door.

It was evident from the commencement that there was going to be a crush. Everybody who had been invited seemed to be arriving. It was to be one of those receptions to which people eager to be seen at the house of a celebrity come in shoals.

As he watched them trooping in, Johns thought, "What sheep they are!" for, in spite of his elevation to the upper strata of society, he had scarcely lost the secret rancour of his class against the aristocracy.

Oh, it was a delightful thought to think that he, John Johns, had forced these buckramed mortals to open their doors to him, to provide him with a wife, and to shower wealth upon him!

One by one he heard announced the names of men who had done vastly more than he to earn their meed of fame—names of officers who had served their country or whose ancestors had done so, of scientists who had made discoveries, of statesmen who had governed England, of writers who had written masterpieces, of painters who had painted them, of eminent ecclesiastics of whose dogmas he didn't believe a word, and of famous doctors whom he wouldn't trust. And they all came to his house (for it was *his* house) simply because he, the son of old David Johns, had managed to fascinate a silly woman! Well, it was a curious world, and what a lot of puppets these people seemed to him as they made their little bow, and then disappeared amid the crowd! Life was full of contrasts and of contradictions!

Lord Stanfield arrived early, accompanied, not by his wife— his wife never went to receptions of this kind—but by a dark-haired young man with a thin face of some intelligence.

"I have taken the liberty," the peer said, "of bringing Mr. Le Neve, of whom I spoke to you a little while ago."

Johns shook hands with the young man.

"My dear Lord Stanfield," he said, "I'm only too delighted and too charmed."

They chatted for a few moments, and presently Le Neve recognized a friend with whom he spoke.

Lord Stanfield took advantage of the opportunity to say to Johns, "Mr. Le Neve has just left the University and is in want of an employment. You would confer a great favour on me if you would take him into your office as a species of sub-editor. I think he would be quite competent."

Johns answered, "Certainly, if you recommend him, I will at once. You can tell him to come to me to-morrow."

Evidently anxious to obtain a post for the young man, Lord Stanfield thanked Johns warmly, and as they separated after a few moments, Johns reflected, "I can even oblige a lord to-night!"

The guests continued to arrive. The bare arms and necks of the women vied with each other in a contest of pink beauty. It seemed as if the women, by a tacit understanding, had, in dress and looks, done their utmost to dazzle and to charm. Had the sombre coats of the men been absent, the room would have seemed ablaze with brightness and with colour. Presently Miss Douglas, tenderly graceful in her simple frock of white surah silk, came in, accompanied by her father.

Johns had heard what had occurred in Switzerland. St. George had met them there, had asked her hand and been rejected, and ever since, the poor fellow had been looking thin and miserable. As soon as he caught sight of them, Johns abruptly left three American ladies who had attacked him, and advanced to meet the old Colonel and his daughter.

"How kind, how charming of you to come! Colonel, I

have never seen you look so well, and you, Miss Douglas, it is so long since you have graced us with a visit!"

The Colonel, a tall, erect old man, with snow-white hair, replied, "I have the greatest trouble, Mr. Johns, to induce my daughter to pay visits. She's terribly remiss in what seems to me to be the first of social duties."

Miss Douglas, without answering, glanced at Johns with a meditative smile.

Johns thought, "I must separate them."

"Colonel," he said, "I'm going to take your daughter from you. I want to introduce her to some people who will perhaps induce her to be less cruel. Come, Miss Douglas, you are in my hands to-night."

As soon as they had left the Colonel, he said, quickly, "Let us go downstairs to the refreshment room; I want to speak to you."

Without answering, she let him lead her to a room on the ground floor where a long table full of delicacies was being served by half a dozen solemn waiters.

At one end of the room was a small recess which was furnished with a velvet-cushioned bench.

Johns said, as they sat down, "Miss Douglas, now that I am married, I'm privileged to speak paternally."

Then, lowering his tone, he asked, "Couldn't you like St. George?"

Startled by the directness of the question, for which she was unprepared, she answered, "I didn't know that marriage gave a right to ask such questions."

"It does to me, Miss Douglas, because I take an interest in your welfare, a greater interest than you imagine."

She gave him a rapid glance.

"Ah, your interests are very wide."

Without appearing to perceive the drift of this remark, he said, "Do you know, Miss Douglas, that when I saw you for the first time, I was reminded of one of those perfect models of Greek art which have come down to us from the time of Phidias? It seemed to me that you were the true expression of that great man's brain, the incarnation of his rich fancy. Later I heard that my friend St. George had been as deeply struck as I. When he told me that he meant to ask your hand, I thought him the most enviable man in the whole world, for I imagined that he would find favour in your eyes. But it seems I was mistaken. It seems that poor St. George had built his hopes in vain, and that now he is obliged to live with his regrets. And what regrets! Ah, were there ever such regrets?"

"Are you grieving for your friend?" she asked.

"For my friend?" he repeated, "I scarcely know; I scarcely like to think"; and he gazed at her deeply, earnestly.

She said, "Two years ago if I had asked you that question, would you have known what to answer?"

"Two years ago I would have pleaded for myself."

She said, "Fate settles things so badly."

"It does," he echoed, sorrowfully.

"And some day," he added, with a sigh, "you will meet the man who will be more fortunate than St. George, and then we will be divided by a double bar."

She was silent. Presently she said, "I don't know why we have talked of this."

He answered, "I will tell you why. It was because we were impelled to by that fatal magnetism which no one can escape, which no one can resist. I felt when I saw you enter this evening that I should betray myself; I knew that I was under the influence of a great, an irresistible attraction. Ah, Miss Douglas, the fire that I see in those beautiful dark eyes of yours, tells me plainly why St. George was unsuccessful. St. George, with his leisurely and quiet ways, was not the husband you deserve. You were born to be the solace of a man of action, of a man who can force his way to the position which he wants. And some day perhaps, you will meet that man, you will marry him, and I shall be obliged to be a mere witness to the marrying!"

"Who knows!" she said, "things happen strangely sometimes."

He glanced up at her suddenly and searchingly, seeking to guess her meaning. Then they were both silent for some minutes.

Presently the strains of a violin penetrated to the recess where they were sitting, in irregular cadences of sound, now plainly audible, now dying away completely in the passage from the floor above.

Johns, who was beginning to fear that his absence from the drawing-room might be remarked, explained, "That's Señor Fernaflor, whom my wife enlisted the other day at the Duke of Dorset's. He's a prince of violinists. I suppose we must go up to hear him."

"As you wish," she said, listlessly.

But as they were going up the stairs, he whispered, "Will you come and see us often?"

She answered, "What would be the use?"

He said, "Come all the same," and then, stopping suddenly

before they reached the last stair, he murmured, "Promise me that you will consult me before you accept another man?"

Again she answered, "What would be the use?"

"I don't know. I can't quite say. I might advise you. I scarcely like to think. But promise me, I entreat you; promise me."

"Very well," she said, "I will."

As they reached the door the violinist, a thin man with a fine thoughtful face surrounded by a thick mass of brown waving hair, had just finished the first part of his performance, and was bowing to acknowledge the applause which greeted him. Johns took advantage of the interval to conduct Miss Douglas to her father, where he left her.

"I guessed as much," he said to himself, as he moved away from them. "What a wife she would have made!"

He had embarked on the little intrigue from his natural liking for such things, from a real admiration for the beautiful young girl, and in obedience to his principle of never neglecting an opportunity. He felt regret that so much beauty should be beyond his reach, and also a vague desire to speculate upon the future. But at that moment he was recalled to a sense of his host's duties by his wife, who was making him a sign to come to her.

As he reached the place where she was standing, the violinist resumed his playing. Mrs. Johns whispered in his ear—

"Those Dawsons have arrived, John. You had better help me to speak to them."

Suddenly, as he looked up, he saw Dawson and his wife upon the landing, listening to the performer.

But what a change in Lucy! Instead of the florid, healthy blonde, with her fresh face and her almost girlish look, he saw a woman with drawn pale features and an air of languor. She was standing at her husband's side, listening to the music, and looking down. Her hands were crossed over her black dress. Johns thought, "Lucy *has* changed."

The Spanish artist was playing a rhapsody with great feeling and expression, and the whole room was visibly impressed. Johns himself, as he listened to the rich sounds which were being given out with masterly precision, muttered, "Poor little Lucy, how thin she's looking!"

When the piece and the prolonged applause which it elicited were over, Johns advanced to receive the Dawsons, and to introduce them to his wife.

As he shook hands with Lucy she looked away from him and

returned his greeting with a mere word. Even Dawson, apparently impressed by the splendour of his ex-reporter, seemed subdued. The two ladies spoke together, and Johns said to Dawson—

"You've often received me at your house, Dawson; now I'm pleased to be able to welcome you to mine."

"And what a house!" said Dawson.

Johns smiled complacently.

"Ah," said Dawson, "we've missed you in the Strand. The man who followed you I didn't keep a month; and the present one—well, I won't mention him." They talked about the paper for a few minutes, and then Johns whispered, "Speak to my wife, Dawson, and I'll take yours down to the refreshment room." Johns offered his arm to Lucy, who took it half-reluctantly, and they went down. Neither spoke. When they reached the room, as she declared she would take nothing, he led her to the small conservatory which was entered from the extreme end, and which was lit with coloured lamps.

They were alone, and he said at once, "It was good of you to come to-night."

"I came," she answered as if with an effort, "to please my husband."

"Only for that?" he said, adding, after a slight pause, "you're not looking well. What has been the matter?"

She was silent.

"Have you been ill, Lucy? Tell me!"

She answered, "Do not be more cruel than you've already been!"

"Cruel? Was I really cruel?"

"Oh, how can you ask that!"

"I was obliged to marry, Lucy."

"Were you obliged to deceive two women at the same time?"

"There were circumstances which prevented me from being frank."

"Ah yes," she said bitterly, "men say those things!"

"Come, come Lucy, this will never do. This solemn tone, these sombre looks! You must forget all about the past and think only of the present. You must not spoil that pretty face by melancholy."

"Yes, you've taught me to be callous."

"Lucy, you're mistaken. I acted really for your good, as some day you'll understand. There was no issue from the position in which we found ourselves. It was bound to come to an end some day."

"That, then, was the kind of love you had for me!"
"Oh, but, Lucy, all that's over now!"
"It is indeed!"
"And perhaps I can do something for you. I'm able now to help my friends, and if you wanted to go into society, for instance, where you might meet someone who would love you more than you imagine I did ——"

But she interrupted him—

"Oh, this is too much! I have loved you with all my heart and soul. I've dreamt of you, I've even prayed for you. I would have given up my life for you, and you talk to me of another man! I don't want to upbraid you. You have done what your inclination made you do; you have followed your ambition, but do not speak to me of a second treachery towards my husband, who was so good and kind to me when I was ill."

"Have you been ill, Lucy?"

"Yes, very ill; but do not let us talk of that. I'm better now, and all I desire is to make the man who loves me happy."

He looked at her attentively. Her face was so intensely sorrowful that suddenly he grew serious himself.

"And do you think," he asked, "that *I'm* completely happy?"

"Have you not all that should make you so?"

"It would seem so," he said, meditatively, with a sigh. "But it doesn't matter about me. I am of the more common clay, a servant of ambition. I can only live as long as I can climb, and if there were nothing left to climb for, I could not go on living. Don't regret me, Lucy, I wouldn't have made you happy."

"You're a strange man!"

"I am, Lucy, I am; but you must forget all about me and my strangeness."

"Ah! if I only could!"

"You can do it, Lucy, if you try. All women can. What, after all, is this love but an illusion of the senses, a matter of chance and circumstance, of time and latitude and opportunity? The lovers of to-day, for all their youth and ardour, are the old men and women of to-morrow! We are all of us undergoing change. It's not a year since you quitted me that afternoon in Jermyn Street, and yet we are both changed already. We could no longer, if we wished, love with the same feelings as before. Time has already altered us. Love is of the present—of the present only. Think of the countless couples who marry in the enthusiasm of a brief moment of delusive passion. All the world is love for them. Nothing else exists! And yet in a few short years they have settled down to a vulgar life of egoism, and their love has cooled into a mere feeling of conjugal companionship. Sometimes it has changed to enmity. We are all the sport of chance! What do you think that room-full of people up above are doing? They are existing merely for the pleasures of the hour. Some have not yet experienced love; some are tasting its delights. For others it is a mere memory. But all are living on the solace of some present pleasure, well knowing that present pleasures are the only ones that count. Lucy, there's a law in nature which makes us hedonists—all hedonists!"

She said, "How different our natures are! You little know a woman's heart."

Johns thought, "I do, though"; and he answered, "No, Lucy, I'm afraid I don't."

By this time he had satisfied his curiosity. He had felt her pulse, and had poured what little balm he could upon her troubled feelings, and now he was getting tired. There wasn't enough variety in Lucy. She was too much of a piece. The best thing she could do was to go on consoling Dawson. That was in reality the part she was fitted for, and it was weak of him to waste philosophy upon her. She had had a shock, no doubt, but she would easily recover now. There were no such things as broken hearts except in the imagination of the sentimental novelist.

"Well then, Lucy," he said, "it's understood. You're going to be reasonable; you're going to devote yourself to that estimable man your husband. In a few years you'll tell me that everything has happened for the best, and that you're very happy."

"In a few years!" she repeated slowly. "Ah, yes, in a few years!"

"And now," said Johns, rising, "we had better perhaps go back."

She rose at once. He offered her his arm, and they returned in silence.

Mrs. Johns, as they entered the room together, gave them a sharp, somewhat suspicious glance, which Johns did not fail to notice.

Leaving Mrs. Dawson, therefore, with her husband, whom he discovered speaking to an acquaintance, he returned to his wife's side.

"Oh, John, everybody is asking for you. How long you've been!"

And Johns, who had by this time satisfied all his curiosity, and who was now disposed to enter heartily into his duties of host, replied, " I couldn't get rid of that Mrs. Dawson, but now I'm at your service."

The evening progressed brilliantly, and the violinist was twice again applauded. The room was animated, the reception was successful. The guests seemed pleased to find themselves together under the Johns's roof.

Johns occupied the remainder of the time in chatting with them, and he noticed with satisfaction that the merest witticism he made, was received with twice the favour it deserved.

" What sheep they are !" he thought again, and as he moved about the room, greeted by smiles and compliments, he felt as he fancied Napoleon must have felt when the women waited for him in the corridors and the men coveted his merest word.

" How they worship their God—success ! " he thought, as he stood amongst the bevy of bare, sparkling necks and listened to fair literary aspirants, distributing the while encouragements and smiles.

When it was all over, when the last couple had departed and the last leave-taking over, Johns and his wife were left alone in the great empty drawing-room.

Leaning her head upon his shoulder, and with her eyes half closed, she murmured—

"Oh my darling Johnnie, how proud I was of you to-night. How well you looked and spoke. If you had been born a prince you could not have seemed more princely !"

Then, placing her arms around his neck, she drew his face towards her and kissed him gently on his eyelids.

CHAPTER FOURTEENTH

THE season was drawing to its close. The series of receptions which the Johns had given had been entirely successful, and the newly-married couple had continued to mount so rapidly the social ladder, that Mrs. Johns herself, whose circle of acquaintances had been singularly enlarged by the attraction which her husband exercised, had been surprised. Although Johns took very little trouble now to court society, he was always in demand, and hostesses considered themselves fortunate when they had been able to secure him. They even pardoned him his rudeness in failing to appear when a superior interest prevented him.

One afternoon, however, in the middle of July, the Stanfields, St. George, and a few intimate friends had been lunching at Grosvenor Place, and were sitting chatting in the drawing-room. Johns, who had partaken freely of his own champagne at luncheon, was in one of his expansive moods. He was describing to his guests the visit he had had the previous day. A man had come to him with an introduction from a friend, and had wished to write in his Review to prove that the curse from which the nation suffered was the hereditary Chamber, which stifled progress and imposed upon the people the will of a degenerated aristocracy whose minds and bodies were alike corrupt. And Johns applied himself to show that the mainstay of the nation was the caste which had made it great, the caste whose moral influence was still enormous, the caste which in reality was the greatest friend of progress.

His guests were naturally of his opinion.

"When I was a boy at school," Johns commenced ——

"At Harrow," Mrs. Johns explained, drawing on her imagination for the benefit of those present.

P

"I remember," continued Johns, without taking any notice of his wife's elucidation, "the son of a commoner who used to preach democracy as he had learned it from his father ——"

But he had scarcely pronounced the last word when the door was opened and a servant entered.

"Mr. David Johns has called to see you, sir."

Johns stopped short and turned at once towards the man who brought him so extraordinary a piece of information.

"Mr. who?" he asked in a low voice.

"Mr. David Johns, sir. I told him you were engaged, but—he says he is your father, sir, from —— I didn't catch the name, sir."

The man, whom Johns had found wanting in intelligence and who was about to leave, spoke loudly enough for everyone to hear.

The Stanfields and the other guests looked up at once, while Mrs. Johns grew serious.

Johns, who thought his father safely at St. Martin, was completely taken by surprise. Quickly he realized that he could not refuse to see his father. Yet it was impossible to ask him in. In his embarrassment, he hit upon the expedient of going down to see him.

Excusing himself, therefore, to his guests, he hurried to the door. But he had no sooner opened it, than he found his father waiting on the threshold. The elder Johns was a short, thick-set man, with a round face the upper lip of which was shaved. He wore whiskers that curled like short crisp waves on a sea-shore, and stretched from ear to ear, passing beneath the chin. His little peering eyes stood out in relief upon the weather-reddened skin, and his reddish curly locks, which were becoming white in patches, although he scarcely seemed more than fifty, completed an essentially seafaring countenance. He was dressed in a suit of black glossy cloth, the vest of which was adorned by a thick watch-chain of pale gold. In his brown freckled hand he was holding a round and soft felt hat.

He had followed the man upstairs and was standing on the landing looking about him at the vastness of the place, apparently abashed at his temerity.

"Well, John, my boy, 'ow arr you? You're surprised to see me, but you know there was an excursion from St. Peter's Port, and the missis said ——"

But in the middle of his speech he suddenly perceived the majestic drawing-room in the background with its velvet hangings, its air of greatness, and in it the group of guests who were looking towards the door with faces of amused wonderment. Abruptly he ceased speaking.

Johns, who felt himself between two fires, and who realized intensely the awkwardness of the situation, paused a moment to collect his thoughts after pressing his father's hard brown hand. He knew that it had been given out industriously by his wife that his father was a gentleman who never left his property in Guernsey, and this apparition of the old mariner was therefore doubly disagreeable.

But there was no time for much reflection. Everybody in the room had heard and seen. It would look worse now to try to hide his sire than to produce him. He *would* produce him. He was strong enough to do so now, and it would be amusing to force the old man upon them. If they came to his house, the silly fools, they must take it as they found it.

Having arrived at this determination, he said, loudly enough for all to hear, "Come in, father."

But the elder Johns remained upon the landing hesitating, glancing alternately at Johns and at the guests, uncertain what to do.

Johns, seeing his embarrassment, encouraged him.

"Come along, father, it's all right."

Slowly, then, the old man followed his son into the room.

As they were advancing, the expression of Mrs. Johns's face would have formed a study for a physiognomist. Fear, offended pride, humiliation, were all depicted on her countenance, which had become as red as the silk bodice she was wearing.

Johns, who by this time had quite regained composure, assumed his most Napoleonic attitude, and, designating his father with a wave of his hand, he addressed his wife.

"This, Rose, is my father, whom you have not yet seen, and who has wished to give us a surprise."

Then, turning to the old mariner, he said—

"Father, this lady is my wife."

The old man timidly held out his hand to Mrs. Johns.

"Good afternoon, ma'm."

Mrs. Johns gave him the tips of her fingers without replying.

But Johns, taking no notice of his wife's evident disgust, now introduced his father to the other guests, and to each of them the old man said, "'ow arr you, sir," or "I 'ope you arr quite well, ma'm." When, however, it came to the Stanfields' turn, and Johns said, "Lady Stanfield, Lord Stanfield, let me introduce my father who has just come from Guernsey," the old man looked bewildered. Never having been in the presence of nobility before, he fumbled nervously with his hat, and finally made a species of obeisance which raised a smile on the lips of Lord Stanfield and his wife.

"I'm pleased to see you, sir," Lord Stanfield said, with an amused expression, which further disconcerted the old mariner, and then, addressing Johns with an almost imperceptible touch of irony, "I didn't know, Johns, that your father was so hale and hearty."

But Johns, unwilling to be outdone, replied—

"My father has a constitution of iron, Lord Stanfield; neither heat nor cold affects it. I have seen him lie on the deck of his boat at night in mid-winter with nothing but an oilskin over him to protect him from the cold. I have seen him remain a whole night at the helm when the wind was blowing in a hurricane, and the waves were soaring as high as mountains. In the whole island there isn't a man so hardy. Shall I tell you a story which his modesty prefers to hide? One night, which is still fresh in my memory, although I was then a lad, a terrific storm burst upon our coast. It wasn't a mere gale of wind, but one of those hurricanes which carry all before them. Suddenly it was rumoured that a ship was in the bay struggling in the dark heaving mass of water. The whole parish gathered on the beach, and soon we saw a rocket dart into the inky sky. There was no doubt then. A ship was there, and in distress. But who could render her assistance on such a night? The men who were accustomed to man the life-boat looked at the night, and shook their heads! They couldn't go! It was nothing short of madness to attempt it. It was risking their lives in vain, they said. No, it could not be done. My father then appeared among them. He listened a moment to their talk, and then he said, 'We must do that job, boys,' and he persuaded them to do it! They got the boat and manned her, and my father took the helm. The first push was unsuccessful: the boat was filled by the huge crashing waves. They tried again and yet again until at length she was launched on the mad sea. Then they rowed as galley slaves have never rowed. Ah, how they rowed! And my father cheered and steered them, although his voice was often drowned in the great roar. The rockets continued to ascend. The ship was drifting rapidly towards them, but the battle with the waves was terrible. The boat was like an ant trying to fight an elephant. All on shore were certain she must be destroyed. It was so dark, so wild! But suddenly the moon came out from behind a bank of clouds just as they reached the ship, and they were able, after a struggle as heroic as an epic combat, as fierce as a death duel, to rescue, how many do you think? to rescue fifteen of the crew!"

A murmur of admiration greeted this anecdote, and Mr. David Johns, surprised at the praise which was being bestowed upon him by his son for an act which he had well-nigh forgotten, was more confused than ever. St. George, however, out of friendship for his son, endeavoured to encourage the old man by asking him a question.

"Do you get many such storms, Mr. Johns?" he asked.

The old man, so questioned, and finding himself entirely in his element, replied—

"Well, not often such as that, sir, but it do blow 'ard in the winter time. I've seen as many as three ships ashore one Christmas."

The guests looked at each other and agreed that that was a great many.

Mrs. Johns maintained a rigid silence.

"Take a seat, father," Johns said, noticing that his father remained standing.

The elder Johns turned and looked at several vacant chairs, but no doubt thinking them too gorgeous with their gilt and their crimson velvet, he chose a kind of stool of inlaid oriental make, and slowly lowered himself into it, as if doubtful if it would bear his weight. As it was very low, and as his legs were short and thick, he had a doubled-up appearance which added nothing to his dignity.

But the conversation, which had been interrupted by his arrival, now continued on other topics, and he became a listener.

A fair young man, with a blank ugly face and an exceedingly high collar, whom Johns invited because he was known to be phenomenally rich (the possession of great wealth placed a man, Johns thought, on a kind of level with intelligences higher than his own), began to relate to Lord Stanfield a carriage accident he had had a few days previously. Johns and St. George chatted about art. David Johns and his daughter-in-law were silent.

Thus the time was reached when luncheon parties which have extended far into the afternoon break up.

Lady Stanfield was the first to rise, and the others followed her example.

In a few moments they had all left. Mrs. Johns had disappeared, and the father and son were alone together.

Johns said, "I'm glad to see you, dad, but you should have written that you were coming. My wife, you know, is a big swell, and doesn't like to be surprised—swells don't."

"I didn't know, Johnnie. It was the missis made me come on that excursion boat. I didn't want to, Lord knows."

"When does it return, dad?"

"In fourr days."

"Where are you staying?"

"Well, you see, Johnnie, it was very late when we got to London, and some of 'em were going to the Cooper's Arms—that's over by the station—so I went along with 'em."

The old man spoke slowly and with hesitation, in a kind of half French accent. He looked down most of the time, seeming timid in the presence of his son.

"And how are you off for coin, dad?"

"I've lots of *that*, Johnnie, thanks to you, my boy."

"And how are mother and cousin Kate?"

"The missis has had rheumatics, but Katie's very well."

Then he went on to tell his son all the village news, the marriage of Peter Luce, and the death of John Lebas, mentioning a host of names half English and half French, which Johns remembered hazily, and speaking in English, either because he guessed that his son had forgotten the Guernsey patois, or because, being in reality of Welsh origin as his name implied, the English tongue was equally familiar to him.

When he had finished, Johns said, calmly, "Well, now, dad, I must go out. I'll come and see you to-morrow at the Cooper's Arms to take you out to dinner. But look here, dad, don't come here again. The missis mightn't like it. Do you understand?"

"All right, my boy, don't mind me. I won't trouble the good lady."

Johns led his father to the front door, and they parted, after agreeing to meet again next day.

Then he returned to the drawing-room, where his wife was now awaiting him. Immediately, as he glanced at her face, he saw that she was in high dudgeon. He had never seen her look so glum.

Preparing himself for a contest which seemed inevitable, he took a seat and waited for her to commence. She was not long in doing so.

"John," she said, "before our marriage it was agreed that your family should never come here, and yet just now, when your father appeared upon that landing in an incomprehensible kind of way, you actually brought him in, and introduced him to our friends. I have never felt so frightfully ridiculous before. You know as well as I that we gave out he was a country gentleman, and yet, in the face of that, you deliberately tell everybody that he is a—a seafaring person. It's monstrous. I shall never recover the humiliation!"

Johns, who was rather in a bad humour himself at what had happened, answered rather sharply, "It was the fault of that fool, James. What was I to do, I should like to know, when he said, before everybody, that he was my father?"

"You should have said he wasn't and refused to see him, or something of the sort. Anything, I should think, would be better than making your wife ridiculous!"

Vexed at the tone she had suddenly adopted, he replied, "I did what occurred to me to do, and after all it wasn't so very *terrible.*"

"It was a perfect scandal! You had no right to bring such a person here."

Johns was stung to the quick this time. His father was his father, and if he chose to acknowledge him, by God his friends must accept him, and his wife too!

He said, "Is that the first scandal, Rose, in which you have been concerned?"

"What do you mean?" she asked, angrily. "What do you insinuate?"

"Nothing in particular; only I've been accustomed to think that one scandal is as good or as bad as another, that's all."

"Oh!" she muttered, I didn't expect that of you!"

He answered, "Everything is to be expected from everybody."

"It seems so, indeed!"

Presently she added, "After what has happened I should think you would see the necessity of our going away from London for a time."

"I see no such necessity, and I don't intend to go."

"Ah," she exclaimed, "I'm beginning to think I didn't know you."

"Perhaps not," he answered, carelessly. "As for my father, whom you are pleased to call a seafaring person, I may tell you that he won't come here again. I shall lunch with him at a restaurant to-morrow."

Saying this, to put an end to the discussion he rose and left the room with a decided step.

This was their first quarrel of any gravity. They had had some little scenes of jealousy at different times, when Johns had been too attentive to his wife's lady friends, but they had led to nothing since there was nothing to be discovered in that direction.

But this time Mrs. Johns had been deeply wounded in her pride of caste, and for some time afterwards, although she had not reverted to the old man's visit, she was colder towards her husband, less demonstrative in the cult which she professed for him. Frequently a troubled, almost sorrowful expression would cross her face, and she would look at Johns as he sat opposite to her at table.

Johns, who wished to commence asserting his independence, did nothing to restore her peace of mind. He regarded the visit of his father as a fortunate event, since it had caused the exact measure of estrangement between his wife and him, which he found necessary to his own comfort, and which he was quite resolved to endeavour to maintain.

It was so delightful now, to indulge his liking for Mrs. Weber to its full extent without having to render an account of the hours which he spent while doing so—the happiest in his existence, and so different from those conjugal moments which he considered as official or as a tax that he had to pay for the position he had reached. As long as his wife would be satisfied with the present state of things, they might go on living pleasantly together, for, after all, she *was* a necessary factor in his life, and she gave him a social status which he would not care to lose, even in order to gain his liberty.

He made it a rule, also, to be excessively polite to her, and to speak well of her before strangers. So that, when Mrs. Weber would jestingly allude to "his antiquity," he would merely remark gravely that Mrs. Johns was very well preserved, and he would refrain from joining in the laugh which greeted this description of his helpmate. "She's not an Ellen," he would say, "but she's Mrs. Johns, and there's no getting over that."

And she would answer, "And I, who *am* an Ellen, am not Mrs. Johns!" and as that was equally undeniable, Johns would content himself with smiling.

In the meantime he had become a frequent visitor at the house of Colonel Douglas in Lexham Gardens. On Sunday afternoons he would spend an hour there, taking, as he called it, a bath of freshness in the beauty of the Colonel's daughter. These visits afforded him a weekly taste of pure idealism, of a different, more interesting feeling, in a sense, to that which he experienced in the society of Mrs. Weber, and they were undoubtedly a great relief from the companionship of Mrs. Johns. He would keep some of his best anecdotes for the young girl, and, when with her, would exert himself to be particularly brilliant. As his wife never came with him, preferring to remain at home to receive her friends on Sundays, he was the more free. Thus an intimacy grew up between them which increased as the months went by, and, faithful to his combative instincts, Johns would make a point of being disagreeable to the aspirants (and they were many) for the young girl's hand, defeating them in argument, using against them the power of words which he now possessed, to their discomfiture, so that they went out vowing that he was the worst cad they had ever met, and strongly regretful that duels had been abolished in this country.

Colonel Francis Douglas, her father, was a retired engineer who had left the service with the rank of captain after inheriting a little fortune, which permitted him to live in moderate ease and comfort. His wife had died a few years before Johns's marriage. His only son had been killed in Africa, and Edith Douglas was now his only child. He allowed his daughter a certain amount of liberty, but as he was adverse to the modern notions of emancipation for unmarried women, he generally accompanied her when she went into society. Several times, incited by her beauty, Johns had hinted at a meeting in a church or picture gallery, for the sake of music or of art, but each time she had told him that it was impossible. And her inability or unwillingness only served to whet his appetite. She was the first woman he had met who took the kind of interest in him he liked—a sensible, consistent interest which never flagged, which could not fail to be sincere, since not only he could not wed her, but he was really standing in the way of her matrimonial prospects.

He loved her youth and her girlish ways, and he recognized in her a bright intelligence, perceptions quite beyond her years. What a wife she would have made! Ah, if Rose, by some enchantment, could be transformed into such an Edith!

One Sunday afternoon at the end of July he was with her in Lexham Gardens. The father had left the drawing-room to show an old friend of his his trophies. Edith and Johns were left alone together.

"And so," he said, "you're going off to Switzerland!"

"Yes, but why that solemn tone?"

"Each time you go away, I think of you so often! I imagine that you are surrounded by a bevy of admirers, and that one perhaps will carry off the prize!"

"Have not I promised to let you know before that happens?"

"You have, you have, I know, and yet I dread to receive a letter telling me that the time has come for you to make a choice. I scarcely like to think what I shall answer!"

"You had better wait until the day arrives," she said, with a little laugh.

"Ah, but it *will* come. It cannot always be delayed."

"It may. I have no wish to marry unless —— Must I tell you?"

"I entreat you."

"Unless I meet someone who resembles you."

He cried with rapture, "I feel like a man who has suddenly been saved from drowning, who has suddenly been brought back to life! Ah, why is there that cruel bar between us? True, the time may come when I shall be free; but years may then have passed, and we shall both have entered deeper into the cave of life. It is now when we are in the full possession, of divine youth, when we are, as the poet says, in the aurora of existence, that we should taste the ineffable delight of love. Forgive me if I speak like this, but I know that with you I may be frank."

"You must not," she said, with a quiet smile, "make love to me. You must wait, Mr. Johns, you must wait with a great deal of patience. You may think me very visionary; but I have a kind of presentiment that if we wait we shall be rewarded."

She seemed perfectly collected as she sat there facing him in the declining light of the afternoon, and she appeared to him so perfectly, so overwhelmingly ideal, so absolutely beautiful, that with difficulty he restrained himself from rising to seize her in his arms.

"You are," he said, in an outburst of enthusiasm, "the most marvellous expression, the most perfect incarnation I have ever met of all that is bright and sweet and lovable. Oh, if I said all that I have at heart to say! But no, I must not, I must go on living with your image stamped indelibly upon my mind and heart."

"Oh," she said, "with me it is not necessary to be quite so enthusiastic, although of course it's very kind of you. Yes, I will confess I like you for your brilliancy and pluck, and I want to see you rise to the height of your ambition. You will always find a sympathizer in me—always."

"By God!" he said, in his bluff way, "with you I could have gained an empire!"

At that moment her handkerchief fell from her lap upon the floor, and before she had time to stoop to pick it up, he sprang upon it with a sudden bound.

"Oh, let me keep it," he exclaimed, as he pressed it to his lips; "let me have it with me always as a souvenir of you!"

"You may have it if you like, but I warn you I don't care for you in a sentimental vein."

Johns was not abashed. He knew women well enough, he thought, to know that no admiration, homage, no matter how excessive, was ever really uncongenial to them. This girl *might* be one of those rare exceptions which are sometimes heard of but never met, yet he didn't think so, and he continued to pour out the hyperbolic phrases which flowed from his lips so readily, until he was interrupted by the entrance of the Colonel. Then, after a few words with the old engineer, he left, saying good-bye until the winter.

When the time arrived for leaving town, Johns and his wife had a serious discussion.

Johns suggested Switzerland, but immediately she said, ill-humouredly, "I will *not* go to Switzerland."

"May I know why?"

"I have my reasons."

Johns bit his lip, thinking, "She's jealous now of Edith."

He said, "Then where *will* you go?"

"I should prefer Bath, where I want to take the waters."

Johns answered, "Then I'm afraid, my dear Rose, I shan't be able to accompany you. I would die of ennui in a week."

"Ah," she said, bitterly, "a year ago you wouldn't have talked of ennui."

"Probably not, but honeymoons cannot last for ever. There must be reason in all things. We cannot be always as young doves."

As he said this he glanced at his wife's face, and scarcely repressed a smile as he noticed the skin which shone in some places with the shine of maturity, and the furrows which endless massage had been unable to remove.

"You lose no opportunity of reminding me of it," she said.

"My dear Rose, one must think of these things."

"And you mean to say that if I go to Bath you will not come?"

"I do."

"Yes, *now* I'm beginning to understand you! You're acting just as I might have expected a man like you would act."

"What do you mean by a man like me?"

"I mean a man of your—well, since you must have it—a man of your *class*, you know."

Johns, who had been leaning against the mantel, drew himself up with great dignity. It was time, he thought, to assert himself. This time he would bid for his independence.

"If you've made up your mind to be rude," he said, "the less we say to each other in future the better it will be, as I don't intend to be insulted. We'll travel separately."

Saying this, he made for the door, striding with an air of offended pride. But just as he was going out, she cried—

"Oh, Johnnie, this is impossible! We cannot live like strangers and go to different places. It would be too dreadful. I could not do it. I should be always thinking of my Johnnie. You know I don't want to say unkind things, but my nerves are bad to-day, and you were not very kind, perhaps, just now, and I felt a little hurt, and I —— Oh, forgive me, Johnnie."

The poor woman was sorely troubled, and the words came out with difficulty. She seemed in pain.

Johns hesitated, with his hand on the handle of the door. He did not want to quarrel outright with his wife just then, neither did he wish to be too easily conciliated. He waited to hear more.

"Don't go, my Johnnie," she said, supplicatingly. "Come and sit here near me as you used to do — at first. I've been feeling so weak and ill for the last few days.

And he, with a half-reluctant air, went back to her and took a seat upon a low stool beside her, looking up and noticing the paleness of her face.

"We'll make it up," he said; "but you *must* go to Bath. Your health needs it, Rose. I won't go to Switzerland, since you don't like my going there, but somewhere else, and I'll come to fetch you when the treatment's over."

"Very well, then," she answered, sorrowfully, "if it must be so!"

And she tried to look contented.

When the time arrived, Johns, after seeing his wife off at Paddington, started for Dieppe, the next day, with Mrs. Weber. He would, no doubt, have liked to go to Switzerland alone, but he had come to the conclusion that it would be wiser to refrain from doing so. Miss Douglas, whom he would have met there, would, he knew, be closely guarded by her father, and he might not enjoy himself at all. All things considered, Mrs. Weber would be the best companion he could have just then.

They crossed together from Newhaven, and arrived at Dieppe after a calm trip across the channel.

In order that they might not run the risk of meeting friends, Johns had engaged, by letter, a villa on the cliffs, at some distance from the town, and thither they repaired at once. It was a bright and pleasant little house—one of the many let to bathers for the season—and it was surrounded by a garden railed off from the road on one side, and from the downs upon the other by a high railing.

Here the time passed peaceably enough in bathing, reading, and in idling.

Johns, however, after a few weeks of this secluded life, began to feel a lassitude, a langour. Whether it was that they were too constantly together, that he was growing hypercritical, or that the beauty of Miss Douglas haunted him, he was beginning to find defects in his companion. She was older than he had at first thought, and though she had never confessed her age, he had a strong suspicion that she was within a measurable distance of five-and-thirty. It was particularly after bathing, when they returned home by the cliffs, that he noticed how fatigued she looked, and how her features had become accentuated, and he would think, "My worthy Ellen, you're going down the hill."

One afternoon they were sitting together in the little *salon* of the villa, rocking themselves in rocking-chairs before the open window. The day had been fine and warm, and the channel sea was stretched before them like a placid lake. Insects were flying about the room buzzing loudly.

Johns, who was affected by the heat, was in one of those tempers which made him feel inclined to vent his spleen on somebody. He was smoking cigarettes, with his feet upon a chair, contemplating Ellen as she turned over the pages of a French novel.

"Ellen," he said suddenly, with a curious smile, "what's your game in life?"

She looked up suddenly.

"What do you mean?" she asked quickly.

"I mean, how do you intend to finish up?"

"To finish up?"

"Yes! Some day or other, I suppose, we shall have a row, or get separated in one way or another. Then what do you intend to do?"

"What a question!" she said, frowning. "Why should we quarrel, why should we separate? I presume you're not contemplating our separation?"

"Of course not, Ellen; but I've always noticed that unless men and women are linked together by the law, they invariably fall asunder. I don't know why it should be, but they do—always."

"Always when one of them desires it."

There was a silence. Johns went on smoking his cigarette. Presently she said, "I suppose you mean to play me a trick, as you play everyone who knows you."

"My dear Ellen, you're getting as bad as if you were my wife."

"That is what I should have been, had I not been so foolish."

"Don't regret it, Ellen. It's a queer sort of post to be Mrs. Johns."

"How well you know yourself! You know how treacherous you are."

"*You* know very well that it's just because I'm not a silly fool you like me. You yourself, dear Ellen, once wanted to play me a little trick, you may remember."

"I wish I had."

"Of course you do; but the combination fell through lamentably. I wasn't to be fooled so easily."

And they continued in this strain, half in earnest, half in bandinage, until they both grew tired of it.

"The fact is," Johns said at length, "we're like two augurs meeting. We can't take each other seriously."

Although they bathed together daily, they refrained from being seen together on the promenade or in the town, because both were afraid of meeting English friends; but the day after this little argument, they were sitting under a kind of awning in front of the villa before the garden and not far from the long white road which led from the town. It was five o'clock in the afternoon, and they were enjoying the cool breeze which had sprung up since the previous day. Mrs. Weber was making cigarettes of a special blend of tobacco of which Johns was fond. There were few passers-by in the road beyond, but those there were, could see into the garden through the railings.

Suddenly a portly figure, dressed in a dark grey suit with the clerical collar of an English clergyman, and accompanied by two blonde young ladies with thin, narrow faces, and mouths which did not close sufficiently, appeared on the other side of the high railings.

The portly person adjusted his eye-glass, stood still for a moment looking first at Mrs. Weber, then at Johns, after which he moved off with great dignity to overtake the ladies, who had continued on their road.

"By God," said Johns, "it's that old sneak the Dean!"

"Well," she answered, "and if it is, you needn't be so overpowered."

"It's very fine for you to talk," he said, roughly, "but it's a damned nuisance. He'll go and write it to my wife, as certain as he's a dean."

"Well it's as bad for me as for you, I fancy."

"*Is* it?" he said, sneeringly. "What have you to lose beyond a pennyworth of reputation, I should like to know? With me it's a matter of three thousand pounds a year."

"Ha, ha," she laughed derisively, "it would be too funny if you were to figure in a divorce case."

"Perhaps you wouldn't find it quite so funny when you were called upon to explain in Court the nature of our arrangement."

"Oh," she answered, carelessly, "nothing matters much now to me. Once I thought that I could some day have been your wife, but all that's over now. You're not the kind of man to marry for anything but a heap of gold, my rapacious Johnnie. I know you well. You'd imagine yourself a poor man if you were a Rothschild!"

He said, "You think it's wealth alone I want?"

"I'm sure of it."

"Just as you like, Ellen; since you know me so well I won't contradict you. It doesn't alter the fact that I'm going to have the devil's own trouble with my wife, and all on account of that silly mania of yours for sitting out here in public. He didn't even bow!"

She said, "You're making a great deal out of nothing. As if you mightn't have been calling on me as a friend!"

"Ah, yes, that's one of those Saxon notions for which they've tried to make Plato responsible, and which they don't really believe themselves. Anybody who knows me knows that I don't indulge in vagaries of *that* sort. Remember that that old person has been disinherited, and he's ready to be spiteful."

"Well," she said, composedly, "that's what comes of what is called an irregular position." But Johns burst out—

"An irregular position! As if anyone cared for regular positions except mediocrities. I should have thought you'd seen enough of life to be aware of that. Regularity means stagnation, and only fools stagnate. Life isn't long enough for that. We've got to get the best we can out of it before we're fifty. It's a rum sort of farce afterwards. Up to thirty a man's groping, so he's only got just twenty years of strength. Do you think that if he shuts himself up in a regular position, as some people call it, he ever gets a chance of knowing what life is? Never. Life, my worthy Ellen, is infinite, and no one ever gets to know it thoroughly. The man who explores it, best is he who takes a crooked course and forces it to tell its secrets! What do those staid and sober puritans who form the majority of the inhabitants of that island over yonder know of the plenitude, the magnitude of life? They treat it as if it were a great, dull, lumbering machine, which could only go on one changeless plan. They know about as much of their existence as the cab horse of the people in the cab he draws. Well, that sort of life wasn't made for me. I want emotions. I want my pulse to beat a little faster than the snail's pace of mediocrity. *I* want to take a deeper draught of the liquor of existence!"

"Well, my dear John," she said, "you're likely to have plenty of emotions if the Dean acts as you think he will."

But Johns had risen from his chair.

"Come, Ellen, let's go in, I want emotions now."

CHAPTER FIFTEENTH

TWO years elapsed. After many bickerings, Mrs. Johns, who had lost her last illusions as to her husband's conduct, had resigned herself at length to a life of passive acquiescence, conscious of the legal strength of her position, which not all the rivals in the world could injure.

As can easily be imagined, she was not happy. Every day, almost every hour, she was reminded by the smiles, the reticences, the hesitations of her friends that the sad collapse of her married life was known, and though with a touching display of ingenuity she endeavoured sometimes to invent excuses for her husband's absences at times when his place was at her side, the excuses were generally so manifestly weak, that she felt that no one was deceived by them. And yet in spite of all she loved her husband, and when she spoke of him to others it was in a tone of admiration, almost of respect. Whatever Johns did or said that was fit to be repeated, such as his editorial work or the latest of his epigrams, she would relate with pleasure, deriving a kind of satisfaction from being the wife of a man whose strength of character and natural ability seemed to be so universally admitted.

But now, however, a little fearful for the future, she evinced for her friends—for those who had known her almost from her youth—much more affection than she had shown before.

With feminine prudence she endeavoured to conciliate them, lest she might some day find herself alone, and even the Dean (who had been so instrumental after the discovery he had made at Dieppe in opening her eyes as to her husband's conduct) she managed to appease by paying for the education of one of his many sons.

Gradually she had come to be somewhat pitied, to be

considered as a woman undeservedly in an unfortunate position, and this was the view taken of the case by both Lord Stanfield and his wife, in whose estimation Johns had fallen, as they did not fail to make him realize.

In the meantime Johns had gratified his wish to test and to explore life fully. His ample means permitted him to take pleasures which previously had been denied him, and for some time he indulged in every hedonistic freak his fancy could suggest. Not only did he become an epicure, a connoisseur of wines—in which at one time he indulged so freely as to come perilously near earning the reputation of a drunkard—but he led for a period somewhat the life of a Turkish Pasha, with Mrs. Weber, who had resigned herself to the inevitable like Mrs. Johns, as his chief lady.

It was not that he cared for the facile conquests which he made, or found much pleasure in moments passed in the company of the flatterers and boon companions he had grouped around him, but he was travailed by a strange desire to show society—and especially that section of it which had been the means of elevating him to the prosperity, the eminence, he now enjoyed—that he was superior to the laws of conduct governing ordinary mortals, and that his will was the only master of his acts. If he wished to leave his house in the afternoon and not return till the next morning with dirty linen and reddened eyes, it was not the same as if an ordinary man had done so. If he chose to give luncheon parties which lasted from two o'clock till midnight, it was because he, John Johns, the editor of the *Centenary Review*, for high reasons of his own, thought fit to do so. And hence he came to be considered as an exceptional personality to whom the ordinary rules of life did not apply, who possessed a genius for singularity which was not to be disputed.

All kinds of legends were gradually formed as to his career in the past and in the present, and these (as usually happens) were full of errors and exaggerations which caused him to exclaim, when he heard of them from a friend, "The fools; they've the impudence to judge me by their own standards!"

But when he had tasted every pleasure which came within his means, exhausted every source of novelty, he relapsed into a satiated state of disenchantment. His body wanted nothing, but his mind was filled with a great vague longing, and with a huge contempt for the men and women whom he saw around him, and whose vanities and vices he knew so well. He had tested the virtue of the women, and he knew the value of the men and the price at which they could be bought. He had explored the aristocracy and found it not one bit more scrupulous in actual reality than he, and if he was to have respect for people, they must not be his counterparts. Those men and women, too, had no reason for not leading an ideal life, such as he deemed might perhaps be possible, for they had their places in the social scale all ready found for them, while he had had to conquer his by his own "grit." It was thus impossible to have respect for anybody in this world of cant and ignorance, in which men were but mere clothed animals with a gift of thought and speech, serving to render them the more worthy of contempt. The earth would roll eternally and they would know no more about their origin, or about right and wrong, than a nigger knows of Botticelli or a Bedouin of Wagner.

And his lassitude and discontent extended now to art and literature, and he waged a war in his Review against the British public, which by its want of taste and of discernment had allowed bad paintings and bad books to multiply. He did this with so much spirit, too, and showed so much discernment in selecting writers capable of laying on the lash with firmness and ability, that, instead of alienating, he gained readers, owing, he thought, to the public's fondness for strong criticism, even at its own expense. Foreign art and letters he alone permitted to be praised, and the resentment he excited in the breasts of English writers of the Saxon school, was very bitter, although it could not be expressed, since Johns held the literary reputation of most of them in a great measure at his mercy.

If he chose to be convinced that contemporary art was an abomination, and that English fiction had been gradually declining since the time of Shakespeare till it had descended to the lowest depth of artificiality and incoherence, all who wished to gain his favour must profess to think so too. One, indeed, of the few satisfactions which remained to him was his sense of power. But even this satisfaction paled when he reflected that it was only in one rather narrow sphere that he could make his power felt. At one time he had thought of trying to obtain a seat in Parliament, but after a few evenings spent in the press gallery, he made up his mind that politics were almost as great a weariness as acting the part of husband to an ancient wife. No, he wouldn't be the servant of a lot of fools who might criticize his acts. Ah, if he had a young and pretty wife to return to after a midnight brawl at Westminster, after he had told them plainly what he thought of them, it would have been very different. But, with Mrs.

Johns, all the poetry would disappear, and, after all, there was poetry, he found, in his composition. He couldn't climb with a perspective such as that. His wife! Really it was perfectly ridiculous to see the care she bestowed upon her person. Her diet was a complex study, and all the morning the house was full of manicures and pedicures and masseuses and complexion quacks, and once a week her doctor called, whether she were ill or not. To what age would she live, he wondered? How *perpetual* she seemed in spite of the wrinkles which massage could not conquer, and the voice which had grown too deep! How eternally he seemed linked to her! For now that they had settled down to a life of conjugal aloofness, now that she had ceased to question him as to his doings, and that a semblance of married harmony was maintained before strangers, for some reason which he could scarcely have defined, he felt himself to be more than ever tied to her. There she was with her constant smile of half-sorrowful indulgence, and her little simpering ways, ready to receive the prodigal in her arms again should he become repentant, and resolved to go on living in the comfort to which she had been accustomed. At the dinner table, no doubt, she was an attentive listener when it pleased him to be expansive, to talk of men and books; but he knew full well that as she looked at him while he spoke, her thoughts were occupied with something of a different nature to the genius of a French writer, or the literary style of a review contributor. She was a woman, a typical and ordinary woman with all the little vanities distinctive of her sex, and with an intellect which did not stretch beyond the limits of the strictly commonplace. On her, his eloquence was wasted; her mind was practically *nil*. "She has intuitions, the good woman," Johns muttered to himself one evening as he strolled down Piccadilly, "but not an ounce of brains." He compared himself sometimes to a wandering knight upon a chessboard unable to escape a queen, or his wife to a sentinel in permanence at Grosvenor Place. And when he thought of Edith Douglas, who had not married, though she had had offers, and who was in the full blossom of her beauty, he felt that, rich though he might be, his lot was hard.

Most men who fall into disorder endeavour to preserve some kind of an ideal, some friend whose life is the opposite of theirs, and Johns found in the Colonel's daughter the ideal influence he needed. In the midst of his gallant adventures, whether he was gratifying a passing fancy for an actress or laying siege to the affections of a duchess, he never failed to spend three, sometimes four hours every Sunday with Miss Douglas, to the annoyance of her father, who had warned his daughter unavailingly of the imprudence of receiving such a man so often. Johns would tell her all his little worries, and endeavour to enlist her sympathy for him in the helplessness of his position, fettered as he was to a wife who could not understand him, who loved him chiefly for his fame. And she would listen smilingly to all he said, and give him her advice on questions of literary policy—advice which he often acted on out of compliment to her. Sometimes, however, she was serious and inclined to fret as if she had at length begun, as season followed season, to realize the hopelessness of their relations to each other, and was taking leave of the illusions which girlhood forms of the destinies of men and women in the world, and the fatality of marriage.

At other times, when they were alone, she would tell him that she had heard some ugly stories of his gallantry. He would reply that they were partly false, that she was the only woman in the world who could force him to be faithful; that if ever they once were married, he would be the most perfect of reformed prodigals. He knew very well that he liked her all the more because she resisted him, and the regret he felt at not being able to possess her, drove him sometimes well-nigh into a frenzy.

No, there was no way out of the situation—no way whatever unless—unlesss the illness of which his wife had complained now and then of late were really serious. Oh, but she was so robust, so remarkably robust, and there was nothing but divorce to have recourse to. And to obtain that, his wife must bring a charge against him, which was precisely what she would not do. Had she not told him so one day with that air of settled purpose which he knew from long experience a woman never used except when resolute? He couldn't force an issue by being brutal. It wasn't in his character. For, after all, the poor old girl had been very good to him, and even now cared for him as a mother, showing herself untiring when he was unwell, spoiling him by every means she could devise. Yes, undoubtedly, that increased the difficulty of the position.

Then, again, there was the question of finance. If he were divorced from her, half the fortune would remain to him, no doubt, but the household would be broken up, and he could not, on his own share, afford to live in such a house or upon so large a scale. He would have to reduce his style of living, and that was a thing he was very much disinclined to do. Life was dreary and dull enough even when one lived it in the fulness of its possibilities, but when lived otherwise it was a very poor game indeed. And then, as he reflected over the position, and realized how thoroughly checkmated he now was, he fell to making accusations against society in general, creating a sort of virtue for himself by exposing its shortcomings in a Socratic kind of way, but becoming cordially detested, and dubbed a bore, a cad, by those who accepted society as it is constituted.

But for them Johns cared nothing. He knew that by giving frequent luncheons, fastuous dinners, he could always chain to him a number of acquaintances whose stomach-gratitude would at least prevent them from becoming enemies. He could always count upon a band of staunch supporters who were, from long practice, habituated to listen patiently to enunciations of opinions which grew less and less orthodox as the time went on. Often, indeed, for the mere delight of "startling the Saxon," as he called it, he would propound some theory subversive of one or many of the rules by which society is governed. He would try to prove the necessity for what is known as sin, showing how wrong it was to think that sin was not a useful factor in the world since it preserved it from the calm stupidity of universal goodness. What was there that was great which had not sprung from sin? When sin had been successful it grew respectable, underwent a metamorphosis, became virtue. The world without it would be a mill-pond of sobriety and of inanity. Sin was the salt of life. It required twice as much pluck to practise it as it did to lead an exemplary existence. All who had made a deep mark in history had recognized this principle from Hannibal to Napoleon. And then sometimes he would tilt at received religion, lapsing into bad taste, calling the Trinity a one-legged tripod, enquiring the composition of an angel's wings, attacking bishops and *tutti quanti*, proclaiming himself a devout materialist.

It seemed as though some demon of combativeness were prompting him to act as he was doing, were pushing him on to fly in the face of received opinions. Whither this tendency would lead him, he did not care. He felt he was a power, and he wanted to impose himself upon society as such.

Matters had been going thus at Grosvenor Place all through the winter when one day, in the early spring, an incident occurred which gave Johns a sudden thrill, and awakened him from the state of lethargic indifference into which he had been drifting.

He had gathered round him four friends at luncheon. All save one, who was a needy Viscount whom he sometimes helped, were journalists more or less of the second magnitude. Two of them were men of about his own age, and one, a dramatic critic, was ten years older. He had met them all while he conducted Dawson's journal, and of late he had shown a temporary affection for old friends, many of the new ones having recently shown signs of shyness. Mrs. Johns, looking somewhat pale, occupied the end of the table, and was doing her best to smile pleasantly upon her guests, and to listen with them to the praise which Johns was bestowing upon Spanish art, of which he spoke almost as if he had discovered it. " Velazquez," he was saying, as if he were for ever consecrating him, " was a giant, a colossus, a genius of superhuman strength ! Spain must have been steeped in art to bring forth such a prodigy !" And he was in the act of casting his eyes upwards to emphasize his admiration when, suddenly, a stifled cry was heard, and Mrs. Johns fell backward in her chair.

" By God !" Johns muttered, as he rushed to his wife's side, " she's fainted !"

The three journalists and the Viscount rose at once.

" Ring the bell," Johns said, and the youngest journalist touched the knob in the chimney corner, while the Viscount dipped his finger-napkin into water and handed it to Johns, who applied it to the lips and forehead of the unconscious woman.

The others, rigid in their long frock coats, looked on in silence.

Presently the servants came, and Johns, who was in a state of great excitement, seeing that, in spite of the Viscount's endeavours and his own, his wife did not return to consciousness, cried out to them—

" Go one of you and fetch Dr. Mead."

But presently, when the lady's-maid had unfastened the collar of her mistress's dress and chafed her hands, Mrs. Johns's face became less convulsed, a little colour came back to her lips, and her eyes slowly opened.

Her gaze rested first on the pictures on the walls, then on the round silly face of the young Viscount, and at length upon her husband's.

" Oh, my Johnnie," she sighed, feebly ; " oh, my John ! "

And Johns, whose excitement had suddenly subsided, pressed her hand, exclaiming kindly—

" Why, Rose, what is all this about ? You weren't tired of listening to me, were you ? "

A faint smile overspread her countenance, accentuating the lines of age.

While leaning back against the woodwork of the high chair

in which she generally sat, because it formed a dark background for her face, her hair had been disarranged, and one short lock, released from the knot which held it, was hanging down above her ear. In it a few grey hairs were visible.

But soon, with a woman's apprehension, she raised her hand and tried to adjust the wandering lock which the maid at once attached. She was better; but as she complained of nausea, Johns urged her to retire to her room, whither he promised he would follow her. Almost reluctantly she consented, leaving slowly with her maid.

The party upon this broke up, and the guests, as they left, pressed Johns's hand as if to show their sympathy. Johns, with an expression suited to the occasion, took leave of them, saying, with an air of quiet patronage, "Good-bye, Jameson, good-bye, Charlton; I'll see you again soon, my boys."

When his guests had left, Johns went up to his wife's room. He seldom entered this room now (for more than a year had passed since his wife and he had lived conjugally together), and as he crossed the threshold he thought of the first days of their marriage, of the parody of love he had had to play there. Two objects caught his eye—the vast carved oak bed in which his wife now dreamed of her lost illusions, and above the mantel a portrait of himself in water-colours which he had given her before their marriage.

Stretched in a sofa-chair, Mrs. Johns, wrapped in a rich, pale orange gown, surcharged with lace, was inhaling salts. Her maid was spreading a covering over her feet.

Presently the maid withdrew, and they were left alone.

"Come and sit near me, John," she said in a low voice, as if she were still suffering; "I've something I want to tell you."

He took a chair and placed it near the head of his wife's couch.

"What is it, Rose?" he asked indulgently, almost tenderly, as he sat down.

"Ah," she said, "how I love to hear you speak to me like that!"

The poor woman was so much in need of kindness, that a kindly spoken word came like balm to her troubled feelings. It was a few moments before she said—

"Come closer, my own John, and listen. You remember that I've sometimes told you I was not well."

He nodded.

"Well, my John, I'm afraid it's more serious than I thought."

She paused a moment, glancing at him as if seeking to read

his thoughts, but his face betrayed nothing of what was passing in his mind.

He made a gesture which was meant to reassure her. He was waiting to hear more.

"John, I'm in great trouble," she ejaculated; "I don't know how to tell you what it is. I can't believe it possible! Dr. Mead has not told me all, but I fear it is not difficult to guess."

He looked at her with a glance of rapid scrutiny. Taking her hand, he said, in a serious tone, "What is it, Rose? Tell me all about it. You're needlessly alarmed, perhaps."

"No, John," she answered, sorrowfully, "I fear not."

Still she hesitated, reluctant to speak plainly.

At length, almost in a whisper, as if she feared that someone might overhear her woman's secret, she told him of her grief.

Yes, she had sensations which were unmistakable. The malady had taken root, and already, in spite of the treatment she had undergone, it was making itself felt; it was asserting its power over her. Soon perhaps—ah, must she confess it? soon she would be unable to wear a low-necked dress!

"Really!" said Johns, astonished beyond measure. "I'm sure, Rose, you exaggerate. It's not so bad as that. I'm sure it can't be."

In the surprise which the news caused him, he forgot to show more sympathy, and she glanced at him with tearful eyes.

"Ah," she said, "how I wish it were not!"

"But this is all so sudden, so unexpected, that I cannot realize it, Rose. Tell me more about it. Show me."

But she shook her head regretfully.

"No, John, don't ask me that, not yet!"

He guessed that one of those instinctive feelings which no woman is without caused her to shrink from saying more. He thought it best not to insist. He would know the truth in another way.

"Perhaps," she said, "it may not be so bad as I imagine; but, John, some fearful operation will have to be performed."

He answered, somewhat dubiously, "No, Rose, I shouldn't think so."

But raising herself in her couch and turning towards him, she exclaimed, "John, promise me that whatever happens you will be good to me! It would be too terrible to suffer without a little sympathy, a little love. It's not much I ask you, John, but I want a little, just a little! For the last year I have been so unhappy, for you have turned away from me, from me who loved you so! I have said nothing, believing that my Johnnie would come back to me when he had found that there was no woman in the world who could do so much for him as I, and now, who knows what is to be my fate!"

Suddenly, as she sank back again, her eyes filled with tears and her breast began to heave with suppressed emotion, the muscles of Johns's face gave a nervous twitch.

"Rose," he said, kissing the hand he held in his, "I don't believe you're half so bad as you suppose. In any case, you know that I'm your husband, and that, of course, you can rely upon my care. It would be a little *too* bad if it were otherwise."

She took a sidelong glance at him again as if trying for the second time to guage his thoughts, but he had no intention of betraying them, and for many minutes they remained silent. Johns was thinking of the new aspect which things had taken. His wife was going to be an invalid, and possibly to ——

Suddenly he had a kind of foretaste of approaching freedom, such as prisoners experience on the merest rumour of release, and he closed his eyes, indulging in a dream which, though vague and a little sombre, was yet strangely soothing. Life, after all, was planned for the benefit of those who could enjoy it best. It was singular how mundane matters were ordained. Singular indeed! And his musing ended in a vision of the Colonel's daughter as she had appeared to him on his last visit in the richness of her beauty.

But when he opened his eyes again, and saw his wife pale and sorrowful before him, he thought, "Poor woman!"

And as if she had divined the passing feeling of compassion, she whispered softly, "Kiss me, Johnnie."

He bent over her and placed his lips upon her forehead; but eagerly, as though she wished to prolong the pleasure so visible upon her countenance, she offered him her lips. This time, after a little pause, he kissed them. If what she said were true, he could afford to be more clement now. A knock at the door was heard and a servant entered. He came to say that Dr. Mead was out. But Mrs. Johns declared that she no longer needed him.

As soon as the servant left, Johns said, "Rose, we must see a specialist."

"Oh John," she answered, "I'm so afraid to learn the truth!"

And Johns, who wanted to ascertain, replied, "I'm afraid there is no help for it."

Throughout that evening Johns was untiring in his attention to his wife, dining with her alone in the little boudoir on the ground floor, spending the evening in her company instead of going to the club, answering some letters for her, and speaking to her kindly.

He did this so well, indeed, that Mrs. Johns seemed almost to forget her trouble in the joy of this reconciliation, and when they parted for the night at the door of her own room—for Johns slept on the floor above—she whispered, "Perhaps, John, I may get better."

And Johns thought, as he mounted the flight of stairs, "How they love illusions!"

Yes, it was always so. There was eternally the same striving on the woman's part to obtain man's sympathy, to occupy a man's attention, to bask in the sunshine of a man's tenderness and care. Here was this poor old woman who, by this little kindness, had been made to forget his infidelity and her own ills! Really she was touching in her naïveness and the adoration which she showed him. But it was the old story, the constant striving of Nature to assert herself, the undeviating bent of the woman's mind, filled ever with one central thought to which all others gravitated! All, from the highest to the lowest, wanted to be loved, to be caressed. Incapable of taking any real interest in what men do to become heroes or to earn fame, they rejoiced to be the wives of heroes or celebrities, chiefly because the world envied and admired them. And the love of being envied and admired was sister to the love of being loved. Strange instinctive creatures were these women; but, by God, how useful!

Busied with these reflections, he went to bed.

The next morning he rose earlier than usual. As soon as his valet came, he sent him to inquire if Mrs. Johns had passed a good night, and as the reply was that she had, and would like to see him before he left, he dressed and went down to his wife's room.

He found her still in bed, although a glance told him that her facial toilet had been made in anticipation of his coming.

"And how goes it, Rose, this morning?" he inquired, as he took a seat upon the counterpane.

She had slept, she told him, but was still in pain. Why did he not kiss her?

"She wants," he thought, "to go on where we left off yesterday," and he gave her a kiss upon her forehead.

"I'm going to see the doctor this afternoon," she said, "and entreat him to tell me the whole truth."

"It won't be as bad as you think, Rose, I promise you," he

answered by way of saying something, for his own plan was formed.

"Do you know, John," she said, "I dreamed of you last night. I dreamed I was very, very ill, and that you were nursing me so tenderly that I felt it was almost pleasant to be ill! Say, my John, that if I am to be an invalid, my dream will have come true! Tell me again, with that beautiful deep voice of yours, that if the worst should happen, you will not desert me!"

He thought, "She really gives too much of that," and answered, "Have confidence in me, dear Rose. Have confidence!"

Then, as he was afraid of being forced to listen to more sentiment, he told her he must be at his office early, and left her to her thoughts.

Quickly he breakfasted in the great dining-room, and then left in a hansom, not for Bedford, but for Harley Street.

He wanted to see his wife's practitioner himself, and he thought that at this early hour he had the greatest chance of finding him.

Somehow or other the streets looked gayer, brighter, than they had seemed to him of late. There was a mysterious air of promise in the aspect of the thoroughfares, almost as in the days of his first successes when he began to feel that he was on the road to fortune.

There was promise in the delicious air of spring, promise in the bright blue sky above. Even the loaded omnibuses going citywards with their freight of clerks seemed full of life and action. As he passed a flower shop, a girl with a pretty face and a lithe figure, was arranging bouquets of delicate white roses in the window, and he was about to stop his hansom and alight, so that he might ask the maiden to fill his button-hole when he reflected that, for the visit he was about to pay, a flowered button-hole would be out of place. No, there was a fitness and a time for all things. As the hansom, passing through Cavendish Square, entered the long and sombre street which the Faculty have chosen as their abode, he wondered what this medicine man was going to say. *Was* his wife attacked as she supposed? Yes, he fancied women did not often make mistakes in matters of that kind. But what, after all, if she were? Those doctors had brought their art to such perfection now that very few people died except from accidents or from old age.

The hansom stopped before a house in the middle of the street, and Johns alighted.

The servant who answered the door said that the doctor was at home, and would see Johns presently.

He was shown into a lofty waiting-room furnished with a wealth of morocco and mahogany. A Turkey carpet lay upon the floor, and the walls were hung with mezzo-tints. He took up a copy of the *Times* which was on the table. But almost immediately he threw it down again.

"Curse him, it's yesterday's," he muttered.

And then, thrown into a bad temper by the disappointment, he occupied the time as best he could by walking up and down the gloomy room, swearing that it was a dungeon, vexed that he should be imprisoned in it, thinking that he should not be made to wait like the merest mediocrity.

And at length when, after half an hour, he was ushered into the study of the Æsculapius, he was by no means in an even frame of mind.

Without preamble, after a mere good morning to the tall elderly man with a shaven face who received him affably, he said, "I've not come for myself, doctor, but for my wife. I want to know just what's the matter with her. She says you don't care to tell her."

The doctor, who seemed surprised at the peremptory tone of Johns, opened a book which was before him on his table, and turned over a few pages. He stopped at one which he read over to himself.

"Am I to tell you the exact nature of the case?" he asked.

Johns answered, "If you please."

Johns had taken a chair opposite the window from which a ray of sunlight streamed, brightening the bindings of the books with which the room was lined. The doctor scrutinized him closely as he continued slowly—

"Has Mrs. Johns told you what it is she fears?"

"She has."

"Then I'm afraid I must confirm her apprehensions. The case is serious, and I am glad you've come to see me, for something should undoubtedly be done and soon. We have a rapid growth which it *may* be possible to eliminate, though I am by no means confident. Without telling her the exact nature of the disease, I have mentioned the necessity for an operation. She recoils from the idea."

Not a muscle of Johns's face moved. It was quite useless, he thought, before this scientist, who was a man of the world as well, and who had once dined with them at Grosvenor Place, to simulate emotion.

He answered, "Of course, doctor, whatever you advise will have to be done."

"Quite so, I take it that you will obtain your wife's consent."

"She will give it of her own accord if you explain the danger to her."

"Very well then, Mr. Johns, if you prefer it so, I shall speak to her to-day, when I notice she is coming here to see me. It would be well if you could accompany her."

"I'll come."

And the physician rose to intimate that he was busy, that the interview was over.

Johns, as he was going, asked, "Are such operations dangerous?"

"To be frank with you, they are, although in this case I hope we shall be successful. Whether the operation will be effectual or not, is another matter."

Thus enlightened, Johns left the study.

In a meditative mood he walked to the nearest post office to send a telegram to Rose. He would call for her, he telegraphed, at three.

"By God," he muttered, as he made for Bedford Street, "Rose is in a bad way, a damned bad way!"

Life, he reflected, was marvellously full of change! Who would have suspected, a few days previously, when his wife appeared to him in the light of a perennial tree destined to resist the blight of years, that on this fine spring morning he would be returning from a visit to a doctor who had given him to understand that her life was jeopardised? Ah, well, things were moving quickly for him now!

CHAPTER SIXTEENTH

JOHNS'S uncertainty was set at rest a few weeks afterwards. The operation performed upon his wife had been so far successful that it had not ended fatally, although the doctors had expressed some doubts whether it had proved effectual.

During the days immediately preceding it, Johns had been unremitting in his solicitude. But when the ordeal had been gone through, when it was known that the issue was not destined to be fatal, when he had seen his wife restored to consciousness and heard her murmur, with livid lips and gasping breath, "Oh, John!" he felt as though something had suddenly gone wrong with him, as if some spring of his organization had given way. Ah, there had been strange moments! When the life of the woman to whom his own was linked was trembling in the balance, when none of those who were standing at her bedside, not even the doctors who had used their skill, knew whether she would live or die, he had gone through many a sensation, had experienced many an emotion! And when the result was known, when it was decided that Rose was going to continue living, he had felt but one desire—that of fleeing from the house, of getting away from there! As soon as he had beheld his wife, haggard and aged, as she appeared after she returned to consciousness, he could no longer stay beside her. Quickly he had fled, and had spent the evening with a band of journalists at a tavern in the heart of Fleet Street, celebrating, as he told them with a dubious grin, his wife's recovery. And he had done so with so much vigour, that they had brought him home long after midnight in a state of alcoholic torpor.

The next day, with an aching head, he realized the situation. Now he would have to lead the same old life with a wife who would think herself more interesting than she did before, and who would imagine, like the naive and silly woman that she was, that her illness had been the means of uniting them again. As if he could ever really be the husband of a dilapidation! She would understand *that* when she recovered, surely. The doctor, no doubt, had said that she was not completely out of danger; but who could tell? Doctors were so often wrong!

All through the summer, Johns, tired of making love, sought new sensations in old vintages, and he soon became renowned among his cup companions for his extraordinary capacity for ingurgitation. After a little practice and a strong exercise of will, he was able to absorb large quantities of alcohol without apparent inconvenience. He wanted to be remarkable even in insobriety. For it marked superiority, according to his way of thinking, to have the power of resisting the effect of alcohol. "By God," he would say to those who endeavoured to keep pace with him, "your heads, my friends, are made of a rum sort of stuff!"

One evening, however, he was leaving a restaurant on the Embankment in the company of an erotic poet whose mind was a strange mixture of wit and incoherence, and who had attracted the attention of the public by his eccentricities. Both had been indulging freely, and as they walked arm-in-arm, leaning affectionately towards each other, they indulged in rhetoric.

The evening sun was shedding a mellow light upon the Thames, softening the outlines of the buildings on its banks. The air, after the rain which had fallen in the morning, was light and fresh. It was an ideal afternoon. Pointing to the left bank of the river, Johns, in a tender mood, was saying—

"I tell you, Horace, that there is beauty in those chimneys over yonder! Look at them. Behold the gentle smoke issuing in majestic clouds from the stately orifice. See how it ascends upwards in the most beautiful of spirals, soft and delicate in its shade of tender grey. Horace, why are there no poets to sing the beauties of that smoke, to immortalize that land of industry which looks from here so placid? Ah, Horace, Horace, why is it that you never paint the real, the incomparable real?"

But the friend whom Johns addressed as Horace, a tall man with long curled hair and a shaven face, beside whom he looked strangely dwarfed, replied—

"John, dear John, reality does not exist. Reality is one of those chimeras which are forged by the middle classes to account for elephantine dulness. Reality, dear John, is like that obelisk, an ugly thing, a thing inimical to art. Do you think Praxiteles or any of the divine Greeks descended to the real? No, dear John, they worshipped at the perennial font of fantasy. Ah, no! ah, no! In this land of grocerdom it is not substance we must cultivate, but artifice. We are surfeited with realism. Our lives in this city of brute commerce are made burdensome with the hideousness of trade; we are submerged in a repugnant sea of barter. Our sense of beauty is ever lacerated. Look at the lovely flower which for a brief day is living with me in my button-hole! Do not its tender petals, so reposeful in their pallor, seem to shrink from the crude brutality of yonder land of ugliness? Is it not so perfect that it deserves the praise of being called unreal?"

As he said this, he thrust his large fleshy hand beneath the lappet of his coat, and raised the flower to his lips, exclaiming rapturously—

"Sweet emblem of immaculate perfection, no stockbroker possesses you! You are resting your sweet beauty on the breast of culture! Your radiance is enjoyed by one whose senses vibrate only for true loveliness, whose soul lives on Parnassian slopes, for whom the common herd must ever be as dross! Ah, there's nothing in the world so beautiful as the unreal!"

Johns had listened to this panegyric patiently. He knew, like everybody, the nature of the man; that he had a band of followers who worshipped him, a woman here and there in London whose thoughts and feelings he had utterly capsized, and for some reason which no one had ever clearly understood, he professed to think him a great genius, and supported him in his habitual arraignment of the middle classes, at whom he had, himself, so often tilted. He answered—

"My good Horace, I agree with you. In principle I myself detest vulgarity, but what I meant to say was that there was beauty in that Turneresqueness. Those chimneys, as I see them now, seem anything but mean. Look at them once again, Horace. Observe the majesty with which they rise up to the sky, the grand unrolling of the smoke-cloud which issues from the orifice, and tell me if you do not think those chimneys are suggestive of idealisms such as not even that narcissus in your button-hole can give."

As he said this, Johns made the poet stop. Then, waving his hand in a wave which embraced all that was visible of the other bank, he cried in a vinous voice—

"Say, is it not superb?"

The poet, clutching his companion's arm and leaning on it, looked across the river, down which a steamer, full of passengers, was gliding rapidly.

"John, dear John, I see but chimneys, chimneys—ugly chimneys and a nasty boat."

"Then, to-day you're blind, Horace."

"I'm not blind, John, to-day."

"I say that they're ideal chimneys!"

"And I that they are not!"

They stood gazing at the river, unable to proceed further with their argument, when they suddenly became conscious that an old man in black, with white hair and a shrunk face, carrying a volume under his left arm, was contemplating them.

Recognizing Tarte, Johns said—

"Well, Tarte, what do *you* think of the artistic merit of those chimneys?"

"I think," the old man said, "that you're both looking at them through the spectacles of Bacchus."

"Ancient," the poet said, "you may be right, but know that the rare Falernian we have both been quaffing at that palace of delights above, is of such potent virtue that its effect should be to call forth from its votaries the choicest of their faculties. To-day, I regret to say, its effect upon my friend has not been good. This afternoon it has impaired his vision. Mine, worthy ancient, it has improved."

The old man looked at them for a moment silently. Then, with his arms crossed and the volume brought more forward, he commenced—

"Oh, Sybarites! Oh, Sybarites! You for whom life is one long fête, you who taste the pleasures which are said to make life sweet, do you know that I, an ancient as you call me, hanging on to life by the slender thread of a daily wage, am inclined to pity you?

"I find you here on this sunny afternoon, with your faces flushed and your minds adrift, disputing about chimneys!

"Blind? Yes, certainly you're blind. You can see no farther than the narrow bounds of your magnificence. You can conceive nothing which exists outside your luxury. It has never occurred to you, my friends, to go into that land of industry to see how life is lived there. You have never guessed that there is poetry in that place of toil. No, you could not see it if you went. You could not see it, because you have not measured life with the true measure—the measure of necessity. To you it seems of moment whether there is or is not an artistic motive in that smoke, but I tell you that life, hard, struggling life is there, that poverty is there, that misery is there, and that is what makes it of more interest than smoke.

"Will you ever learn that there is something more than art in life, that the vast majority of men and women do not know it, that they only live to feed and clothe their bodies? Ah, yes, I say to you that if you let art take too much room in life, you will fall victims to it. When the tree of culture has been climbed until the top is reached, a fall is imminent, and that fall is often into the pond of incoherence. Sometimes the road of the cultured hedonist leads to Bedlam, sometimes it leads to Newgate, and in neither of those places are the muses wooed, my friends. If either of you take one or the other of those roads, you'll be worse off than I, the Philistine, whose days are destined to be ended in a select establishment of paupers.

"If you knew how empty life can seem to a man like me who knows it! If you knew how useless all of you appear to me, and how I see the pleasures which you prize—I who yet have never tasted one of them! Do not think that envy prompts me. I envy no man. Life passes before my eyes as a race to annihilation. I don't know whence I came; I have no knowledge whither I may go when my organism ends. I desire nothing, I hope nothing, and I fear nothing. Long ago I would have retired from the game had not my meagre pittance served to keep alive another, more attached to life than I.

"But yesterday I buried her, and now death is not far from me. I feel it in the air, it whispers warnings in my ears. I see it in my mirror, and I feel it in my gait. Perhaps it will overtake me before I reach that home of indigence in the sweet Surrey hills where a man can feel himself decay in ease. Whenever it may be, I'm ready. If there be a God, as this old missal, which I've bought for sixpence, says there is, he ought to think me a deserving person; for I have never sinned. My body will leave the world as pure as it came into it. Oh, Sybarites, remember that pleasure, culture, art, are mere delusions fraught with peril!"

Saying this, without even taking leave, and after placing his russet volume under his arm again, he moved away, leaving them to their reflections. After a moment the poet asked—

"Who is that melancholy person?"

Johns answered, "Oh, only an old devil on an evening paper."

"He is an example," pursued the poet, "of the infirmity of sense-perception which afflicts some men who have never known the higher things. I shall write a poem on his singular perversity."

Johns did not reply, and they resumed their walk.

In a few moments they reached a turning leading to the Strand, and here they parted.

But the words of Tarte had caused Johns to stop and think, and to take himself to task. He was slipping into foolish habits, into habits which, if not stopped in time, might make a slave of him. Rather than be tied to liquor, he would put himself upon cold water. There was some truth in what old Tarte had said; there was a danger of getting soft in leading this emollient life of pleasure. He must pull himself together, discipline himself. He wanted to climb higher, not to descend lower. He realized that there was something wise enough in the practice of respectability, and that Bohemianism was a dissolvent he would do better to avoid.

Horace was very well in his own way, but he wasn't a man to be seen with often, for though he had the thoughts and bearing of a genius, and though he (Johns) had pronounced him to be one, there was an instability about the man which made him a person to be frequented with caution. Moral unconsciousness might be very well, but there was a way in things, and Horace, with his vices and his mannerisms, went too far. In short, he recognized that there was danger not only in the companionship of Horace, but also in the band of casual inebriates whom, in his *tædium vitæ*, he had gathered round him. A change there must be. Johns ordered it, and it was Johns's duty to obey.

Henceforward he placed himself upon a régime of a pint of claret daily, and when his cup companions called, he was invariably "out."

In the meantime his wife's convalescence proceeded slowly. Each day he was forced to spend a few hours with her, listening to the projects for the future which she was always making as she lay upon her back in the French sofa-chair. They would not leave England for the Continent until the winter, when they would spend six months on the Riviera. There she would soon regain her strength, and he would see how much better she would look now that a weight was off her mind. He had not known her as she could be, because, at first, she had fancied he was cold towards her, and a woman never looked her best when she was troubled. But he had been so good when she was ill that she forgave him gladly now. She felt that he would never be unkind again. He knew how much she loved him. And he would listen to her, smoking indolently, wondering whether there were any bounds to the credulity of women, and thinking that, after all, it was not a very great achievement on his part, to have persuaded such a silly woman to become his wife.

And during the weeks which, at the end of the summer, he was obliged to pass at Eastbourne with his wife, Johns occupied himself in riding, in conducting his Review, and in writing long letters in his finest prose to Edith Douglas, whose father had taken her suddenly to Norway before they had had time to say good-bye. He put into those letters all his admiration, all the longing of his youth for a consort who should be young and beautiful. He told her of the illness of his wife, but without exulting over it, and with good taste, letting it be seen, however, that he was sorrowful and lonely. And as he poured into these letters all the tenderness he knew, and as in writing he could be particularly tender, he produced epistles that were calculated to arouse the young girl's feelings to the utmost. He told her he was jealous of the people she would meet in her journey to the North, jealous of the merest stranger who would be struck with admiration at her beauty, jealous of the midnight sun which was destined to behold it. Ah, why had he not met her sooner? Why was there this barrier between them? For how long would they be separated thus? He was tortured at the thought that she would be induced to become engaged in spite of her resolve, and he vowed that if she did, he would break his bonds, and then—ah, then——! But yet there might be happiness in store for them. It was not certain that he would be for ever tied. He had some information which he could not well impart, but which contained a possibility of something happening which would make him free. But he scarcely dared to think of it. The issue was too great.

And in reality he was in love with her, far more in love than he had ever been before, chiefly because she resisted him, because of her quiet air of candour, and of her bright intelligence, which was so distinctly feminine. Yes, she was the true embodiment of the ideal he had always formed.

She answered him with more fervour than she had shown before, letting her strong attachment be apparent in every line she wrote, but delicately, and with a half malicious coyness. Her descriptions of the places she had visited and the incidents of the journey they were making were full of charm and freshness, and they were made with that woman's touch which men can never imitate. This correspondence was a change for Johns, tired as he was of easy conquests, and it served to render life endurable at an hotel full of uninteresting people. His wife, delighted at the resignation which he showed, made brave attempts to regain her health. But her recovery was slow, and neither the long drives she took each day on the coast roads and along the front nor the care she bestowed upon herself advanced it much. She still looked aged and worn, and she was so well aware of this that when Johns assured her she was looking better, she shook her head—a circumstance which caused him to reflect, " She *can't* be well if she isn't ready to admit it." But after they had passed six weeks thus, Mrs. Johns declared that Eastbourne did not suit her, and that she would like to return to town. Johns acquiesced, the more readily as Edith Douglas was returning the same week, and he wanted to see her before he left with his wife for the Riviera.

They returned, therefore, in the middle of September, and during the month preceding their departure, they lived very quietly, receiving only their most intimate friends. Mrs. Johns did not want to undergo fatigue, and Johns was busy with his own affairs. He had consented to this long absence, partly because the idea of the Riviera pleased him, partly because he did not know how he could decently refuse to accompany his wife in her condition. There were always the Stanfields to be thought of, and though, at the bottom of his heart he cordially detested them, he recognized that they were a power, and he had a kind of respect for them as such.

But Edith Douglas did not return as soon as he had expected. Her father had been taken ill on the journey home, and she had had to remain many weeks at Christiania with him. Johns, in the meantime, consoled himself in the society of Mrs. Weber, whom he was always glad to see after an absence of some length, although he tired of her when he saw her too repeatedly. She, on her part, had become reconciled to his infidelity, and would often say to him, "John, you're a faithless wretch, but you'll always return to me." And he would answer, when he was in a mood to be pleased with her, " By God, Ellen, I believe you're right."

She represented to him the perfection of ripe womanhood, and by comparison he had come to know her staple value. She knew his habits also, and he was well aware that she admired him sincerely. Altogether he was glad when the Wednesday came—the day when they generally met. Was she faithful to him? He didn't know. He had been told that an ancient baronet was a frequent caller at her house, and that they had been seen together in the summer on the river; in fact, that the baronet had succeeded Parker. But he refrained from asking her, feeling that, after all, she had a right to make provision for herself. He didn't want to stand in the way of her doing it. Besides, a man of over sixty! What *did* it matter?

The remainder of the time preceding his departure for the South was occupied in making arrangements for a lengthy absence, in giving instructions to his lieutenants for the conduct of the Review, and in winding up some little love affairs which had previously diverted him in moments of caprice.

At length, shortly before the day fixed for the flight to the Riviera, he received a note from the Colonel's daughter, acquainting him with her return, and bidding him come to see her on the Sunday.

Johns did not need to be asked twice, and when the Sunday came, scrupulously dressed, after a lengthy consultation with his valet, for whose experience in great houses he had respect, he jumped into a hansom and was driven to Lexham Gardens.

As he ascended the stairs, preceded by the maid, his quick eye was attracted by the threadbare patches in the stair carpets which were more or less in keeping with the want of luxury he had previously observed throughout the house, and he reflected, "It's a pity they're so poor." But the thought was soon dispelled when he reached the drawing-room and found the young girl waiting for him alone.

Never, since he had known her, had she looked so beautiful. A flush of health was on her slightly sun-browned cheeks; the oval of her face was firm and perfect; her eyes were full of lustre, and her figure, which had been somewhat over slight before, had become a little rounder, a little more pronounced. She seemed to Johns the fairest woman he had ever seen.

Advancing to where she was seated on a low sofa, he took her hand and pressed it to his lips. She said, with a happy smile, " I'm truly glad to see you. My father is in his room, and I expect no visitors, so we can have a long, long chat."

"For ten weeks," he answered, "I have been looking forward to this day." Then they exchanged confidences. She told him all the little incidents of travel which she had omitted to narrate in writing, and of the indisposition of her father—a chill caught in an excursion—which had detained them at Christiania, and she ended by confessing that the day when she had found his letters waiting for her there, was not the least delightful of the trip. He wrote such admirable ones! She liked his letters as much as his little tales. They were full of the same personality and the same charm. It was alone worth travelling to receive such treats.

Then he told her of his wife's convalescence, of his projects for the conduct of his magazine, of his resolve to drop his bibulous companions as she herself had advised him once to do. But when he announced to her that he was leaving with his wife next day for the whole winter, a look of disappointment overspread her face.

"For the whole winter!" she repeated.

Yes, they would not return until the spring. What was he to do? His wife was still an invalid, and had entreated him not to leave her to the care of strangers. And his wife *was* his wife, and had, he supposed, some claim upon him. But perhaps he would come back before her. Perhaps, if she made progress, he would return alone in a few months' time, and then they would see each other often. Then he would give a party at his house—an original kind of party, at which there would be no hostess, only a dowager for propriety—but to which he would invite none but pretty women, so that she might be the queen among them—she whose beauty was so unsurpassable. But whether he returned or not, she must not despair. He had written her that he possessed some knowledge which might alter destiny for them, and she would understand its nature when he told her that it proceeded from the doctor. He knew she would not like him to say more.

"You understand me, Edith, don't you?"

"Yes," she said, reflectively, "I understand, and you need not explain. But, tell me, supposing that that 'something' happened, will you promise faithfully that you would marry me?"

"Promise you?" he repeated, bending forward and speaking low, "I pledge my life that nothing upon earth would then prevent me from making you my wife."

Then, drawing nearer, he continued—

"Could you for a moment doubt it? Ah, you do not know how I have thought and dreamed of you as the only woman who could complete my life, the only woman I could ever love! You do not realize that you have chained me with the gentlest, yet the strongest of all chains, to break which would be a crime! You have not learnt how deep my passion is, or you would not ask me that!"

He looked so earnest, so sincere, as he murmured this in impressive tones, that, apparently convinced of his sincerity, she said—

"Forgive me, I believe you! You need fear nothing while you are away. No one shall supplant you, John."

Oh, how he wanted to thank her for that word! What could he do to express his gratitude? How could he put it into words?

Had she been an ordinary woman, he would have been already by her side reciting his little formula, but Edith Douglas was not an ordinary woman, and he feared lest he might spoil all by a false move. He looked at the vacant place upon the sofa, and then entreatingly at the young girl; but she, interpreting his gestures, rose from the place of danger on the couch and took a chair, in which she seemed to feel in safety.

"Why are you so hard?" he asked, his face convulsed with unassumed emotion. "Why, on this last evening for so long, am I not allowed a respite from that cruel discipline?"

"Simply because I happen to possess my own notions of some things, and they forbid me to become what is called a semi-maiden. It may be that I'm old-fashioned, but I've made a very firm resolve, if I ever marry, to do so without a single active flirt upon my conscience."

He knew these cases of feminine scrupulosity, and was aware how hard they were to deal with.

"Well, well," he said, "I must continue to regard you as a picture too rare and beautiful to touch."

Without noticing this last remark otherwise than by a little frown, she said, "Tell me, have you been good to your wife while she was ill? I could not bear to think that you were not. Poor woman, I have felt so sorry for her!"

But he protested that he had done all that a model husband could, "even," he said, "at the risk of earning too much gratitude."

"How she must love you!" she exclaimed.

"Yes," Johns answered, with a queer expression, "and that's the worst of it."

She said, "You see ambition must be paid for."

"It must indeed! When I was younger I imagined that wealth could give me happiness, but I was quickly undeceived. Since I met you, Edith, I have realized that money counts for very little, that beauty such as yours is the only good. Ah, why did we not meet sooner?"

There was a pause, during which she looked into his face intently as if she were trying to gather an impression from it. At length she said, "I hope that those strange dark eyes of yours are truthful."

And he remembered that evening in the early days when Mrs. Weber had asked him the same question. It was curious how women's minds all ran in the same groove.

"Is it possible," he answered, "that you should still have doubts?"

Again she asked him to forgive her. She ought not to be so distrustful. She would try to mend. She wanted earnestly to have confidence.

Then, in an accent of subdued passion he began to tell her of the bright dreams he sometimes formed. With her as his wife, he dreamed of a great political career, of places conquered rapidly and brilliantly, of the delights of power, of the joys of influence, of distinctions which would shed a halo round her beauty, which would make her the most envied of the women of her time. Oh, it was all planned! Their party wanted a man like him, a man who wasn't afraid to speak his mind, who could hit hard when hard hitting was required, who could beard the lions of democracy and socialism. And in the life which he imagined, it would not be all work. They would travel frequently and far—not as mere superficial tourists, but as persons to whom all doors were open, for whose intelligence there were no sealed books. He would show her the old world and the new—Italy with her Cæsarean and her Papal Rome, her Veroneses and her Botticellis; Greece with her memories, her inalienable classicity; Spain with her semi-Moorishness, her marvellous Escorial, her Murillos, her Velazquez. Later, when the conquest of a great position was achieved, they would explore the East and make it yield to them its secrets and its charms. What a life of infinite expansion, of boundless satisfaction, it would be, and how he loved to dream of it!

She closed her eyes as if to realize the picture he had drawn, and then she answered, thoughtfully—

"Yes, it would be glorious!"

"It will happen, Edith. I have a presentiment it will."

"Perhaps," she murmured, dreamily.

Johns stayed talking to her until late in the afternoon, and when at length, his rhetoric exhausted, he was leaving, she said with more earnestness than he had seen her show before—

"Write to me often, very often!"

Keeping her hand a prisoner in his, he promised that he would. He would tell her everything, his thoughts, his acts, his joys, his sorrows—every little incident, all that happened, and as often as he dared he would send her roses from that land of flowers.

But just as he was bidding her adieu for the last time, he fancied suddenly he detected something in the lustre of her eye, in the intense expression of her face, which seemed encouraging.

Then suddenly, without a word of warning, and before she could resist, he caught her in his arms and kissed her.

"Now," he exclaimed, as she disengaged herself, "now, whatever fate may have in store for us, I shall know that I have been the first to press those lips."

Flushed and serious, she said—

"You would have done better to have refrained."

"You're not angry with me, Edith!"

"Not as angry as I should be, but not pleased, and don't think you have gained anything. My resolution is unchanged."

Falling on his knees before her, he implored forgiveness. He had been unable to resist a sudden impulse which had come upon him like an avalanche, against which his will was powerless. Ah, the fault was not altogether his. Beauty such as hers was not without its perils. It could not be always passively beheld. But he would place a curb upon himself in future. She would have nothing more to fear. Only he would not go from there until she had absolved him.

With a smile she told him that she would not absolve him unless he rose at once. Then, springing to his feet again, he thanked her warmly, and, after pressing her hand for the last time, he left.

A few minutes later, as he was rolling in a hansom back to Grosvenor Place, he thought, "I *have* been laying it on thickly *this* time. She's so superb! It's a pity, though, that they're so poor!"

The next day Johns and his wife crossed the Channel.

After a night spent in Paris, where Mrs. Johns wished to rest, they took the train the next evening at the Lyons terminus for Cannes.

Carefully wrapped in furs, although the weather was not cold, and thickly veiled, Mrs. Johns, as she stood upon the platform, looked more than matronly, and Johns thought, as he glanced at her amid the gay and fashionable crowd of people fleeing from northern skies to the land of sunshine, that everyone must take her for his mother. Well, so much the better if they did!

The platform teemed with notabilities in travelling costume. Near them Johns recognized the tall figure of an ambassador whom he had once met, and who returned his bow with cold politeness. A little further off, he saw an eminent French, novelist whose works of keen analysis he knew. He was accompanied by a young and rising poet of whom the French Parnassus had great hopes. An English lord, with a numerous family of sons and daughters, was standing before the bookstall, gay with its wealth of yellow covers, and was buying the London papers. An English general, who had lately earned distinction in South Africa, accompanied by a young and pretty wife, was surveying the scene with an expression of amused contentment. At the carriage doors, friends and relatives were taking leave in many languages, and amid the bevy of French ladies, fitly and elegantly dressed for travelling, there were one or two whose grace and beauty made Johns sigh. What would he have given at that moment to have been standing on that station with a young and pretty woman with whom he was to spend some happy months at Cannes!

But the hour of departure was at hand, and the officials were calling upon the travellers to take their seats. Those who had lingered on the platform now clambered up to the high carriages to take their seats. In a few minutes, after a brief discussion between the stationmaster and the guard, the signal was given, and the train crept slowly off.

Johns, who had been looking out of the window, amused at a parting scene between a young Frenchman and his wife or mistress, felt himself touched upon the shoulder. It was Rose who wanted to know which of the berths in the sleeping-car he wished to occupy. What did it matter to him? he answered, rather roughly. She must take the one she liked. And then, as they were alone in the compartment, he sat down discontentedly, and watched her make her preparations for the night. The sight of the fair women on the station had put him into a bad temper, and he saw her open her dressing-case and take from it an infinity of pins and puffs and cosmetics, which told their tale so plainly, with a feeling of irritation. Truly, he thought with bitterness, truly it was lamentable to see her thus exhibiting the accessories she used to hide her age, which he had ascertained was nearly fifty, just as though he had been a husband who had grown old with her, and from whom she did not take the trouble to hide anything. Oh, what tactless creatures, after all, these women were! But she, as if she had guessed his thoughts, suddenly replaced the objects in the dressing-case, and continued to prepare for the night's journey by taking off her cloak and shoes, loosening her corset, and taking off her skirt. She had refused to let her maid travel with her in the sleeping-car, and therefore she was obliged to assist herself.

Presently, when she had loosened her golden locks and sprinkled some scent upon the pillow, she laid herself in her berth, and, with a tender accent, asked Johns to spread a rug upon her.

Slowly he arranged the rug, and as he was doing so she

gazed at him tenderly, saying in the voice which since her illness had grown weaker—

"Ah, John, I feel I shall get strong again down there."

He answered carelessly, "Why not?"

He resumed his seat, and, drawing from his pocket a packet of Parisian newspapers, began to read them by the faint light to put an end to further conversation.

But after a while she said, "I feel so sleepy, Johnnie. Kiss me before I go to sleep," and he, suppressing an imprecation, was obliged to rise again and pretend to touch her forehead with his lips. He knew that he might have refused to do so, but his experience had convinced him that nothing is more foolish than to offend a women for a trifling cause. There was always danger enough in doing so when great issues were at stake. For the second time he resumed his seat, and as the train, which had now acquired speed, was flying southward, shrieking in its course, he was left to his reflections.

This, then, was the kind of happiness which was to be derived from a marriage such as his! Here he was, in the full vigour of his manhood, condemned to travel and to live with a woman who seemed to become more frivolous, more stupid, as the days went by. This was what riches without liberty implied! If she only had been young, he would have forgiven her, even if she had been plain! A young woman had always freshness in her favour; she spread around her the subtle perfume of her youth, was never altogether without charm, while Rose, that faded rose whose bloom had lasted for so long, was wearisome to see. And riches were, after all, so relative! It was true that he possessed enough to gratify his minor whims and fancies; it was true he lived in a big house and was waited on by many servants, but he knew scores of richer men than he, whose scope of influence was immeasurably greater than his own. Had *he* that potent prestige which men possessed whose fortunes caused them to be respected, flattered, feared for the benefits that they were able to bestow on those who won their favour? Did he enjoy that kind of second royalty which enabled such to force their tastes, their prejudices, upon the crowd? No, certainly, he didn't—he who could not properly afford a yacht!

Tired at length of these reflections, he continued reading the *Gil Blas*, a journal whose Gallic salt amused him; and as he read, he became engrossed in a little story of Parisian life told by one of those brilliant artists of the salacious style who weave impressionisms on the theme of love. The writer had depicted in vivid and alluring colours an episode in the existence of a beautiful young peasant girl in one of the valleys of Touraine, a lass who had conceived a passion for a mere lad too young and naïve at first to be responsive to her longing, but whom, by displaying all the grace and beauty with which she had been gifted, she succeeded at length in dazzling and winning. The little narrative breathed nature in its most unvarnished state, and had a flavour of rustic freshness which, rendered with unerring skill, threw Johns into a pleasant reverie, from which he was aroused by a dry, grunting sound he knew too well.

His wife had fallen into a profound sleep, and in spite of the noise which the train was making as it rattled on the rails, her snore was audible.

"Sweet soul!" he muttered, as he folded up the paper, glancing at his wife, who was breathing with her mouth wide open; "truly she's divine."

Upon this, with a smile of irony upon his lips, he divested himself of his outer garments and turned into his own berth.

The next morning when he awoke he looked out of the window of the car.

The dawn had broken over the brown land of Provence, and the first rays of the rising sun were shedding a weird light upon the olive groves, upon the pale-grey rocks and wastes of the fleeting landscape, upon the leaves of the giant aloes. Dispelling the dark shadows projected by the trees and hedges, the rays increased in their intensity until the whole country was bathed in light—in light which was softened by the sombre green of the dark foliage and the brown parched vegetation.

Now it was a peaceful village—stone-walled, red-tiled—which the train flew past with a rapid whisk, now the ancient town of Provence with its fortress, its cathedral, and its bridge, then the country appeared again.

Upon Johns, who found himself in it for the first time, this land of troubadours and eclogues produced a great impression. He felt as if he had emerged into a region full of promise. It seemed to him as if the swift express were bearing him towards joys he had not known before, towards some new and bright experience which had not come to him as yet. Illusion, it might be, but as he gazed at these southern landscapes, he felt himself invigorated.

But the spell, alas! was broken when a familiar voice in the next berth murmured—

"Where are we, Johnnie?"

CHAPTER SEVENTEENTH

ON the afternoon of their arrival, Johns, leaning over the railing of the balcony of a suite of rooms on the first floor of the hotel, was looking at the scene before him.

At his feet were the grounds of the palatial building, with their tall, thick pine trees diffusing aromatic freshness, their fan-shaped palms glistening in the sun, their flower-beds and lawns. Beyond, and plainly visible through the opening amid the trees, the great calm lake, placid as a mirror, vied with the sky in blueness. At a short distance from the land, the island of St. Marguerite, with its romantic castle, its air of solitude and mystery, was peacefully reposing in the waveless sea, oblivious of the white-sailed fishing-boat beneath it, waiting for a breeze to take it past the group of the Lérins. A little to the right, the mountains of the Estèrel, partly hidden by the foliage, exhibited their peaks bathed in a thousand shades of purple and of blue. The air was full of fragrance, and a grateful stillness reigned.

To Johns, this azure coast appeared as an earthly paradise. It was the spot designed, he thought, by nature, to be the most perfect of all lover's nooks—a spot where life could be enjoyed by all the senses in the highest measure of enjoyment, where women's beauty must be doubly beautiful, where the tedium and the banality of life must be unfelt. Ah, if ever he were free, how often he would seek this favoured corner of the world!

As his wife, indisposed after the night journey, had retired, he entered the room again, intending to take a stroll, when a servant came to say that a gentleman named St. George had called. Somewhat surprised, Johns said that he would see the gentleman at once. The man left, and a moment afterwards

St. George, attired in a light grey suit, appeared. He said, as he advanced into the room—

"I saw your name just now, dear Johns, on the list of visitors downstairs, and I came up."

Johns, who had not seen or heard of his friend for many months, pointing to a seat, replied—

"So this was where you were, you truant! What are you doing here?"

"I'm merely basking in the sun like everyone."

But Johns eyed him narrowly.

"I don't believe, St. George, you're only here for that. Are you sure you're quite alone?"

"Oh, quite."

"You're mysterious, St. George!"

The young man laughed, and by way of answer, asked, "How is Mrs. Johns?"

"She's pretty well, thanks. She's resting after last night's journey. But you've not yet told me what you're doing here, you rogue!"

St. George looked round the little room, with its gilded clock upon the mantel, its fluted ceiling, and its yellow hangings and upholstery. Then, after a few moments' hesitation, he burst out—

"Why should I hesitate to tell you, Johns? We're old friends and can trust each other. Listen. Things have not been going very well for me of late. Since I was refused by Edith Douglas, I've been floating about the world in a rather moody frame of mind, and spending and losing a lot of money. At Monte Carlo I lost £7000, and a dramatic lady, of whom I was naïve enough to be enamoured, relieved me, in one way and another, of nearly half as much again, so that, as I was never a rich man, I'm reduced now to the bare necessities. But a little while ago, as I was finishing the summer at Montreux, thinking what a fool I'd been, I met a family who interested me greatly. The family was composed of two—a father and an only daughter. The father, I soon learnt, was a financial person who had retired from business with a million. The daughter was a little girl of about twenty, with a pleasant face and plenty of accomplishments. Well, to cut my story short, I did my best at once to enter into the good graces of these favoured people, and I was so successful, that when they announced their intention of passing the winter at Cannes, I announced mine of following their example. At the present moment we're all staying at this hotel, and as I've become a convert to your doctrines about money, and the little heiress is.

not altogether unattractive, I'm laying a patient siege to her affections. *Now* you know why I am here."

Johns had been listening to this speech with marked attention, moving once or twice in his chair restlessly while doing so, conscious of a feeling of uneasiness, almost of envy, for the prize which was perhaps about to fall to his friend St. George. Without letting his thoughts betray themselves, however, he said—

"Well, St. George, I wish you luck."

"I knew you would, Johns. But not a word to anyone of what I've told you."

"Of course not. Not a syllable."

And then St. George, carried away by his enthusiasm, told his friend of the excursions he had made with Miss Wilson and her father, of the evening talks upon the terrace, and of their games of draughts in the *salon* afterwards—of his hopes, in short, that he would be accepted when he judged the moment opportune to ask her hand. Johns smiled approvingly, and remarked with apparent unconcern—

"And you say the father is a millionaire?"

"More than a millionaire. He made a colossal stroke ten years ago, and he's lived like a prince since then. Besides a fine house in Park Lane, they've a perfect castle in Northamptonshire, and she's the only child."

"And so you think you're on the right track, St. George?"

"I hope so, Johns; there's only the father, who is a little hard to please."

For a few moments Johns was silent. Then he handed to his friend the box of cigarettes which was lying on the table. St. George took a cigarette, and they resumed the conversation, which drifted to other subjects. But when St. George had been there half an hour, he looked up suddenly at the clock upon the mantel and exclaimed, as he rose from his chair—

"It's time for the promenade. She's sure to be there this afternoon, and I wouldn't miss her for the world."

Johns, rising also, answered—

"I'll go with you, St. George. I'm curious to see this little person."

St. George expressed himself delighted, although he scarcely looked so, and they left.

Passing out by the side door of the hotel, they took the road which led to the old town, and walked along arm-in-arm. St. George, chatting gaily, pointed out the celebrities they met—the princes, the grand dukes, and the heirs-apparent (some of

s

whom Johns knew by sight), and the galaxy of minor stars who follow in their wake.

About each he had an anecdote to tell, some little scandal he had heard since he had been at Cannes, or some gossip he had gleaned about the Prince.

And Johns listened, interested, for, at the bottom of his heart, he had a lurking admiration for royal persons—the respectful admiration of the lower classes for people of high birth. At the street corners, and at different points along the route, they met ambassadors and statesmen, potentates and artists, poets and financiers, some accompanied by ladies, and all wearing that indulgent, self-contented air which the Riviera seems to lend.

Johns, amid this collection of celebrities, felt himself suddenly belittled, and realized acutely, for a moment, how very small his own position was, compared with that of the majority of these great people. If he were only really rich as they! But no, he felt he was a very minor figure there.

Passing by the old harbour, they reached the commencement of the Croisette, the crescent-shaped promenade which curves so picturesquely.

The first person whom they met was a lady they both knew well. She was middle-aged, rigid in her bearing, and her face, the colour of old parchment, wore a judicial look about its lower portion and was curiously relieved by a pair of light blue eyes. The two friends recognized the semi-comic physiognomy of Lady Vieille, who, they both knew, bore a well-earned reputation for excessive rudeness. She was accompanied by a girl of about sixteen, who seemed to be her daughter.

Johns whispered to his companion, "Don't stop," and they passed along, raising their hats and bowing rather low, for they both knew that Lady Vieille, who dabbled in literature and who had some sort of a literary drawing-room, was apt to be vindicitive.

And St. George, after they had passed, told Johns laughingly of the lady's latest freak, that of inviting stray acquaintances to lunch any day they liked to choose, and then, when anybody not of primary importance was foolish enough to go to Harvey Street on such an invitation, to request him, through the butler, to be good enough to come again another day.

Johns shrugged his shoulders.

Then they met the owner of a New York journal, a tall man with a red face, who was leading by a string a little dog whose body-cloth was studded with precious stones. St. George explained that if this eccentric millionaire was there that evening, "the Prince," whom he worshipped, must be expected on the promenade.

Contemptuously, Johns said, " Poor snob ! "

But the sun had begun to set in a conflagration of intense beauty. Its glowing rays penetrated far into the deep blue sky above, and were reflected on the leaves of the palm trees in the plantations, upon the walls of the old fortress in the distance, and upon the faces of the promenaders. Everything which met the eye was softened, was transfigured. For a few moments of extreme splendour the scene was of such striking beauty that it caused Johns to ejaculate—

" By God, how fine ! "

St. George said, " Isn't it ! " and they walked along in silence for some distance. Then, as they were approaching the extremity of the Croisette, St. George suddenly pressed his friend's arm and said in a low though excited tone—

" Here they are. They're coming."

A few yards in front of them, a young girl, rather below the average height, with a round healthy face, a little nose inclining upwards, a small and rather well-arched mouth, a pair of inexpressive dark-brown eyes and hair to match, was accompanying a short stout man of about sixty, whose light, pointed beard, was turning grey and beginning to give a stamp of age to a somewhat plebeian set of features, mainly expressive of prudent foresight. The daughter was admirably dressed in a perfectly-fitting brown costume, with a straw hat of the same colour half-hidden beneath a veritable garden of well-blended flowers. The father wore a short dark double-breasted coat, rather light check trousers, and a soft felt hat. St. George shook hands with each in turn, cordially with the young girl, but rather timidly with the father. After this he introduced his friend.

" My friend, Mr. Johns, the editor of the *Centenary Review*."

Johns made a profound bow to the father and the daughter, which was returned politely. Then, after a few words, as they were all returning the same way, the party divided itself naturally into pairs. St. George and the young girl went on in front ; Johns and the father followed.

Johns, not knowing with what theme to break the ice, started that of Cannes, asking the father's opinion of the hotel at which they were both staying, what he thought of the climate of the Riviera, and which were the best drives in the vicinity. He appeared to attach much weight to the answers he received, although he kept his eyes fixed upon St. George and his companion, trying to discover, from what he could see of the expressions of their faces, on what terms they were. The father, Johns noticed, maintained a species of reserve which somewhat disconcerted him, and made him wonder if the millionaire had heard any of the stories which he knew were floating about London as to his career. But no, most probably he was a dry Saxon whose words had to be pulled out of him one by one. He knew the type, he fancied.

"Are you here alone?" the elderly man inquired, after they had exhausted local topics.

"No," Johns answered calmly, watching the effect his words produced, "my wife is with me, only she's somewhat indisposed this afternoon."

After a moment, when he had seen Miss Wilson look up at St. George with a glance of sympathy, he added—

"My wife, Mr. Wilson, is very fond of young society, she will be glad to make the acquaintance of your daughter."

Wilson answered, in a more amiable tone than he had hitherto adopted—

"My daughter will, I'm sure, be pleased."

They continued thus, until they reached the end of the Croisette. By this time the promenade was nearly empty, and the island of St. Honorat was beginning to look dark in the waning light.

Consulting his watch, Wilson said that it was growing late, and they started on their way back to the hotel still in the same order. During the walk Wilson sufficiently unbended to give Johns a description of the visit he had paid to Egypt the previous winter, when he had been decorated by the Khedive for the presents he had made of English cattle to improve the native breed, and Johns, who knew something about cattle, was able to make apposite remarks.

When they reached the hall of the hotel they separated, agreeing to meet again at dinner.

"Well," said St. George, as soon as they were alone, "what do you think of them?"

"Oh, merely ordinary people, apart from what you say they're worth. I should think, St. George, she'd be an easy conquest."

St. George looked slightly dubious. He said, "With the daughter I'm getting on very well, but the father's a terrible old man, and gives me hints sometimes that he has higher aims. He positively makes me nervous."

"Timid fool!" thought Johns, and saying that he must go up to his wife, he left St. George to his reflections.

Johns found his wife still in her room, a large square room, elegantly furnished, where he had left her in the afternoon.

She was lying on her bed covered over with a rug, and her face, as Johns observed it against the dark red curtains of the French bedstead, looked pale and worn.

"Well, Rose," he said, indulgently, "how are you feeling now?"

She said that she was better, that she would be quite well the next day. But she would not dine with him at the *table d'hôte* that evening, as her mirror told her she was not looking at her best.

"We women, you know, dear John, are a little sensitive about our looks."

He said, "Quite right, Rose, it's better to rest to-day, and surprise us all to-morrow."

Then he told her of St. George's visit, of his walk with him, and of these Wilsons to whom he had been introduced, whom he was certain she would like, and who owned one of those fine fortunes which gave them, in spite of their mediocrity, a certain standing. The little girl was not exactly pretty, but she seemed to have pleasant manners. It would be well to make friends with them.

Mrs. Johns said she would be glad to know the Wilsons, especially as they were staying at the hotel.

Johns then passed into his own room. There he dressed. And he hurried down again as the hall bell was ringing.

At the entrance to the long and lofty dining-room, with its high curtained windows, its palms, and its lengthy table decked with fruit and flowers, Johns met the Wilsons and St. George. He explained his wife's absence on the score of slight indisposition, and Wilson said—

"We have a reserved table in the corner, Mr. Johns, and if you will share it with us we shall be pleased."

The daughter, with a pleasant smile, seemed to second her father's invitation, and Johns readily accepted. The Wilsons' table was a small one at the extreme end of the long room. Johns, seated on the right hand of Wilson, faced the dark young girl, who was tastefully attired in a high dinner dress with a profusion of bows and ribbons. From where he was was placed, he could see the entire room. More than two-thirds of the visitors, he perceived at once, were English. The remainder, chiefly French, were clustered together as if for mutual support at the end of the table near the door, looking like travellers in a strange country—the sound of their native tongue being drowned in the greater din of English voices. The men among them were particularized by being in frock coats, while the Englishmen were nearly all in evening dress.

Johns saw, to his satisfaction, that a little sensation had been caused in the English section on his entrance, and that many a glance was directed towards him. He had been recognized, was known. Nothing could cause him greater satisfaction.

During the dinner, while the long *menu* was being served under the stern eye of the *maître d'hôtel*, Johns allowed the conversation to drift on generalities, often engaging in a colloquy with Wilson upon finance or agriculture, while St. George talked with his neighbour upon what was happening at Cannes.

Throughout the meal, however, Johns glanced at Miss Wilson, now and then with a sympathetic, half-melancholy reflective glance, as if he were thinking over the destiny in store for her in life, and sometimes, as their eyes met, she would look down quickly, shyly. Johns had come to the conclusion that the nature of the ordinary woman resembled that of the well-bred domestic cat, wrongly considered spiteful. The furry puss was charming; exhibited her playfulness and pretty ways to those who took the pains to win her confidence by appearing to be kind and just to her, not disturbing her too much in any of her little comforts, never being harsh or boisterous, always natural. But if by chance she once lost confidence, then she recoiled into her own self like a snail into its shell, and it was a hard matter to win back her favour. And so, Johns had come to think, it was with women who were really women—women who had the instincts and the foibles of their sex. So, at least, he had always found them.

To create a good impression, and in some speculative way he wanted that evening to create one, was always a delicate, nice task. A single error, a single breath of ridicule was often fatal —so intuitive were women. Thus he desired to tread cautiously, and it was not until the dessert appeared, and the theme of books had been introduced, that an opportunity occurred.

Miss Wilson, in her little girlish voice, had laughingly enquired of anyone who cared to answer, what was thought of Clara Baroletti's novels. She, for one, did not like such visionary books. She had plainly told the authoress as much when she had met her a few days before in the villa of some friends, and she feared she had offended her.

Johns, sitting upright in his chair, as he did when he meant to be impressive, said, "Ah, Miss Wilson, how well can I understand that you, with your evident good sense and clear perceptions, should repudiate such mystic vagaries. For you, as I judge you, there can only be one style, the old and ever new, the bright and charming tale of nature. You love the style which elegantly renders all the primary affections, joys, and sorrows of our lives, always without affectation, without pose. Your taste enables you to readily distinguish what is frank and fresh, sincere, harmonious in art, from what is artificial, forced, unfelt. You are able to enjoy the perfume which all real works of art give forth as surely as a rose gives forth its scent. Ah, Miss Wilson, that style will live when the books of all the Barolettis that our island rears, are relegated to the limbo of forgotten things!"

"Oh!" exclaimed the young girl, with a smile of pleasure on her face, "you say exactly what I think, but so much better than I could say it!"

Johns, once started, was in no mood to stop.

"Yes, we should seek the natural, and cast aside the weird, the ghostly, the fantastic, as too facile and too tame, not fit even for the nursery. If I wrote novels instead of spending my time in the ungrateful task of conducting a Review, I should love to draw a graceful and bright-witted girl with a charming nature like your own, Miss Wilson."

He glanced at the father as if to ask permission to take his daughter as a type, and then continued —

"I would paint her mischievous, delightful, coy, always with a laugh upon her lips, gay, light-hearted, young, and yet with a little head which knew well what it wanted, with a judgment which wasn't to be imposed upon.

"Then, as nothing is of greater interest, of greater charm in life than a love's idyll, I would create for her a handsome cavalier, one after my own heart, with dash and spirit, who knew his own mind well, and who, being very much in love, meant to win her in spite of all the obstacles which I, as novelist, would place before him. And in the end they would be happy, extraordinarily happy, and their lives would be destined afterwards to flow as smoothly as a summer's dream. That would be all my story!"

In drawing this portrait of what he meant to be an idealised Miss Wilson, Johns had glanced alternately from the father to the daughter, apparently oblivious of the presence of St. George (who was listening with a half-satisfied expression), and his eyes had become moist with the enthusiasm he had contrived to conjure up. Miss Wilson, when he had finished, looked more pleased than ever, and exclaimed, "Oh, Mr. Johns, how charming of you! That's just the kind of book I like."

Johns said, "I thought it was; I guessed it must be from your face."

Then, turning his gaze upon St. George as if he had but now perceived him, he exclaimed —

"But here we have, if not a novelist, at least a poet whose modesty I must unveil. St. George, do you remember those bucolic poems I published for you in the *Planet?*"

St. George had been endeavouring to make a sign to Johns to stop, but seeing that he would not, he expostulated—

"Oh, don't let us talk of *those!*"

Miss Wilson said, "I didn't know, Mr. St. George, you were a poet!"

St. George declared that he had merely written a few verses which were not worth speaking of, but the young girl said—

'Oh, but I want to see them! I'm curious to see them."

St. George protested that he hadn't kept them, that he would not know where to find them even if he were in London.

But Johns gave out that he knew how to procure the pieces. He would write to the office for the numbers of the paper.

"Do, Mr. Johns," the young girl cried, apparently enjoying St. George's evident confusion. "That *will* be fun. I'm dying to read your friend's poetry. Fancy being a poet and keeping it so secret! Mr. Johns, I shall rely upon you to get the verses."

St. George, seeing that it was useless to object, was silent, trying to look pleased in spite of his evident annoyance. After this, the dinner was soon over. The party rose at the same time as the other diners at the long table, and left the room with them.

In the vestibule—a large hall paved with marble and furnished with basket chairs and little bamboo tables—they took seats, and were served with coffee. But they had not been there more than a few minutes when Miss Wilson, whose chair happened to be a little apart from the rest, found herself surrounded by three young Englishmen whom Johns judged quickly to belong to the money-seeking class for whom the Riviera has always been a hunting ground.

Sipping his coffee leisurely, and smoking a cigar, Johns amused himself by watching them, speculating on their chances, glancing at St. George occasionally to study his discomfiture. To do her justice, Johns admitted that Miss Wilson did not seem to give any of them much encouragement, and she answered a dark man of about forty, with a scar upon a rather handsome face, with much indifference.

"Who is that man?" Johns asked St. George in a low tone.

"His name is Blanchamp. He's a baronet," St. George

replied, with evident disgust. The other two were younger and somewhat less assiduous.

But after listening to their conversation for a little while, Johns came to the conclusion that they were very clumsy, and, setting down their chances as extremely slight, he began to talk to Wilson about the state of trade.

A little later, however, Miss Wilson, having dismissed her trio without much ceremony, exclaimed—

"Oh, father, we don't want to speak of business. We want to settle what we're going to do this evening."

St. George at once proposed a walk, but Wilson shook his head. He had walked enough that day. St. George next proposed the Casino, but the young girl declared she was tired of the Casino. Nothing that evening was taking place there. Johns made no proposal, and there was a short pause.

At length Miss Wilson, who had been reflecting, suddenly clapped her hands.

"I have it! Mr. Johns will tell us one of his little stories. I've heard so much about them from a friend, and I'm dying to hear one of them. Now, Mr. Johns, you won't refuse me, will you?"

Johns, thus appealed to, said that nothing would give him greater pleasure, and, after a moment to collect his thoughts, he told them the best of his little narratives, one that he knew by heart, and which he related with so much skill, alternating so cleverly between humour and subdued pathos as he progressed, that the end was greeted by a prolonged murmur of admiration on the part, not only of the young girl, but of her father also.

"Oh," said Miss Wilson, naïvely, "how I wish I could tell such beautiful, such charming little stories!" and she looked at Johns half-shyly, as if impressed by his subtlety, his knowledge of human nature.

And Johns, who felt as though he had returned to the early days when his little stories were his only capital, pleased at the effect he had produced, told another tale, which was received with almost as much favour as the former.

This occupied the greater portion of the evening, and after half an hour spent in the little *salon* which adjoined the hall, the party separated. The Wilsons retired to their rooms, and the two friends were left together.

St. George, who had plainly not enjoyed himself all through the evening, said—

"I do think, Johns, that you needn't have promised Miss Wilson you would show my verses to her. It wasn't exactly kind. It might prejudice her against me. Girls are so peculiar!"

Johns, who remembered the amateurish lines he had published once when he wanted to oblige St. George, replied—

"My dear St. George, believe me, there is a flavour, a literary merit, in those verses which cannot fail to advance your cause. You saw how my little compositions pleased. Yours, which are better, will be even more appreciated."

But St. George was not convinced. He said—

"At all events, of *you* I've no reason to be jealous. You're married, my boy, as married as you can be."

Johns repeated, thoughtfully, "As married as I can be, St. George, as married as I can be!"

Then they chatted, and after a last cigar each retired to his room.

The next day Mrs. Johns made the acquaintance of the Wilsons. The young girl was not sufficiently good-looking to cause Mrs. Johns the uneasiness she felt when in the presence of a beauty, and as her manners were pleasant and engaging, they were soon on the best of terms. The acquaintance ripened. Mrs. Johns, in her delicate state of health, was not able to accompany her young friend for walks, but Miss Wilson, from the first, evinced a readiness to sacrifice her inclinations to the comforts of the invalid—for such she still remained— driving with her when she would have preferred to ride or walk, staying with her often in her room—in this way winning her affection. The father was not too much pleased with the arrangement, which deprived him of some of his daughter's company; but as it kept her out of danger, he refrained from making an objection. St. George, seeing the course which things had taken, at once endeavoured to enter into the good graces of Mrs. Johns.

Thus, life at Cannes for the little party was soon organized upon a more or less settled plan. In the morning, before the mid-day breakfast, and after the visit of the doctor, Mrs. Johns would take a drive, either through the town when she wanted to make purchases, or along the sea front, or a short way into the adjoining country. Frequently Miss Wilson would accompany her, and sometimes, too, St. George would be invited, though not often, for Johns had told his wife that, as Wilson was entirely opposed to the notion of a marriage between his daughter and St. George, they must be careful not to give the young people too many opportunities to meet. In the afternoon the programme was generally undecided. On certain days the Wilsons had to visit friends, or the father wanted to take a ride in the country with his daughter, or, if Mrs. Johns was not indisposed, a drive was organized in the Johns' or the Wilsons' landau, both of which being constructed only to contain four, St. George was excluded by the mere force of circumstances. The evenings were spent in the drawing-room, where Johns was soon a favourite with both the English and the French, or at the Casino where Mrs. Johns indulged her fondness for mild gambling.

Johns, in the meantime, watched events in a curious, undecided, speculative, semi-philosophical frame of mind. A portion of his days was devoted to his Review, and he spent the remainder in answering the long and admirably-written letters which he frequently received from Edith Douglas, and in amusing himself as well as he was able under the circumstances in which he found himself.

One day, after they had been a few weeks at Cannes, the Wilsons asked St. George and Johns if they would ride with them that afternoon. Miss Wilson had heard of some new views, and she wanted very much to see them. Mrs. Johns would come a part of the way with them in the carriage, and they would have a pleasant afternoon.

The invitation was at once accepted with enthusiasm by St. George, whose chances that week had been growing somewhat dim, and who hailed this opportunity to endeavour to advance them.

The Wilsons had had their saddle horses sent from England, but the two friends were obliged to hire the best that could be procured in Cannes, from stables which had previously supplied them with fair mounts.

After breakfast, therefore, the party assembled in the hall before the start. Miss Wilson wore a light grey habit which showed her small, though well-proportioned figure to the best advantage, and on her happy little face the glow of health was softened by a coat of down which lay upon it like the bloom upon a peach. She was looking at her best, and her points of modest beauty were admirably shown, as her mirror, to judge by her high spirits, must have told her.

Mrs. Johns, on whose face the powder puff had been extensively employed, whose cheeks were drawn and pale, whose eyes seemed to betray the artificial means that had been used to give them brilliancy, made a sad contrast to this youth and freshness. In spite of her desire to appear light-hearted, there was an anxious look upon her countenance which her smiles could not dispel.

Wilson, somewhat indisposed that afternoon, had decided

that he would not join the party, but he was in the hall to witness the departure.

When the trap and the horses came, Johns, St. George, and Miss Wilson mounted, while Mrs. Johns took her seat in the landau with the wife of an English general who was staying at the hotel.

While they were going through the town, Miss Wilson, St. George, and Johns, riding side by side, followed the carriage, trotting a few yards behind, and in this order they reached the Antibes road.

But it soon became apparent that the original order could not be maintained. The long and parched white road was covered with a thick layer of fine dust, which rose in such dense clouds as the carriage dashed along, that the riders following, soon became as white as millers, and were well-nigh choked and blinded. They tried to ride in front, but the cloud raised by their horses' hoofs was again so great that Mrs. Johns in the landau, distressed by it, made her coachman stop. The rest turned back and came to see if anything had happened, and she asked them to take their ride independently of her. The roads were far too dusty for them to keep company, she said. They would meet when they reached the forest. Miss Wilson was quite safe in her husband's hands.

The riding party therefore halted for a few minutes until the landau was nearly out of sight. Then they continued at a walk.

But it seemed that the commencement of their ride was not destined to be without interruptions, for the horse St. George was riding—a tall lean bay, with a long sinewy neck, which, in starting, had shown signs of restlessness—now began to give him trouble, and to take him away frequently from his companions for a mad gallop upon the hard road, the dust rising after him like a long wall of cloud. St. George was a good rider, but he was mounted on an imperfectly-trained beast which required his whole attention, and prevented him from remaining long at Miss Wilson's side.

Johns, who was riding a fine Norman mare, reflected that St. George had got no luck, for he knew well that Wilson's sudden resolution to stay at home that afternoon had deprived his friend of an opportunity of riding alone with the young girl, since four might have paired and three could not—three certainly could not. Presently, as Johns and Miss Wilson were advancing, looking in front of them at the place where St. George had disappeared in a cloud of dust, they reached a turning which the young girl said was the best to take. Mr.

St. George, she said, would know that road, and would see that they had taken it. If not, they would meet when they reached the forest.

"Poor Mr. St. George," she said, laughing, as she turned her horse's head, "he's so unfortunate to-day!"

Then, confidentially, as if she had been speaking to an accomplice, she continued, "It was such fun to read his poems. I had no idea he could be so sentimental. 'The marriage of Belinda' was wonderfully soulful."

Johns asked, smiling, "What did you think of them?"

"Shall I confess? I will if you promise not to tell."

"I promise."

"Well, then, I think they're rather silly!"

They both laughed, and Johns replied, "You're a sagacious critic!" Then he pursued, in a comiserating tone, "Poor St. George, he's got no luck to-day, and yet in some respects I envy him. If his poetry is bad, perhaps he is appreciated for other qualities he may be thought to have, by one whom every man must wish to please. And St. George is free, a bachelor, while I—oh, I—well, never mind. *I* do not count."

"Why do you speak so regretfully?" she asked, becoming serious.

He gave her a rapid glance, and as he fancied he detected the trace of an incipient emotion on her countenance, he asked himself, "Why not?" and after a moment's pause, exclaimed—

"Miss Wilson, I feel impelled to ask you, to entreat you to allow me to confide in you. You are one of those rare persons who call forth confidence."

He looked round quickly to ascertain if St. George were coming, and, seeing no one in the narrow lane they were passing along, continued—

"We are such good friends now that I am going to confide in you as I have never yet confided in anyone before. I have such absolute reliance on your discretion!"

"Of course," she said, deeply interested, "whatever you tell me I will not repeat."

"I know it! Well, then, Miss Wilson, dear Miss Wilson, let me tell you what you may have guessed—I am not happy; no, not happy!"

He paused a moment to collect his thoughts. Then resuming—

"A few years ago I married a woman whose kindness touched me, whose great solicitude for me, coming at a time when I was fighting against many obstacles in my profession, and had need of sympathy, caused me to feel doubly grateful, and at last to mistake my gratitude for love. My friends persuaded me that the difference in our ages need be no bar to happiness, and as I was then inclined to be convinced, I married. Our married life flowed smoothly. My wife continued to be kind and—motherly. I endeavoured, as you may have seen, to make her life (that of an invalid) as pleasant as I could, but, alas! I have gradually and painfully become aware that I was reckoning without human nature, that I had linked myself to one who could never be more than a friend to me, a companion. And day by day the dismal thought has grown upon me that I had made one of those mistakes which cannot be repaired, which embitter a career. For at last I came to own that my ideal, the ideal which we all form, had not been achieved, and that I could only dream in vain of a young wife, bright and gay and sympathetic, without too much sentiment, but with that charming magnetism which one feels so subtly, with that delightful little girlish malice, those delicious ways which are the salt of feminine attractiveness, above all possessing a character, a nature akin to mine, linked to it by mutual affinity. And I have been living with a great regret, trying to forget it by hard work, disdainful of the lying stories, some of which you may have heard, invented by jealous mediocrities about me. And so the time has passed, until at length fate willed that my wife's health should bring us to this place, and that here I should meet one who, from the moment I beheld her, seemed to be the absolute realization of the ideal I had formed! And then my trouble was increased a hundred-fold. Never had I felt so keenly that I was not free!"

They had passed the little chapel of St. Antoine, and a turning of the road had brought them to an eminence commanding a superb view of the azure coast. Before them lay the Gulf of La Napoule, slightly ruffled by a light breeze, and presided over by the town of Cannes, gleaming white in the strong sunlight. Farther still, the islands of St. Marguerite and St. Honorat were dotted as if fallen from the sky. A little to the right, appeared the iridescent peaks of the changeful Estèrel. In the same direction as far as Bordighera, the rocks and promontories alternated in bewildering succession, and on the other side, across Cape Antibes, Nice, whiter still than Cannes, was resting calmly, as if protected by warlike Toulon, a speck in the far distance. In the rear, the snow-clad summits of the Alps lent to the scene a note of peaceful dignity.

After Johns had finished speaking there was a pause. Miss Wilson, playing with her reins, was looking seawards thoughtfully.

At length she asked, with a slight tremor in her voice—

"Who was she?"

"Oh! can you ask me that?" he cried. "Who might she be but you? You and you alone."

Looking away from him, she said—

"You ought not to have told me!"

"It was inevitable! I knew that I should tell you the first time we were alone. There are inclinations which can never be controlled. I felt, I knew, that there was sympathy between us, and that must be my excuse."

"How did you know I liked you?" she asked, ingenuously.

"Then you do! you do!" he cried. "Oh, I was not quite certain, but now that you have told me so, I almost feel as if, in spite of all, I could be happy!"

"Of course I do," she said, in a low tone. Then she added—

"Why is it, I wonder, that nice people are always married? Since I have been out, I've had eight offers, and not one of the men was as nice as you, not one. Most of them wanted to marry me simply for my money."

"The curs!" said Johns, with a deep frown.

"And I hate a man who only worships that! Money isn't everything!"

"No one knows as well as I how true that is!"

They rode along in silence for some distance in the direction of the pine woods, and just as these were coming into sight, darkly green against the blue, cloudless sky, she said—

"But it's no use to think of impossibilities. We ought to have met before."

He answered, "I shall never cease to regret we did not."

Presently they reached a cluster of old pines spread like panoplies between the earth and sky, giving the impression of huge black mushrooms guarding the entrance of the woods.

She said, as they passed into the shade—

"But we must not be miserable about it, and you must be very good to poor Mrs. Johns, who seems so ill!"

He reflected once again that they all said the same things, and then replied—

"I shall never forget that she is my wife; but, oh, if I could see into futurity!"

The young girl was silent, and they advanced along a narrow forest path, barely wide enough for their horses to walk abreast. Johns hesitated for a moment, undecided upon what chord to strike. The situation was extremely delicate. She was not of a sentimental nature, he knew that well, but yet experience had taught him that women are apt to judge men sometimes by the way they act towards the weaker sex. He must be cautious, therefore, as to what he said about the future. Several times the word divorce was on his lips, but when he thought of his wife's health, and of the extreme measures he would have to take to force her to break the marriage, of the scandal which must inevitably be caused, he quickly saw that the idea must be abandoned. And yet what a prize she was! And how neat her little figure looked in that grey habit! Above all, how young! Presently an inspiration came to him.

Leaning towards her in his saddle, he gently placed his arm around her waist, and murmured—

"Gwen, my little Gwen, promise me, at least, that while we are here together, you won't accept another man. It may be selfish, but I could not bear to see another win you. We shall only be together for a few months, and I am so fond of you, so fond! Oh, promise!"

Disengaging herself quietly, she said—

"Of course I will, with pleasure. I'm not in a hurry to get married, and none of the marriageables here can tempt me."

He thanked her warmly, vowing she was the kindest and the most delightful nature in the world, the sweetest and the best.

Then he said, "I almost feared, you know, St. George had been successful."

But she gave a little laugh.

"Oh no, good Mr. St. George is rather nice, and at first I might have had a little liking for him, but lately—well perhaps, he doesn't bear comparison. Besides," she added, "pa has some notion in his head about a title."

"A title," he repeated, "and do *you* care for that?"

"Scarcely a bit."

"How quickly I would have obtained one for you had I been your husband! There is nothing I would not do, no place I would not conquer!"

She answered, enthusiastically—

"I'm sure you would, and if you had been free, no one would have prevented me from marrying you. I don't believe what people say about you."

"How good, how kind you are!"

They had reached the end of the narrow path and were emerging from amid the trees into an open space which joined the road beyond when they perceived the carriage. St. George, his horse still foaming at the mouth, was at the side of it.

The young man was speaking to Mrs. Johns as they came up. He replied to Johns's "Well, St. George, have you tamed your steed?" by a mere "yes, thank you," in a dry tone, without looking at his friend.

But Mrs. Johns exclaimed —

"Oh, John, I was so afraid you might have had a horrid beast like poor Mr. St. George, and that something might have happened!"

Johns answered, with a laugh, that his mount was a pretty good one, and that they had left the road to see the delightful view from the heights beyond.

Then, presently, after a little conversation, as no one wanted to dismount, and as Mrs. Johns confessed that she was not feeling well that afternoon, the party started homewards.

The riders took the lead, but owing to St. George's taciturnity, the ride back was an almost silent one.

CHAPTER EIGHTEENTH

TWO months after the visit to the pine woods, Johns was sitting by his wife's bed-side, watching her features as she slept. It was the afternoon, and the window shutters, closed to exclude the sunlight, had plunged the room into a half obscurity, throwing into cold relief the pallor of the bed-clothes, and the white wimple of the grave Sister watching on the other side. On a table near the bed, a large bouquet of red roses in a vase, diffused their perfume. The stillness was unbroken, save for the faint sound of a distant piano, and now and then the noise of carriage wheels on the gravel path below.

The fears of the London doctors had been realized. Suddenly the disease which women shrink from naming, had re-appeared, this time with redoubled force, and the poor woman, after concealing its recrudescence with untold suffering for many days, had been at length obliged to yield to the inevitable and to confess. The local doctors, and an eminent practitioner from London, who was then in Cannes, had held a consultation, and had declared that another operation could not be attempted. All that could be done, they said, must be in the way of palliation. They could alleviate the suffering, they could not conquer the disease.

And what a change had taken place ! Instead of the woman, half-girlish in her carefully preserved maturity, whom Johns had married but a few years since at Westminster, a patient, aged and worn, was sleeping a narcotic sleep in the large white bed. The lines upon her face had become deep furrows, rendered the more apparent by the congested aspect of her features. The mouth had sunk, and the chin rested upon the somewhat swollen neck. The golden locks, carefully waved and dressed, contrasted strangely with the ravaged face. Johns, as he looked at her, muttered, "Poor old Rose," for even he, had been surprised at the rapidity of the decay, and at the suddenness with which his own prospects had been altered. Truly, it seemed, he thought, as if fate worked for him, as if whenever he had an end in view everything conspired to help him to attain it. "Poor old Rose," he repeated. "If she only knew!" For it had been thought humane to refrain from telling her how hopeless her condition was.

Presently the patient moved. She turned her head slightly towards Johns, and her eyes slowly opened.

A forced, sad smile overspread her face as she enquired—

"Have I been long asleep, Johnnie?"

"Only a few hours, Rose; how are you feeling now?"

She shook her head with a mournful gesture.

"I'm very ill, my John! I'm very ill! The doctors have not done me any good. No good at all!"

Johns answered, "You must have patience, Rose."

But again she shook her head.

"I love so much to see you near me when I wake, to look at your dear face while I am a little calm, before the dreadful pains return. Ah, how sweet it is to have a husband!"

And she gave him a long glance of despairing love, while the Sister, who had been listening, cast her eyelids down.

But presently she said, "Open the window, John. I cannot breathe."

Johns rose and turned the latch of the folding window opposite the bed. At once a current of pure air, fragrant with the first scents of spring, came into the room as if to give fresh life to the sick woman.

She took a long deep breath.

"How delicious!" she exclaimed. "Do you know, my John, that when I am well again we must take a trip on the Atlantic to breathe the salt sea air? Oh, when shall I be well again?"

As she said this she passed her hands before her eyes as if to exclude a sombre thought, and presently a tear emerged from between the fingers and trickled slowly down her cheek.

"Don't worry, Rose. The doctors say you won't continue as you are."

"Ah, no! Perhaps I may be worse!"

Through the open window now came the sound of singing. A man's and a woman's voices were mingling in a duet, accompanied by the notes of a soft-toned piano. The voices were young and pure, and they thrilled with earnestness and passion as they rose and fell in the cadences of a French love song. It seemed as though the singers must themselves be lovers, and were singing under the influence of love.

The voices were so fine and the song so tender, that they listened silently, attentively, until the last note had died away.

Then, heaving a deep sigh, Mrs. Johns exclaimed—

"Oh, John, how happy they must be!"

And Johns answered simply—

"Yes, Rose!"

But he was thinking, "Ah, yes, happiness—always happiness. They crave for it. They live for it. They give their bodies up to it. They sell their souls for it. And, by God, they're right! Pleasure is the only certain good, the only reason for continuing the dull farce of life. Rose didn't get much of it when she married me, yet now she's bitterly regretting the little she obtained. If she had lived to sixty she would still have pined for it. Pleasure! Pleasure, held before each one of us like a bag of hay before an ass to make him go! Nothing else can make us live. Egoism will ever be the law of life."

Then, moved by a sudden fancy, he drew a full-blown rose from the vase upon the table, and placed it gently in his wife's hair.

And she, oblivious to the incongruity, said almost in a whisper—

"Oh, thank you, John!"

But at that moment there was a gentle knock at the bedroom door.

The Sister rose to open it. Gwendoline, bearing a large basket of flowers, entered.

During the illness of Mrs. Johns she had been untiring in her kindness to the condemned woman. Sitting at her bedside in the afternoon, and attending to her wants with a woman's patience, she had become almost the only stranger whom Mrs. Johns would see, and, severed as the latter was from relatives and friends in Cannes, the kindness of the young girl was doubly grateful.

Johns rose and, giving up his place to her, relieved her of her burden.

"Oh, the lovely flowers!" Mrs. Johns exclaimed, "how kind of you, dear Gwendoline!"

And her eyes filled with moisture, for in her state her sense of gratitude was strong. Johns held the basket near her that she might inhale the perfume of the stephanotis.

"Ah," he said, "we have to thank Miss Wilson for so much!"

The young girl chatted gaily, trying to amuse the sufferer by

telling her whom she had met that morning on the promenade—
Lady Vieille with the Poet Laureate, the Prince with a young
French Jew, the Serene Highness from Monte Carlo with his
wife. Then followed a minute description of the gowns and
bonnets she had seen, intermingled with a little scandal.

Mrs. Johns listened somewhat absent-mindedly.

"Ah!" she said, with a deep sigh, when Gwen had finished,
" I wonder if I shall see all that again !"

Both hastened to reassure her.

But Johns, seated at a little distance from them while they
had been speaking, had been glancing, now at his wife with
her careworn face and golden hair decked with the large red
rose, now at the fresh young girl not ungraceful in her light
cloth dress. And he had muttered to himself, "Two provi-
dences, but, by God, how different !"

During his wife's illness he had seen much of Gwen, but the
young girl, as if guided by a scruple of feminine conscience,
had maintained a slight reserve, avoiding as much as possible
finding herself alone with him, and telling him, when they met
by accident upon the landing or in the corridor, that he must
be very good to his poor wife who was so ill, and escaping
quickly with a little smile at his discomfiture. And even now,
when their eyes met while speaking, she quickly looked away.

Johns understood her feeling and did little to dispel it. He
was certain he could count upon her, and events must take
their course.

But as the afternoon advanced, the patient's face began to
show signs of pain, and she no longer listened to the conversation. A sad, obliterated look came over her, and her head
sank deeper into the hollow of the pillow.

"Oh," she said, in anguish, "it's coming on again ! "

At once the Sister rose and, going to a side table on which was
a phial and a small glass, poured out a potion which diffused a
smell of ether in the room. Then, coming back to the bedside,
she placed the glass to the patient's lips, who drank its contents
eagerly, lapsing shortly afterwards into a quiet sleep.

Gwendoline and Johns then rose and left.

"Oh, Gwen," Johns murmured when they were outside,
"she's very bad!"

"Yes," said the young girl, gravely, " it's terrible to see her."

" Gwen, she won't get over it, the doctors all say so."

"I know they do, you need not tell me. Poor, poor
woman !"

"Believe me, Gwen, I'm sorry for her too !"

"I'm glad to hear you say so," she replied, and without

waiting to hear more, she left him, disappearing down the passage rapidly.

When Johns reached his room he threw himself into an arm-chair, and, after lighting a cigarette, he opened the letter which he had received that afternoon from Edith. She asked him the reason of his long silence, wondering if he might be ill, telling him how much she missed him, how she hoped he would be returning soon. She had never in any letter she had written him allowed her feelings to betray themselves so plainly, and Johns, after he had finished reading, asked himself what he should do, whether he should answer her or not. Edith Douglas, he began to argue, was certainly the most beautiful of all the women he had met, and even then, as he shut his eyes and saw her in imagination, lithe and graceful, perfect, he could not banish feelings of regret. Why was it that he was always forced to make a choice between material things and beauty? His luck even now was not without a flaw.

For a few moments he enquired of himself whether he should write to tell her of the hopelessness of his wife's condition; but he soon decided that he would not. It was never wise to impart knowledge without a purpose, and in this case it would be specially unwise. No, certainly, he would not, and he sat down at his table and wrote a letter full of well-turned sentences which committed him to nothing. His wife was still unwell, he told her in a postscript, and he did not think they would be back again till May.

"Poor Edith," he said, as he sealed the envelope, "she won't like it when she knows!" But what was he to do? Every man was meant to carry out his destiny. The destiny of a man like him was to constantly ascend, and life was much too short to do so when the *nerve of war* was absent.

Ah yes! the nerve of war! The mighty power of the age, the subtle influence before which conscience, virtue bowed; the all-excusing salve; the talisman before which no doors were closed! There might have been a time when other powers reigned, love, religion, and such things, when men fought for something else but gold. That time had passed, and one must be of one's period!

Thinking thus, he lit a fresh cigar, and went out for a stroll upon the terrace.

The days succeeded each other now in the same way, and each day the condition of the afflicted woman grew more grave, each day her sufferings increased. Gradually the definite decline set in. Gwendoline and Johns, as they watched at the bedside in the afternoons, witnessed the progress of the sinking, and at length the poor woman's realization of her state.

By degrees, as the truth dawned upon her, she sank into a dull lethargy, and her face, discoloured and congested, lost all traces of good looks, became forbidding, ugly. Her hair, which she refused now to have manipulated by her maid, was losing its golden hue and turning grey in patches. She was relaxing her hold on life.

One morning, as Johns lay in bed, reading with great interest "Bel Ami" of Maupassant—a story in which the hero's character, he was forced to own, somewhat resembled his—he heard a knock at his bedroom door. A servant entered—a pretty Niceoise, with an Italian face—and told him that the Sister begged of him to come to his wife's room, as madame was much worse.

Jumping out of bed, as soon as the girl had left, he dressed in haste and passed into his wife's room.

As he went in, he heard a low, moaning sound, and a glance at the face upon the pillow convinced him that his wife was within a measurable distance of her end.

The Sister rose and met him before he reached the bed, whispering in French, "The night, monsieur, has been very bad. I fear the end is not far off. You should warn a minister of her religion."

Johns advanced gravely to the bedside.

Taking his wife's hand, which rested inertly on the bed-clothes, he said kindly—

"Well, Rose!"

Slowly her eyes opened, and casting a look of sorrow upon her husband, she murmured in a hollow voice—

"Oh, John! oh, John!"

In the disordered room there was an odour of disease mingled with narcotic fumes. On a side table stood an array of medicine bottles, cups, and glasses, a heap of lints and bandages. The place had an air of gloom, disintegration, and the rays of the morning sun which streamed through the upper rafters of the shutters, fell upon the dark red curtains of the bed almost sacrilegiously.

Johns asked, "And are you suffering, my Rose?"

But she scarcely seemed to hear, for she answered feebly, "Oh, John, I'm going from you now! I did not think that it would be so soon!"

Johns pressed her hand in silence, finding no words for the occasion, and she continued to moan piteously.

Presently the door was opened, and the English doctor, a tall man, with a thoughtful shaven face, came in.

A brief examination of the patient was sufficient. He requested Johns to follow him to the adjoining room. There he said, "I'm sorry to have to tell you that your wife is sinking. She may linger for a few days, but the break-up has commenced."

"Indeed, doctor."

"So that, if you wish to summon relatives or an English clergyman, there's no time to be lost."

"I shall see to it at once."

The doctor left, promising to return later in the day.

"Summon the relatives!" Johns muttered, "the Dean and all the meddling tribe!" No, he didn't intend to do it. The clergyman might come, but the rest might stay in their cloudy England. He didn't want them.

Thinking thus, he took up his hat and left the room.

On the landing he met St. George, and he said at once—

"St. George, go, like a good chap, to fetch the English parson. Rose is getting worse."

St. George, who had been employed of late on a number of errands for Mrs. Johns, chiefly under instructions from Miss Wilson, at once expressed his readiness to go. The unlucky youth had found a further obstacle to his matrimonial prospects in the illness of Mrs. Johns, for he had been excluded from the sick room in which Miss Wilson now passed so many hours of the day. And although, since the visit to the pine woods, he had watched Johns's behaviour towards Miss Wilson rather narrowly, he had not been able to discover anything that might confirm his incipient suspicion. He was waiting patiently for the *dénouement* to make a supreme attempt.

"It's hopeless, then?" he asked.

"Quite hopeless!"

St. George said, "Poor woman!" and went off upon his errand.

In the afternoon, Johns and Miss Wilson were sitting in the room witnessing the sufferings of the condemned woman, and waiting for the arrival of the clergyman. The Sister, not wishing to be present when the latter came, had just retired.

Johns, thinking his wife asleep, was saying, "The morphia no longer seems to give her much relief, Gwen!" when his wife's eyes opened and her gaze wandered from the young girl to him. Whether she had heard her husband call the young girl by her Christian name, or whether her impression was instinctive, she murmured in a voice that was scarcely audible—

"Ah, yes, you're both so young! You'll be so happy soon!"

Then she continued, plaintively, "But oh, John, say that you are my own husband while I'm here!"

He answered gravely, "Always your devoted husband."

She gave a sigh as of relief, and said, "I have not always been considerate for you, my John. I ought to have remembered that we were not—of the same age; that I ought not to have expected—ought not to have hoped for all your love! But a woman cannot help yearning for her husband's love, and you, my John, have always seemed to me so wonderful, so perfect! Will you forgive me, John, if I have been unkind to you?"

That his wife should ask his pardon seemed to him astonishing, but he replied—

"Yes, Rose, with all my heart."

Gwendoline, on hearing this, rose from her seat, saying that she thought they would prefer to be alone; but Johns, who, for some reason he could scarcely have explained, had a strong disinclination to be left alone, entreated her to stay.

"And, John," the sufferer continued, still in the same weak voice, "I would like the Dean to have a little money."

"He shall have some, Rose, I promise you."

"If I really cannot live. Oh, John, can nothing else be done? I did not want to die so soon. Is there no other doctor can be called?"

Johns pretended to reflect for a moment, then he said, "We might send to London for another, but those you've seen are very good physicians."

But the poor woman, again tortured by her pain, had ceased to listen. Her face had assumed an almost livid hue, and she sank back on her pillow with a stifled cry. Gwen's eyes filled with tears.

"How she must be suffering!" she said, and Johns, casting his eyes upwards, answered, "Yes, Gwen!"

Presently the curate came. He was a thin young man, with light hair and a light moustache, having nothing ecclesiastical in his appearance except his clothes. Taking a seat which Johns offered him by the bedside, after a few words exchanged in a low voice, he asked the patient several questions to which she replied somewhat vaguely, although his presence did not seem to cause her much alarm. In a few minutes he produced a morocco-covered book from an inner pocket, opened it at a place marked by a blue band, and began to read a chapter from the Epistle of St. Paul upon the vanity of the present life and the superiority of that to come. Johns, while he read, looked blankly at the floor. Gwendoline kept her eyes fixed upon the sufferer.

When he had finished reading, suddenly, and with some agility, the curate turned in his chair and dropped upon his knees. Johns and Gwen followed his example.

Then, in a drawling monotone, which reminded Johns somewhat of the Dean's, he prayed for Mrs. Johns, asking that her life might be eternally continued up above, and that the good works she had done might be remembered. We poor mortals knew, he said, that the flesh was transient and dust-composed, a garb to be exchanged for a more etherial raiment in a world of light and joy. The pleasures of the world were vain allurements which no good Christian should regret. He entreated the Divinity to show clemency towards their sister lying there upon her bed of pain. As surely as the world had been redeemed, their trust was that her sins would be forgiven. All there that afternoon, he said, had confidence in the divine compassion.

After he had finished praying, he remained so long upon his knees that Johns could not refrain from looking through his fingers to see if he were not about to give the signal to get up. For the moments passed in genuflexion, with his elbows on the cushion of his chair, seemed long to Johns, and he was beginning to wonder if the young man had not gone to sleep.

At length the latter rose; Gwendoline and Johns rose also.

"Good-bye," the curate said to Mrs. Johns, bending slightly over her; "I'll come again to-morrow."

The suffering woman moved her head as a sign that she had understood, and the fair young man withdrew.

Mrs. Johns lingered after this for many days. She declined indeed so slowly that Johns began to feel the strain the daily watching placed upon his nerves. The silence of the sick room depressed him. He shrugged his shoulders at the queer humanity of keeping so long alive a being hopelessly condemned. For his part, had he been in his wife's condition, the sooner he could have ended the better he would have liked it. But no, there was some sort of a tradition that life must be preserved to the last gasp, even at the expense of suffering. It was in conformity with custom to go on giving medicines to prolong the miserable existence of a decayed and useless body. Well, the *genus homo* had its superstitions he supposed, and one must manage to have patience with them.

And yet, when he would awaken in the morning and open his window to the soothing breath of spring, full of fragrance and of promise, he would readily forget that his wife was dying in the adjacent room. The birds were always singing in the pine trees a loud song of love, and the sea was sparkling joyously. A flood of imperious desires, aims, ambitions, would mount up to his brain in a confused medley of aspirations.

Riches, power, station, all seemed wafted on the breeze. Life in its fullest plenitude smiled at him seductively.

Then, when he would remember that his wife was leaving him, a vaguely tender melancholy would come to cast a temporary gloom upon his feelings. It was a slight ordeal to go through, and there were always compensations in this world of accident and chance.

Still, the ordeal was not to be short, for Mrs. Johns, day after day, though sinking visibly, continued to exist, and each day Johns had to listen to the reading and the praying of the curate, to see Gwendoline before him at the bedside, always reserved and thoughtful, and to be present during the brief visit of the doctor.

But the dying woman, in her waking moments, murmured constantly the same two words—

"Oh, John! oh, John!"

And throughout the day they sounded in Johns's ears until he grew well nigh sick of his own name, so greatly the endless repetition increased the tension of his nerves. Sometimes the words seemed almost to be pronounced reproachfully, at others it was as though they were merely an expression of her pain. Whatever they might mean, they disconcerted him, and once, giving way to a semi-conscious feeling of retaliation, he replied, "Ah, Rose! ah, Rose!"

It was not until the tenth day after she had been pronounced to be declining that the ultimate break-up took place.

In the morning, as if she felt that her end was near, she had made a last appeal to Johns in favour of her relatives, and mentioned the names of two distant cousins to whom she desired to make gifts.

"Oh, John," she said, when she had finished, "how hard it is to leave! Pray for me if you can, John; I'm afraid I've not been too good a woman. Try to pray for me, my John!"

There was no one in the room except the Sister, and Johns replied—

"Sister Marthe will pray for you better far than I."

And turning to the Sister, who as usual was looking on in silence, he said—

"Pray for her, Sister Marthe."

The Sister knelt and prayed.

But in the afternoon she sank into a state of torpor, which the doctor, when he called, pronounced to be the last.

Her features towards six o'clock, when Johns, Miss Wilson, and her father and St. George were gathered at the bedside, had assumed the desperate expression which sometimes precedes death. The skin had taken a dark, bluish colour, and the cheeks were hanging flaccidly. The weary face told plainly of the struggle which was nearly over, and the disordered hair, undyed now and streaked with grey, of the abdication of her female vanity.

Already the breathing had become uncertain, hard and deep at times, at others so imperceptible that for a moment once, Johns thought life extinct.

Through the half-closed curtains, the rays of the setting sun were streaming, shedding a golden light upon the face of the dying woman, and the fresh spring flowers, dispersed on every niche and table in the room, lent a note of poetry to the last moments. Gradually the breathing became more intermittent, the features more definitely rigid, and at length, after a supreme convulsion, as if it were taking a last leave of the exhausted body, the breath ceased.

All remained seated, watching. The nurse prayed audibly in Latin. Gwendoline's eyes were filled with tears.

Johns's face betrayed no sign of what he felt.

But finally, when the suspense had lasted many minutes, rising to his feet, he said impressively—

"My friends, the end has come!"

St. George, Gwen, and her father rose, and crossing to where Johns was standing, pressed his hand in turn, as a sign of sympathy. Then, after a last look at the dead woman, they silently withdrew—Gwen, as she reached the door, exchanging an earnest glance with Johns.

As soon as they had left, Johns turned to the Sister, saying —

"Close her eyes, please, Sister Marthe," for the fixed stare of his wife's eyes disconcerted him, and, besides, it was the custom.

When the nurse had complied with his request, he stood for a few minutes by the bedside, thinking.

Yes, it was all over, Rose had left for good. She had departed upon that grim, vague journey from which there was no coming back. She, and all her little troubles and her love, had passed for ever from the world. And whither had she gone? Into that conjectured second state which no one could describe, which none had ever seen? or simply into nothingness—the state to which, for his part, he believed he would return ? Ah, the huge stupidity of not knowing, of belonging to a race of imbeciles, coming they know not whence, going they know not whither, blindly driven by their instincts ! And there she lay, this partner of his life, dissolving rapidly, a mere object, a mass of bones and tissues, soon to be taken away from that large white bed and buried.

Well, she had had her share of pleasure in the world—she had had more husbands than are given to the majority of women. She had known the true beatitude of wealth, and she had gratified a last ambition, a last vanity, when she had married him. Yes, she had had her little strut, and now she had reached the goal—the goal that he would reach in time, after he had made life yield all that it had worth having. Life for anyone who was not influenced by the traditions, who did not allow himself to be allured by the chimeras, who possessed the means of gratifying the greatest of all instincts, the love of power, was acceptable enough, even if it must end in nothingness. It was a wonderful arrangement of human things that Roses were supplied to men like him, Roses who withered in their season !

These reflections over, he looked around, asking himself what was to be done next, when he became aware that the eyes of the pale Sister—large thoughtful eyes which seemed to search humanity—were fixed upon him. Quickly, as they met his, they were cast down.

What was she thinking of, he wondered? What could be the thoughts of this voluntary celibate, this constant witness of the end of human joys, this chaste associate of human misery? Was she comparing his demeanour now with that of other husbands she had seen in the course of her career? If so, he would be curious to know the impression she derived. Probably she thought him callous, but why should he feign grief which he did not feel? And, indeed, if he had yielded to his inclinations, he would have lit a cigarette to calm his nerves. But no, he owed it to the memory of Rose to suffer a little for her sake, and the Sister might nourish whatever thoughts were capable of germinating in her pious brain. Whatever they might be, it mattered very little. The thoughts of a humble Sister were of no value in the world.

Asking the nun to tell a servant to summon the French doctor to witness the decease, he passed into his room.

There he took some sheets of paper from a drawer, and, throwing himself into an arm-chair, began to scribble telegrams.

Although he knew the interment must take place within eight-and-forty hours, he calculated that there would be time for the Dean to come to Cannes if he wanted to, so he added at the end of the telegram, "Funeral to-morrow."

That would settle it. He could not come in a single day, and thus he wouldn't be there to meddle. He might think himself extremely fortunate if one of his extensive brood was sent to Eton.

Two days afterwards, Johns, accompanied by Wilson, St. George, and the curate who had said the customary prayers, followed what was left of his wife to the cemetery of Cannes. As in this town of vaunted healthfulness and pleasure death is concealed as much as possible, the rules of the hotel required that the remains of Mrs. Johns, covered though they were with flowers, should go out by the back door, and thence, accordingly, on a sunny morning, the little party left, marshalled by an official of the *pompes funèbres* in beadle's uniform.

Johns and Wilson occupied the hind part of the carriage, and St. George faced them.

On the journey Johns was silent. He was thinking of the brief meeting he had had that morning on the stairs with Gwendoline, and the plan he was elaborating in his mind entirely engrossed his thoughts. His friends were silent also.

A short drive through back streets and suburbs brought them to the cemetery, and there, in the English portion, in a spot surrounded on all sides by the graves of consumptives from the British Isles, Mrs. Johns was laid to rest by the fair young curate in a white surplice.

The return journey, after the brief ceremony, save for a casual remark made by Wilson and St. George, was as silent as the coming; but when they reached the hotel again, Johns, having parted with St. George, saying that he was tired and wished to rest, followed Wilson up the stairs as he was going to his room.

"Mr. Wilson," he said, "to-morrow I would like to speak to you in private. May I come to you at ten?"

Wilson, who seemed somewhat surprised, replied—

"I shall be pleased to see you, Mr. Johns, at ten."

CHAPTER NINETEENTH

THE next morning when Johns awoke, he was conscious of a delicious sense of freedom. Already Rose had become a figure of the past, and life, that endless chapter which he loved to read, appeared to him, as he lay in bed, in its most alluring aspects. To realize his dream of wealth and influence, the first thing to be done was to make a move at once in Gwen's affair; otherwise, if he delayed, there was a chance not only that the beauty of Edith Douglas, of which his recollections were still vivid, might cause him to neglect his duty to himself, but also that Wilson might take his daughter suddenly away, now that the season was nearly ended. During his wife's, illness he had obtained precise information about the Wilsons. He had learned that the fortune of the father, who was already a millionaire, was increasing daily owing to the productiveness of his land investments in America, and that the daughter herself, when she reached the age of twenty-one, would be entitled to a considerable dowry under the terms of her mother's marriage settlement. Everything, therefore, in that quarter was satisfactory. It only remained for him to play his cards with skill.

Leaping out of bed with the air of a man who has important business to transact, he dressed carefully and without haste, thinking, as he surveyed himself in the wardrobe glass, that he looked extremely well in black, that his well-cut suit of mourning gave him a sober air of reticence that might tend perhaps to mitigate the somewhat bad impression which, he thought, the current rumours had made Wilson form of him.

A waiter brought him coffee as soon as he had finished dressing. He poured out a large cupful and sipped it leisurely.

Then, as the clock upon the mantel pointed to a few minutes before ten, he rose and left.

The Wilsons occupied a suite of rooms on the floor below, and as he descended the stairs, he settled in his mind the way he would commence the interview, the exact words he would employ. He had not had an opportunity of seeing Gwen since the funeral, but he felt quite sure of her. The look which she had given him that day, was too eloquent to be mistaken. Probably her father would have mentioned his request for a private interview, and she would know what to expect. Passing along the corridor, he reached a door bearing the Wilsons' number. He paused a moment to button his frock-coat, then he knocked.

A scarcely audible "Come in" invited him to enter.

Wilson was waiting for him in a parlour furnished like most of the rooms of the hotel in the Louis XVI. style, and draped with yellow damask. There was a round table in the centre, a high-backed sofa against the wall, and a few fauteuils and chairs. The room had the conventional appearance which hotel rooms possess.

Wilson shook hands with Johns affably enough, though his manner was reserved. They took seats upon the sofa, and Johns commenced at once.

"Unusual circumstances, Mr. Wilson, have always seemed to me to necessitate unusual methods. I hope, therefore, that when I tell you what it is that brings me, you will understand my motives and excuse my want of orthodoxy. I know I can be frank with you, and I'm going to speak freely. It would be mere hypocrisy on my part were I to pretend that there existed, between my late wife and myself, anything more than friendly feelings. She was many years my senior, and she was quite reconciled to the life of mere companionship we led. We came here, as you know, because she thought she would recover from her malady. As you are aware, she has succumbed. During our stay, however, we were fortunate enough to make the acquaintance of yourself and of your daughter."

He dwelt a moment upon the word "daughter," and as Wilson remained impassive, he continued—

"For the last few months I have been privileged to meet Miss Wilson often, and I have been able to appreciate her qualities, her graceful nature, her intelligence, her charm. There has grown up between us a tender feeling which could not be expressed for the reason that I was not free. Day by day I saw her watching at poor Rose's bedside with touching patience and devotion, and gradually I became so much attached to her that I resolved, if my wife should die, I would ask her hand. I don't think I am wrong in believing that my affection is returned. When speaking to Miss Wilson, I have always felt that there was a community of tastes, an unfailing sympathy between us. I will go further and confess that, as far as I was able in the circumstances in which I found myself, I have ascertained her feelings. As regards my income, I may say that, though scarcely rich, I am not poor. I have between six and seven thousand pounds a year. Mr. Wilson, you are leaving soon, and there is urgency. I ask you for your daughter's hand!"

A frown had been gathering on Wilson's face while Johns was speaking. Without a moment's hesitation he replied in a firm voice—

"I am sorry, Mr. Johns, but I have other views."

Johns was not altogether unprepared for a refusal, but he did not expect that it would be so decided.

"You have other views," he repeated, slowly, "and you refuse?"

"I regret to say I do."

"You have heard, perhaps, one of the many calumnies which jealous people circulate about me?"

"I'm sorry, Mr. Johns, that I cannot enter into further reasons."

Johns, vexed and baffled, eyed Wilson narrowly. What did this old nobody with his enigmatic answers mean? By God, he'd soon find out the kind of man he had to deal with! He wasn't going to mystify him in that way for nothing.

"But," he said, with emphasis, "what if Miss Wilson doesn't share those views? I suppose you would not thwart her wishes!"

Wilson grew very red.

"I refuse," he said, "to consider such a possibility."

"I think you'll find she'll tell you it's the case."

Wilson rose.

"Have you by chance been working on my daughter's feelings?"

Johns, rising also, answered—

"I have been fortunate enough to be preferred by her."

Wilson reflected for a moment.

"All I have to tell you, Mr. Johns, is that I refuse my sanction."

"That is your final answer?"

"It is."

"Very well, then, Mr. Wilson, we need say no more about it. I'm leaving Cannes to-morrow, and as I shall probably not have another opportunity of seeing you, for the present I will say good-bye. Perhaps the day may come when you'll regret having been so obdurate."

Wilson did not answer, and, after a slight bow, Johns withdrew.

He returned to his room to think. The refusal had been absolute. The taciturn old fellow had simply shown him to the door. Well, that being so, the time had come to act. He had told Wilson he was leaving the next day merely to prevent him from taking Gwendoline away, as he might, under the circumstances, have been inclined to do; but now the plan, of which this announcement was only the forerunner, had to be elaborated.

He thought for half an hour, and at length he went to the writing table in the corner and began to write—

"Gwendoline! This morning I asked your father for your hand. He refused me flatly! Something must be done! I told him I was leaving Cannes to-morrow, but I'm only leaving the hotel. As I don't want to appear at meals to-day, I entreat you to meet me this evening on the terrace after your father has retired. Don't fail to come, my Gwen, my life, my joy! My thoughts are full of you from morning until night."

After he had written this little note, he read it over twice and it seemed to him to contain that mixture of circumstance and naïve enthusiasm which, to a woman much in love, he believed to be more eloquent than the finest phrases.

Feeling satisfied, he folded up the missive and enclosed it in an envelope.

Then, after a few more moments of reflection, he thrust it into his pocket and left his room.

Going down the stairs again, he wandered about the passages, passing the open doors of rooms which were being cleaned, and at length, as he was turning a corner of the corridor, he suddenly found himself face to face with an elderly chambermaid in *coiffe* and apron. As he looked as though he wished to speak to her, she said—

"Monsieur desires something?"

He answered, "Are you not the chambermaid who waits upon the Wilson family?"

"Yes, Monsieur."

"Then," he said, putting a louis in her hand and producing his note, "I want you to give this, in private, to Miss Wilson on the first opportunity you get to-day. But, remember, no one must see you give it."

The woman took the note.

"Monsieur can be quite easy. I'll do exactly as monsieur wishes."

Having thus taken the first step in the execution of his plan, he left the hotel by the side door to avoid meeting St. George or being seen by anyone. The morning was somewhat dull. Large white clouds surcharged with moisture had obscured the sun, and Johns walked to and fro at the side of the hotel for a few minutes, enjoying the cool freshness of the morning air. Presently he hailed a fly that was passing on the front, but just as he was getting into it he was accosted, to his surprise, by a stout man in mourning.

Recognizing Dawson, he exclaimed —

"What, *you* here, Dawson!"

"Yes," Dawson answered, dolefully. "You know, I suppose, the loss I have sustained."

"How should I?"

"My poor wife!"

"Dead, Dawson?"

"Yes, Johns! A month ago."

"Indeed," said Johns, gravely, noticing the man's downcast look, "I'm very sorry."

Dawson then explained that his wife had been a sufferer for some time from an affection of the heart, to which she had at length succumbed. He had sent no cards, but an announcement in the papers had been made.

"Well," said Johns, when he had finished, "we're brothers in misfortune. *My* wife has left me also."

"You don't mean to say that Mrs. Johns is ——"

"Dead, Dawson!"

Dawson's face expressed a mixture of surprise and half-sincere condolence.

It was evident that he was thinking of Johns's stupendous luck.

He merely said, "Dear me, how sad!"

Johns, however, was in a hurry to attend to his own business, and he said good-bye, after telling Dawson that he was leaving probably the next day. His parting admonition, as he shook his hand, was, "Cheer up, Dawson!"

Then, giving an address to the driver of his fly, he took his seat and was driven off.

Poor little Lucy! he reflected. Truly it was a pity, for she was a good little woman after all, and he almost wished he had more time to feel a little sorry for her. Only, she wasn't meant to fall in love with anybody but a husband. She took it all too seriously, and perhaps, who knew? she had fretted herself into the illness by which she had been carried off! Women were fragile creatures sometimes! There was only Ellen who took things with philosophy. What a woman Ellen was, in spite of the mellowness by which she had been overtaken, perhaps because of it! When he returned to town he would see her with a great deal of pleasure. For the present, however, he must not think of Edith. Ah, Edith was going to be lost to him if his plan succeeded!

The carriage followed the Antibes road for a considerable distance until, at length, it stopped before a square white villa in a garden half-hidden by the trees surrounding it. Upon a a board fixed to the railings was inscribed, *Villa Celli, Appartements garnis à louer.* Johns alighted and unlatched the gate. Passing up the gravel path, he knocked at the front door. He was admitted by a stout woman in a dressing-gown, who, on learning that he had come to see the house, showed him into a little parlour filled almost to repletion with ebony and gold furniture, the walls being hung with mirrors, the hangings being of red velvet.

Johns looked around and asked, "Are all the rooms furnished like this one, madame?"

The woman with much volubility assured him that they were, as he would see if he gave himself the trouble to go round.

Johns passed into the adjoining bedroom, also draped throughout with red.

Being satisfied, he said, "I'll take the house."

Then, after agreeing as to the terms, paying a week's rent in advance and glancing at the other rooms, he left, saying that he would arrive next day.

Jumping into his trap again, he was driven back to the hotel.

For the remainder of the day he stayed in his own rooms, causing his meals to be served him there, and telling the waiter to say he was unwell to anyone who called. He wished especially to avoid St. George.

The day passed tediously and rather anxiously. He felt that everything was still uncertain, and that failure in the enterprise he had in hand was quite within the bounds of possibility. Much depended on his meeting with Gwendoline that night.

He wiled away the hours, reading, until dinner time. After dinner he smoked numerous cigars, reclining in an arm-chair with his feet upon the sofa in transatlantic fashion, until the clock struck ten. Then he rose, put on his overcoat and a soft felt hat, and left his rooms.

Descending by a little staircase used chiefly by the servants, he found himself in a courtyard paved with stones and dimly lit by the lights from the windows of the house. He crossed this rapidly, and worked round the building by the shrubbery until he reached the walk in front of the hotel which was called the terrace.

As it was a dark night he was able to place himself in an angle of the building, out of the stream of light which issued from the door of the hotel. He knew he was too early, for although Wilson generally retired at about ten to his own sitting-room whenever they did not spend the evening at the Casino, yet some time must elapse before Gwendoline would be able to quit her father. What if her courage failed her at the last moment! But no, she seemed a pretty resolute young lady, and after all there was nothing so very terrible in the proceeding. The only danger was that in passing through the hall she might meet friends. Surely she would have sense enough to come out by the back door.

He waited for some time, listening to the sound of footsteps, but the hotel was unusually quiet, and the only sounds he heard were an occasional note of music from the drawing-room or a peal of laughter from an open window up above. Had something happened to prevent her coming? He was beginning to grow anxious.

Suddenly, when he had been there nearly half an hour, he heard the rustle of a dress, and a light tread upon the path. In another moment Gwen, her head wrapped in a lace mantilla which almost hid her face, appeared.

"Not here," he whispered, "it's too near the house," and he led her quickly to a dark place beneath the pine trees in the grounds.

"Oh, Gwen," he whispered, encircling her waist, "if you only knew how I have been waiting for this moment! The day has seemed so long, so long! I feared that something might prevent your coming—that your father might have taken you away; I feared a thousand things."

"My father stayed up later than he generally does, and so I could not leave."

"But now you've come, my Gwen. Now I have you near me, now I can hear your voice, now I can tell you all I have to say! Has your father told you of our interview?"

"Yes, he came to me this morning in a dreadful rage and told me that such a reprobate as you, who had only buried his wife the day before, had had the impudence to ask him for me. He warned me that, if by chance I liked you, he would never give us his consent. I said that you were not a reprobate, that

I liked you very much, and that I would marry no one else but you."

"You said that, Gwen!"

"I should think I did."

"And what did he reply?"

"He said that in that case I should have to remain single."

"Gwen, are you ready to take a bold step?"

"What, John?"

"Listen. Your father is a very obstinate old gentleman, and it's no use to try persuasion with him. We must take our destinies into our own hands. Nothing was ever gained, Gwen, by submitting patiently to tyranny. Your dear papa refuses; we must force him to consent!"

"Oh, but how?"

"I'm going to tell you. This very morning I drove out on the Antibes road—the road we took that day when I first told you how you had enchanted me—and I found the prettiest of little villas, a perfect paradise, hidden in a nest of trees, in the quaintest of French gardens, in the quietest of nooks.

"Immediately, as it was to let, I took it, and now I entreat you, I implore you, Gwen, to come with me to-morrow night. No one shall see you come. I will wait for you here at the same time, and we will walk there like two lovers arm-in-arm so joyfully. The people of the house will be bribed to secrecy, and there you will remain with me as though you were my sister for a week—perhaps only for a day—until your father yields, as he *will* to prevent a scandal. And we will be so happy there, so happy, and not a soul will be allowed to interrupt our happiness. Gwen, say that you will come!"

But Gwen was silent.

"Oh," she said at length, "*that* I could not do. Fancy the scandal there would be in the hotel and among our friends in Cannes!"

"You won't brave it for my sake?"

But she repeated, "Not in Cannes! Oh, not in Cannes!"

An inspiration came to Johns. Why had he not thought of it before? Of course, like all her sex, the little girl had local prejudices, as he termed those scruples of environment which sometimes have an influence on women's acts, and she shrank from taking so bold a step, in a place where she was known. Perhaps, with her woman's instinct, she was right, and his little scheme was short-sighted after all! Cannes was not large enough for that. Quickly, another plan suggested itself to him.

Drawing her nearer to him, and whispering softly in her ear, he said—

"Gwen, my little Gwen, I have no other thought in life but to make you happy. If you think you would not like the Villa we'll go to Paris! There, in that great city, where we are unknown, we shall be free. Oh, and it will be so delightful! I will show you a thousand things you've never seen. I will take you through old Paris, with its quaint old houses and its fine old churches. We will explore the students' quarter, we will go to places where we shouldn't, we will see everything, have constant fun. Say, Gwen, you'll come."

"To Paris!" she repeated, " oh, how could I?"

He felt that she would yield, and he continued—

"So easily! We would take the night express, my Gwen, when everyone had gone to bed, and the next evening we would be in Paris! It would be all done so quietly, so well, and afterwards your father would be obliged to give us his consent. There would be no help for it!"

For a few moments Gwen reflected. Presently she said—

"I should like to, for I know that he would never give it otherwise. But do you think I really could?"

"I'm absolutely certain."

"And you would promise that, however long we might be together, you would treat me as a sister?"

"Gwen, I promise."

"Then I suppose I must say yes. But not for a little while. It would be too dreadful, only a few days after your poor wife's funeral."

Rapidly Johns counted up the issues. On the one hand, all delay was dangerous; on the other, a woman's scruples could not quite be set aside. Still, as the balance of advantage in such cases must always be upon the side of actuality, he resolved to urge the need for immediate flight again.

He said, " I'm so distrustful of delay. Your father might suddenly leave Cannes, or something unforeseen might happen. Gwen, let us go to-morrow night?"

But he felt that she recoiled.

"Oh, no, not so soon as that," she cried.

From the instinctive movement she had made, and from her tone, he judged that it would be better to effect a compromise.

"Well, then," he said, decisively, "let us arrange it for a week hence."

"Oh, that's my birthday!"

"Your twenty-first, Gwen?"

"How *did* you know?"

"I guessed. But then, so much the better."

She reflected, and at length she murmured with a sigh—

"Next Friday, then!"

"And will you promise faithfully you'll come?"

"I promise faithfully!"

Then, feeling satisfied at the firmness with which she had said this, he told her how it would be arranged. She would leave the house in the same way as she had left that night, and he would meet her in the road. Together they would walk up to the station. She would be careful to put on her thickest veil and a long cloak. She would want no luggage. Everything would be provided at their journey's end. Each day she would write to him at the Villa Celli, where he intended to remain in strict seclusion the whole week, and he would answer her *poste restante*. Relying on her promise, he was certain, absolutely certain of success.

She answered that she would do exactly as he wished. He need have no fear. She would keep her promise.

He thanked her, earnestly vowing that his gratitude was too great for words, that her happiness would be the study of his life. And how happy they would be! How kind she was, how good!

To seal the compact they had made, he kissed her gently. They lingered for a few moments, during which both were silent, and at length she whispered—

"I must leave you now. It's getting late."

He murmured, "Must you, Gwendoline?" and slowly he released her from his arms. She quitted him after a last assurance that she would keep her promise, and in the dim light he watched her retreating form until it disappeared into the house.

Then, after lighting a cigar, he strolled up and down the lawn. He scarcely knew if he was satisfied. It was a great thing to have induced her to consent; but the week's delay which she demanded would be hard to pass, and there was just a possibility of something happening on which he did not count. On the other hand, on that day she would be entitled to her mother's legacy, and that was a consideration. By God, what a prize she was! Fancy that fool St. George thinking he could win her! No, such windfalls weren't for St. Georges. There was nothing to do for it but to wait. The little girl was thoroughly in love with him, and he was certain she would keep her word. He knew her character, and that it was not wanting in decision. He finished his cigar and then went in to give notice of his leaving the next day.

The next morning he rose early. As soon as he had dressed, and while his late wife's luggage and his own was being taken down to the carriage which was to convey him to the station, he thought he would amuse himself by paying a parting visit to St. George.

He found the young man still in bed.

"I'm in a great hurry," Johns exclaimed, as St. George was opening his eyes, "I'm off at once, and I just came in to say good-bye."

St. George started up in bed and looked at Johns enquiringly at first, and then with a satisfied expression.

"Oh, you're going, Johns!"

"The carriage is waiting for me at this very moment, and as I'm late I haven't time to talk. Good-bye, St. George, and good luck with the little heiress. You'll be a rich man yet, my boy."

St. George smiled half complacently and half sceptically. Johns, who did not want to prolong the interview, pressed his friend's hand, saying that they would meet again in London, and left him to his reflections.

A few minutes later Johns was in the hotel omnibus. As the vehicle was being driven off, he thrust his head out of the window and looked up towards Wilson's suite of rooms on the first floor of the hotel building, in the hope that he might catch a glimpse of Gwen. He saw, to his delight, the young girl standing at her window leaning on the rail. She kissed her hand to him, and in acknowledgment he raised his hat, giving her an earnest glance.

When he reached the station, whither, in order to maintain the fiction that he was leaving Cannes, he had thought it prudent to repair, he told the porters that he would not leave before the evening train, and he ordered them to place his luggage in the cloak-room. Then, after waiting until the train had left, and the station had become empty, he set out on foot for the Villa Celli by the least-frequented road.

Here, for a week, he lived in absolute seclusion under an assumed name, obtaining what he needed from the town in the way of books and linen through a messenger, and keeping up a correspondence with his *fiancée*, who wrote to him each day. The time in this pleasant villa passed more quickly than he had anticipated, and as the letters he had received from Gwen denoted no change in her intentions, he continued to feel confident of the success of his undertaking. No doubt she showed herself a little timorous, and had some qualms of conscience, but then he knew that he was asking her to take a very bold step indeed. The qualms of the female conscience, he considered, seldom prevented women from following what were called the dictates of their hearts, especially when they desired to obey them. What wonderful contrivances for self-deception women were! How admirably they were designed by nature to gratify a man's desires! On the fifth day of his sojourn, the post brought him a letter from Gwendoline which related, humorously, the way in which St. George had made his last proposal. The previous evening after dinner on the terrace, he had unburdened to her his pent-up feelings, and she had answered in her father's words that she had other views.

"Poor St. George," she said, "he looks so sad, and he is going to leave at once."

She told him also in the same letter that her father, although he seemed relieved when he heard that Johns had left, had been very bearish, and had watched her since so narrowly that she had only once been able to call for letters at the post-office. Ah, well, there would be an end of all that soon; but what a daring thing it was to do!

Johns smiled when he had read the note, and as the time of their flight was drawing near, he sat down and indited a letter full of love and promise and enthusiasm, well calculated to sustain her courage.

At length the appointed evening came.

As soon as it was dark, Johns, impressed with a full sense of the importance of the venture, left his villa and set out for the hotel. He had preferred to walk, partly because he had time to spare, partly because the hire of a carriage might afford a clue if an enquiry were made next day, and in cases such as this, it was impossible to be too cautious.

It was a moonlight night, as he saw with dissatisfaction, and the villas which he passed were looking snow-white amid the trees. Cannes appeared proud and peaceful in the day-like brightness. Johns, however, was thinking little of the scene, and scarcely heeded his surroundings. His thoughts were concentrated on the business of the evening.

When he reached the precincts of the hotel, he found, on looking at his watch, that it was still early, and therefore, putting up the collar of his overcoat and bringing his soft felt hat well forward over his eyes to avoid being recognized, he passed the time in walking up and down a lane of aloe trees in the rear of the hotel.

At length, when another consultation of his watch had told him that the time of the meeting was drawing near, he left the lane to saunter round the entrance of the grounds. To his annoyance, when he reached the gate and looked towards the terrace he recognized St. George, who was walking slowly to and fro as if in thought. This threatened to complicate affairs, for how, he asked himself, was Gwen to leave as long as that idiot remained there? He was beginning to feel uneasy, and heartily cursed St. George.

The time appointed soon arrived, and yet there were no signs of Gwen, and still St. George continued to pace the path. Johns felt he could have choked him. Really it would be too much if the plan fell through on *his* account. Of course, Gwen might come out by the back door; but he knew that that was sometimes closed rather early in the evening. There was very little time to lose. The train would leave at nineteen minutes past eleven, and unless she came at once, there would not be time to walk up to the station. Surely his luck wasn't going to desert him now!

His perturbation became so great, that, unable to remain still, he paced up and down in the shadow of the wall. At length as he was looking up at the young girl's room, he perceived a light, as of a candle, held suddenly before the window for a moment. This made his pulse beat faster, though it left him in perplexity. What did the signal mean? That she was, or that she was not coming? He was not able to determine, though it seemed to augur well.

A few moments elapsed, during which the room was lit as by a faint light; then it relapsed again into darkness.

"Now," thought Johns, "if she means to come, she'll come, though it's deuced late."

Waiting until St. George had nearly reached the remote end of the gravel walk, he quitted his place of ambush and ran round quickly, passing over the grass of the flower-beds to avoid noise, to a corner of the building where he had waited once before. If Gwen should come he would thus be able to encourage her.

Almost as he arrived there he heard a hurried footstep on the path. He looked in the direction whence it came, and saw Gwen turning the corner of the house. There was not a moment to be lost. He glanced in the direction of St. George, and seeing that he had stopped at the end of his walk and was lighting a cigar, he darted quickly to the young girl's side and whispered, "It's all right, Gwen. Now, follow me."

He led the way to the entrance gate, and she followed at a few yards' distance. Then, when they reached the road, he seized her arm and whispered—

"Gwen, it's very late, we must simply fly up to the station."

"Oh," she said, "it was so dreadful! A visitor came in and I could not get away. I feared it was too late. Oh, what should we do, then?"

Johns reassured her, and they walked so fast that they had no breath left to speak. It seemed to both of them that they would never walk fast enough; that the houses and the villas they had to pass would never end.

Gwen, being short, could not take long steps, and the road appeared interminable. Carriages passed them, bound also for the station, and each time they were forced to turn away their faces to avoid being recognized. Johns, inwardly, was cursing his bad luck.

Gwen's strength was failing, and he was beginning to bitterly regret that he had not procured a carriage, when suddenly he perceived an empty fly going in the same direction as themselves.

In a moment Johns had hailed it, promised the man a louis if he arrived in time for the express, and was being driven with his companion furiously along the dusty road.

The man lashed his horse to so much purpose, that they reached the station five minutes before the hour of departure.

Quickly Johns caused his luggage to be reclaimed, while Gwen, who had drawn down her veil, waited for him on the platform. Johns took the tickets, and, with Gwen leaning on his arm, soon forced his way through the throng in the station to the *coupé* which a porter had retained. They entered quickly, took their seats, and, after drawing down the blinds, waited in suspense, with their hands joined, for the train to start.

Soon they heard the signal given, and in another instant they were conscious, to their intense delight, that the train was moving off.

Johns, drawing the young girl to him, said exultingly—

"*Now*, my little Gwen, we're safe!"

"Oh," she murmured, "how I love to trust you!"

In a few more minutes, as the express sped on, they were chatting gaily, just as though the journey they were making was in the ordinary course of things.

Johns preserved a tenderly protecting attitude, resolved as he was to respect Gwen's scruples as long as she herself should seem to wish it. She scarcely appeared to realize the step which she had taken, and he, on his part, refrained as much as possible from speaking of her father or their flight.

And thus, after a few hours had elapsed, tired after the day's experience, she went to sleep, resting in his arms.

Then Johns reflected. As he closed his eyes, and was rocked by the swaying train, the whole of his past history, from the day he had landed at Tilbury to the death of his wife at

Cannes, appeared to him distinctly. The women he had known—Ellen, Lucy, Edith, Rose—his many conquests in society; the syrens who had now and then diverted him; even the little friendless girl of Grafton Street, with her pale and weary face; he saw them all in his imagination as though they had been portraits in a gallery. Truly he felt he owed them gratitude, for each in her especial way had been the means of advancing his career; each had borne her share in the work of his apotheosis, which this little girl, whose head was leaning on his shoulder, was to complete. Ah, yes! it was through women that men climbed fastest. Their love was the lever which no barriers withstood. Through them, nothing was unattainable. Had he not learned that poor Society, with its rules, its prudery, its pride, capitulated to the man its women loved? Had he not seen that the virtue of the highest was not more difficult to overcome than the famous pride of caste which had been unable to withstand the prestige of the son of David Johns? Women were the providence of life. How fortunate it was that there should be a sex so bountiful!

As he arrived at this conclusion, he cast a glance at Gwen, who was sleeping calmly, the light of the roof lamp falling on her maidenly and almost pretty face. He muttered to himself, "Yes, yes, she'll do. *She must!*"

Then, to drive away all other thoughts, he disposed himself to sleep. In a few minutes he was soundly slumbering.

When he awoke, the light was streaming through the front windows of the *coupé*. He drew aside the blinds and saw that the train was traversing a rich green country, bright and joyous with spring tints. How well he recollected his awakening five months previously in the old brown land of Provence, which, compared with this, was as a matron to a budding girl! Well, he had left the old existence there. The new life was before him now. He had exchanged the old wife for the young!

He had reached this stage of his reflections, when the voice of Gwen caused him suddenly to start. She was asking—

"Oh, John, where are we?"

And he remembered that these same words had been used by Rose upon the journey down.

"Amid the beautiful green fields, Gwen. Soon we shall be at Lyons."

She sat up in the carriage, adjusted the folds of her light silk dress, and passed her hand over her dark brown hair. It was all dishevelled, and a lock was hanging down. She asked—

"How shall I do my hair, John? I've nothing with me!"

Johns, rising, reached from the hand-rail a leather dressing-case which he had brought with him. Opening it, he said, "You'll find all you want in there, Gwen."

She looked at the open case with its rows of silver mountings, its button hooks, its scissors, and its combs, and presently she spied a hairpin.

"Oh!" she said, "surely it's your wife's?"

He kissed her, saying, "Gwen! it's yours."

They breakfasted at Lyons.

The remainder of the journey was passed pleasantly, and in the evening, to avoid detection (for Johns was not quite sure whether by French law Wilson might not have discretionary powers over Gwen), they alighted at a suburban station before Paris, to which they had caused their luggage to be addressed.

Thence they were driven to an hotel behind the Etoile Arch, which Johns had once heard recommended for its quietness.

Their first act, as soon as they had secured a suite of rooms, was to telegraph to Wilson.

"Your daughter is in my hands and safe," Johns wired. "It's useless for you to object to our marriage now. Please tell us you consent through the medium of the *Times* advertisements. We intend to be married soon.—J. J."

Three weeks afterwards, Wilson, having yielded to the force of circumstances, as Johns had judged he would, they were married quietly in the English Church at Neuilly, having lived platonically, to Johns's amusement, the whole time. Then, after a short trip in Brittany, Johns took his wife to Grosvenor Place.

Wilson had given a princely dowry to his daughter, and the Johns's fortune was sufficient to sustain ambitions of the greatest magnitude.

The Stanfields, however, discontinued Johns's acquaintance, and St. George wrote him a letter in which he called him a mendacious cad.

Johns laughed over the letter with Ellen the first time they met; but when she asked him if he was really happy now, he answered slowly—

"Happiness, my worthy Ellen, is unattainable!"

THE END.

www.ingramcontent.com/pod-product-compliance
Lightning Source LLC
Chambersburg PA
CBHW022105230426
43672CB00008B/1282